Who's Who in Spy Fiction

DONALD McCORMICK

Who's Who in
SPY FICTION

TAPLINGER PUBLISHING COMPANY
NEW YORK

First published in the United States in 1977 by
TAPLINGER PUBLISHING CO., INC.
New York, New York

Library of Congress Catalog Card Number: 77–71599
ISBN 0–8008–8277–6

Contents

Introduction

THE word 'spy', for which there is a single character in the Chinese language, had as its original meaning in ancient China that of 'a chink', 'a crack' or 'crevice'. From any of these meanings one can derive the sense of a peep-hole, so it would seem that the earliest Chinese conception of a spy is very simply one who peeps through a crack.

It is worth while turning to ancient China for some background to spy fiction because it was in this country as far back as 510 B.C. that the earliest textbook, not only on the arts of war, but on espionage and the organisation of a Secret Service, was written. This was the *Ping Fa* of Sun Tzu. It has not only been respected as a valuable guide to the arts of espionage down the ages in China, but an abbreviated, simplified version of the book in English was issued to the RAF in Ceylon during the Second World War.

'One who peeps through a crack . . .': this is really the purist's definition of a spy. It is also what the author of spy fiction must be able to do, for at its best this genre of literature is a peepshow. But it is a peepshow that changes in its images from age to age, from generation to generation. In the early 1900s it was peeping mainly on German spies as seen on the Riviera, in Vienna and Paris (actually the Germans' real spying then was done in Portsmouth, Chatham, Devonport and Marseilles); in the 1920s it switched to watching Chinese and Russian spies. At one time it was essentially high-life espionage, telling how the butler in a country house saw the black-velveted seductress stealing the plans of a new submarine. Today spy fiction is much more likely to feature a rather scruffy, pimply student of electronics working out how to infiltrate the computer which contains the secrets of the round-the-clock anti-submarine warfare watch.

One of the difficulties in compiling a *Who's Who of Spy Fiction* is that it is far from easy either to pin-point the beginning of the genre, or to define who is and who is not of this particular Band of Brothers. There is, for example, a very strong case for including Lo Kuan-chung of the Yuan dynasty (A.D. 1260–1341), the author of that celebrated Chinese classic, *San Kuo* (or *The Romance of the Three Kingdoms*). On some counts he could rightly be called the first spy fiction writer. The *San Kuo* is an extremely long historical novel, its plot being based on events covering the period from A.D. 168–265. It opens with the threatened decline of the Han dynasty in the reign of Ling Ti and the insurrection of the Yellow Turbans. The book shows how the *I Ching* (or *Book of Changes*), that most remarkable of Chinese prediction works, was consulted by directors of spies in the period, and its pages are filled with ingenious spy plots, espionage techniques and double-agents. It contains many examples of the kind of deadlock that often ensued as a result of warring espionage groups of equal astuteness. 'I would rather betray the whole world than let the world betray me,' declares Ts'ao Chen, the villain-hero (*not* anti-hero) of *The Three Kingdoms*. So Ts'ao kills the entire family of his host because he believed—quite wrongly as it turned out—that they were plotting against him. This is not so very far from the situation in Somerset Maugham's *Ashenden* when the wrong man gets killed. But one must rule against including Lo Kuan-chung, I feel, first because his book is as much a classical, philosophical treatise and a work of history as it is a tale about spies, and, secondly, its accounts of espionage ruses are in all probability more factual than fictional. Mao Tse-tung and the Vietcong guerrillas are said on the most reliable authority to have consulted *The Three Kingdoms* as a textbook on espionage.

Others might claim that the spy story in fiction had its origins in the seventh century A.D. in the person of Ti Jen-chieh, mandarin and Intelligence Chief of the Empress Wu of China. His exploits inspired those eighteenth-century stories created around his name, known as the *Dee Goong An*, later to be adapted and fictionalised by the Dutch diplomat, Dr R. H. Van Gulik, in his series of books known as the 'Judge Dee' stories, since popularised on the television screen. But even though spies play a marginal part in some of these stories, they belong more to the category of detective fiction.

To define spy fiction is not as easy as to define detective literature. The latter can be defined in precise terms and has therefore come to be accepted as a branch of literature. But not so the spy story, which has been much more the subject of sneers and derision. Many authors object, sometimes with justice, to the labelling of their novels as 'spy stories'. Even some of the authors included in this book have registered this objection, insisting that their books are novels first and foremost and only incidentally spy stories. As one of them points out, 'once you start pigeon-holing novels and plays I suppose you reach the point where *King Lear* is defined as "regal fiction—Drama".'

Some of the practitioners of the spy story are authors of great distinction in the broader world of literature, Conrad, Chesterton, Dickens and Maugham among them. It cannot, however, be denied that some of the best-known and most prolific writers of this genre have given the spy story a bad name. Indeed, as will be seen in this book, it is sometimes impossible not to give them more space than some of the better writers, if only because in their clumsy and rodomontade manner they have been trend-setters. Curiously, not one of their characters is likely to become one of the immortals of literature. So far there has been no spy fiction hero to vie with Sherlock Holmes for longevity of fame. This may be due to the fact that 'spy story' is in itself a misnomer. A detective story is built entirely around the character of the detective. Without him there would be no story. And he can survive indefinitely. But the main figure in a spy story, if he is technically a spy, cannot be expected to have too long a life: sooner or later he must be 'blown', or 'taken to the cleaners'. But he may not be a spy at all: he may be a counter-espionage agent like James Bond, or an Intelligence Chief sitting at a desk in London, Washington or Moscow, controlling a network of spies, but not doing any spying himself. In fact, when we speak of the spy story we are talking of spy-catchers as well as spies, of double and treble-agents as well as agents, of hired killers, planters of misinformation, or sometimes even of that unassuming little man at the corner shop who operates a kind of letter-box for agents.

Yet for very many years, in the western world, there was another reason why the pure spy story was, if not derided, at least ignored. Spying was regarded as something despicable and no spy could be considered as a hero. Nor was it even considered desirable that the chief villain of a story should be a spy. A thief, yes; a murderer, most certainly; but a spy was the nineteenth-century equivalent of the sexual pervert hero or villain of the pre-1939 period—the most ostracised character in literature. Unlike the Chinese, who have shown a remarkable taste for their own spy literature and have even made this part of their education, the western world has only belatedly learned some of the lessons of ancient espionage. Shakespeare introduced an espionage trick in *Macbeth*, when Malcolm ordered:

3

Let every soldier hew him down a bough,
And bear't before him; thereby shall we shadow
The numbers of our host, and make discovery
Err in report of us.

But it was centuries later before this lesson in camouflage was scientifically adopted by military strategists.

Antipathy to the spy story was presumably as marked in the seventeenth and eighteenth centuries as it was in the nineteenth. One would have expected both Mrs Aphra Behn and Daniel Defoe to have contributed to this form of literature. Defoe admitted that he had been employed by Queen Anne 'in several honourable, though secret services', yet he never drew on his experiences in his writing either in fiction or in fact. Like Aphra Behn, he was more interested in the antics of the bedroom than in those of the informer travelling from tavern to tavern. Aphra Behn was probably the first really effective professional female secret agent in Britain as well as being the first Englishwoman to write plays. She, too, avoided the theme of the spy story.

Yet the links between literature and espionage are considerable, and this applies more to Britain than to any other nation in the world. Perhaps this is why British spy fiction writers so greatly outnumber those of any other country. The Americans can fairly claim to have produced the first writer of a spy fiction book— Fenimore Cooper. Probably this was due to an aroused interest in espionage as a patriotic duty during the War of Independence. The spy was much more of a hero in America in this period than he was elsewhere. But American writers did not follow up this trend in the early part of the twentieth century to anything like the extent to which the British did. The French, surprisingly, have produced few spy fiction writers, even though their talent for espionage can probably be rated higher than that of most nations. Like the Germans and the Spaniards, the French seem quite content to read translations of Anglo-Saxon espionage stories.

In compiling this work one fact stands out clearly—the recurring link between spy fiction (most noticeably among the English-speaking writers) and real life espionage and Intelligence work. Fact begets fiction and fiction begets fact. Fenimore Cooper may well have undertaken some espionage missions himself while serving in the Great Lakes area as a midshipman on patrol in the US Navy. A. E. W. Mason tells us quite frankly that, when on an espionage

4

mission for the British NID (Naval Intelligence Division) in the Second World War, he borrowed an idea for disguise from a story by Conan Doyle. There is an astonishingly long list of authors who have actually been involved at some time or other in Intelligence work and who, unlike Defoe and Mrs Behn in earlier times, have produced spy stories.

After Fenimore Cooper there is a long gap, broken only by Dickens, before one comes to the next real spy story, *The Riddle of the Sands* (1900), by that lovable, if quixotic cavalier from Ireland, Erskine Childers. He based the tale on his own yachting voyages in the vicinity of the Frisian Islands. Intended as an awful warning of the threat of Prussian militarism, the book is said to have precipitated that classic of now established Admiralty jargon, 'As Your Lordships are well aware', which, when translated into plain English, means 'My God, we have forgotten to tell the Admiralty!' For the awful truth was that Erskine Childers' novel, if you please, revealed that the Admiralty charts of the area were not up to date. The NID then sanctioned a real-life spy trip to the Frisian Islands.

Somerset Maugham, A. E. W. Mason, Compton Mackenzie, William Le Queux, Graham Greene, Dennis Wheatley, G. K. Chesterton, Ian Fleming, Sidney Horler, Sir John Masterman, John Le Carré, John Buchan, Bernard Newman . . . the list of spy writers who have been engaged in Intelligence is not merely extensive, but impressive. And this is but the tip of the iceberg. How many others lurk unknown or undetected beneath either their real names or their pseudonyms as writers of spy fiction? While some, like Sidney Horler, may have merely been on the fringes of 'the game' (attached to the propaganda section of Air Intelligence in the First Wold War), others have held key posts and may even have influenced vital events in history. One could probably draw up an effective and highly imaginative mini-Secret Service out of spy story writers alone. There is abundant evidence of Maugham's Secret Service career in the private papers of Sir William Wiseman at Princeton University. Both in Switzerland and in Russia he was a key agent during the latter part of the First World War. There is a transcript of an interview which Maugham had with Kerensky in October 1917. According to Maugham, the Russian leader's message was so secret that he would not put it in writing and asked Maugham to pass it on verbally to Lloyd George. But Maugham was afraid that his stammer might ruin any chance he had of impressing Lloyd George and he wrote the report instead. Years later he blamed himself for the Prime Minister's failure to respond to Kerensky's requests. There is also in the Wiseman Papers a letter to Wiseman, then Chief of British Intelligence in New York, dated 7 July 1917, which makes the point: 'I do not know whether it is intended that I should have any salary for the work I am undertaking. I will not pretend that I actually need one, but in Switzerland I refused to accept anything and found afterwards that I was the only man working in the organisation for nothing and that I was regarded not as patriotic or generous, but merely damned foolish. If the job carries a salary I think it would be more satisfactory to have it; but if not I am not unwilling to go without. I leave the matter in your hands.'

One can hardly imagine James Bond being quite so conciliatory. On the other hand Maugham's perfectly framed hint seems to have produced results, for eleven days later, on 18 July, he signed the following receipt: 'Dollars 21,000.00. Received the sum of Twenty-one thousand Dollars, W. Somerset Maugham.' Maugham even introduced a few literary and publishing names as code-words in his messages. An agent named Tsertelli was 'Hodder', the Workmen's and Soldiers' Council was 'Dent & Co', and Lane, Locke, Fisher Unwin, Harper and Dutton & Co. were all turned into code-words. There is ample documentary evidence that Maugham did most important work in Russia and that he grasped the essential facts rather better than many agents. The GRU, the Soviet Union's earliest Military Intelligence section, discovered the facts about Maugham's work in Russia and, linking them up with his book, *Ashenden*, urged that henceforth a study should be made of all British spy stories by a special section in Moscow. This study is conducted just as thoroughly today by the KGB as ever it was by the GRU. The Russians are always searching for the truth behind the fiction, possibly because so many of their own spy novels—a new trend which sprang up in the 'sixties—are propaganda exercises in which the stories of true-life spies are thinly disguised as fiction. This was part of their campaign for glorifying the Soviet spy in the mid-'sixties. In February 1966, Vadim Kozhevnikoff's novel, *Sword and Shield*, was first published in the literary monthly, *Znamya*. It is generally assumed in Russia that the redoubtable Colonel Rudolf Abel provided the prototype for Kozhevnikoff's hero, Alexander Boloff, whose surname was a transposition of Abel in Russian. Shortly before his death in Moscow in 1971 Colonel Abel introduced a film called *The Dead Season*, a spy thriller about germ warfare experiments in the western world.

The most prolific period of the spy story was between 1914 and 1939, but it was very far from being a golden age of espionage fiction. Hundreds of authors produced thousands of stories, short and long, of this genre during that quarter of a century. The advent of the First World War whetted the appetite of the reading public for this kind of thing and after that the spy story became a habit rather than a cult. Some of the stories were competent, one or two like Maugham's *Ashenden* were first class, the vast majority was mediocre and many were appallingly bad both as credible plots and as examples of the written word. Even the blurbs advertising some of these books were atrociously written. Take this example boosting a Francis Beeding book, *The League of Discontentment*, in 1930: '... another Granby Secret Service story, as exciting and as good as *The Six Proud Walkers*. The good Colonel, while on holiday in the South of France, gets a message to go to the Pont du Gard to interview a miller who has some information to sell—too late, the miller is dead, very dead! The old spider, Caramac, in the château high above the miller's cottage, is weaving new plots; and the flies—Granby and Carroll and Diana—are only too ready to oblige. Breathless Beeding!'

Breathless, indeed! Or, as the French tutor of the period might have put it: 'Have you the secret code which was hidden in the garter of my niece at the château on the hill?' 'No, but I have the invisible ink which your uncle put in the champagne bucket in the left-hand corner of the hayrick.'

No doubt it was all good, innocent fun, appealing to the innate snobbery of the reader who, then at least, had the not altogether unadmirable desire to be lifted out of his mundane environment into the exotic high-life of the 1920s. It was in some ways magnificent in its uninhibited flamboyance and flaunted grandiloquence, but it was not literature until the advent of Eric Ambler at the tail end of the 1930s. Maugham had struck his own warning much earlier, but this message had not yet penetrated to the masses who still lapped up the offerings of Horler, Le Queux, Beeding and 'Sapper'. They were not ready to appreciate the 'new look' at the spy as provided by such a realist as Maugham when he made his character Ashenden ruefully comment that 'the great chiefs of the secret service in their London offices, their hands on the throttle of this great machine, led a life full of excitement; they moved their pieces here and there, they saw the pattern woven by the multitudinous threads ... but it must be confessed that for the small fry like himself to be a member of the secret service was not as adventurous an affair as the public thought.'

It was Ambler who really put over the Maugham message to a wider readership, who successfully changed the pattern of the spy story and paved the way to the emergence of something more adult and realistic. And it was Ambler, paradoxically the one man who had not been mixed up in the Intelligence game, who first produced the most factual, authentic spy stories of the century. He achieved this simply by patient, meticulous attention to detail, by checking and cross-checking on his facts. If I had to nominate a real life 'M', a spymaster-in-chief, and I was restricted to authors of spy fiction for my choice, I should unhesitatingly pick Eric Ambler. He would smell a phoney among his prospective agents at once, and he would detect errors of technique and fact which many professional agents would overlook (note the way in which he has detected errors in Ian Fleming's sometimes hastily researched novels, as revealed in his entry in this book).

Ambler pointed the way, if not to a golden age for the spy story, at least to a far higher standard of work, a genre to which a serious, highly skilled novelist such as Graham Greene could at last contribute. From Ambler onwards the emphasis was on authentic detail and diligent, accurate research. The old school of the 'twenties and early 'thirties really conned its readers more thoroughly than anyone else since the days of Ouida and in some respects not as well as that romantic novelist. (A sociologist of the future may perhaps wonder if this was not a symptom of the slow decline and fall of the British middle classes, for it is improbable that a Victorian readership would have lapped up so much rubbish without demur.) It was possible in 1925 for a writer who had never travelled more than six miles from, say, Pudsey, to produce a spy novel that would be acceptable. Today not only does it require the author to be widely travelled, highly sophisticated, knowledgeable about the technology of espionage and to have some first-hand knowledge of how Secret Services operate, but he (or she) probably needs to spend a holiday in the actual setting chosen for the book, not to mention taking a crash course in electronics and spending an afternoon learning how debugging devices work. Fleming not only travelled far afield in quest of more exotic settings for his own stories, but employed a number of people to undertake research for him. Even so, it is doubtful if his books were as realistic as those of Len Deighton and his readers frequently delighted in catching him out in some tiny detail. John Dee, Queen Elizabeth's astrologer and secret agent, signed himself '007' (he wrote it as $\overline{007}$), but nobody seems to have pointed this out to Fleming. It also happens to have been the number on the door of the ladies' lavatory at the old Commonwealth Relations Office, now incorporated with the Foreign Office. (In conversation Fleming once said that he took the code-name from the zip code for the Georgetown area of Washington, DC, where many CIA agents live—20007.)

The new 'in' thing in spy fiction became a passion for detail. At first it was 'fun finding out' (which, incidentally, was the title of a regular column in the *Daily Express* in the immediate post-war years when people began to yearn for all they had missed learning in those six years of war). But Fleming erred in writing the kind of detail that interested him rather than what might appeal to his readers. At first it did not matter because the reader was flattered that the author should appear to think he appreciated these things and wanted to know more about them. This was particularly true of food and drink in the mid-'fifties after years of wartime austerity, and possibly Fleming did more than anyone to make vodka popular in suburbia. But, as Kingsley Amis has pointed out, this tendency began to reach an extreme point: '. . . the identifying of a Soviet agent in London is the merest peg for a great lump of information about Fabergé jewellery [Fleming's 'The Property of a Lady', *Playboy*, January 1964], Wartski's shop and Sotheby's auction rooms. Mr Fleming lectures as well in fiction as any writer I know, but one expected at least a more energetic pretence that the facts are doing some honest work instead of merely hanging about asking to be admired.'

It was the brief age of the 'super'-figure—'SuperMac', 'Super-Bond'—and there was bound to be a reaction to it. James Bond was grossly oversold as the man who never failed to lay a girl. Statistics show that only twice in thirteen books did Bond fail to seduce the girl he fancied. One wonders whether Fleming acted out his own fantasies in Bond. Not only did the sex-bomb Bond lure a lesbian to change her allegiance to his side, and his bed, but in *From Russia With Love* the dedicated Soviet agent, Tatiana Romanova, becomes so enamoured with Bond's photograph that she decides to double-cross her bosses and bring information with her, if only the irresistible James will enable her to escape with him from Istanbul.

Fleming forgot the lessons of Ambler: he tended to make Bond and his enemies less credible figures in his later books. When the reaction set in the demise of Bond was swift even among his most fervent admirers. But the reaction of other up-and-coming writers was even more pronounced. A new school emerged: these writers actually loathed Bond, seeing him as a neo-Fascist, a propagandist of the Cold War and an awful reminder of the nadir of racialist, right-wing 'Bulldog' Drummondism. Some of them felt this instinctively on aesthetic grounds, while others reacted morally and politically. One could almost picture Le Carré and John Gardner carrying placards in a Chelsea demo, shouting 'Bond Out!' The Communist *Morning Star* gave quite a lot of space to a write-up of an interview with John Gardner. In the United States there was *Alligator*, the Harvard *Lampoon* parody of an Ian Fleming book, while in *The London Magazine* Cyril Connolly sounded a hilariously funny note with his satirical extravaganza, *Bond Strikes Camp*. In this latter story Bond is disguised as a woman, with 'the very latest in falsies—foam-rubber with electronic self-erecting nipples', on the specific instructions of 'M'. His mission is to ensnare a general in the service of the KGB. But the general turns out to be 'M' in disguise, the head of the Secret Service having been a sublimated homosexual all these years, nursing a hidden passion for getting Bond to his bed in drag.

Thus by the mid-'sixties the spy story had become the target of the satirists. For a while the John Gardner method of 'sending up' espionage fiction was highly popular. But by the early 'seventies the pendulum had swung again: this time it settled down to something like a happy mean, an almost imperceptible movement around sober realism. The stories eschewed the melodramatic, the ultra-heroic, the extravagant; the characters were much more like the gentle old man in the antiquarian bookshop, the girl teacher who takes a package-tour holiday to Yugoslavia; the settings for the stories were changed to more distant places and in many instances, in order to heighten the effect of realism, real-life stories were taken as the subjects for fiction. Alan Williams made 'Kim' Philby an important figure in one of his books, while R. Wright Campbell took the incidents surrounding the sinking of the *Royal Oak* in the Second World War as the theme for his *The Spy Who Sat and Waited*.

Looking back, it may now appear that the Ambler, Greene, Fleming, Le Carré, Deighton period was the golden age of spy fiction, say from 1939–69, though most of these books were published after 1955. This era covered a wide range in trends from the

Bulldog Drummond Mark II of the 1950s (Bond) to the Ashenden Mark II of the 1960s (Leamas and Boysie Oakes), though Maugham might wince at the thought of Boysie Oakes being linked to Ashenden. Spy fiction had long been regarded as excellent material for films, but the golden age of this genre brought the spy story into the living-rooms via the television screen. Here was a new medium for the writer of this type of book and the character of Callan, the agent with a chip on his shoulder, became almost one of the family, a favourite erring son who popped back into the sitting-room of an evening.

Any student of the spy story, and indeed any author contemplating writing such a story, could usefully read Edward Weismiller's account of how he came to write *The Serpent Sleeping* in his essay *The Writing of a Novel*. It tells more than anything else what goes on in the mind of an author working towards creating a spy story. If one could have ten such pictures it would provide an invaluable insight into the history of this genre. Weismiller was obviously enormously influenced by his wartime experiences in the manipulation of enemy agents: 'It is a strange thing to learn about oneself [that one might be "the smoothest liar who ever came down the pike"]. It is a strange thing to have wanted to become. It was strange, too, to learn that one had to betray in order to protect one's country against betrayal—really, that this was to be expected . . .' And the most interesting factor that emerges from Weismiller's work, based on first-hand knowledge, is how closely his experiences bear relevance to Ambler who was never 'in the field'.

If one must peer into the future of the spy story, I would suggest that the spy stories of the next decade should be assessed on the developments in real-life espionage. As the cloak-and-dagger tactics of past decades disappear (and Watergate has dealt them a severe blow, not to mention the anti-Castro tactics of the CIA), so will computerised espionage become more important. Here is enormous scope for the spy story writer as the technique develops. After all, the front-line spies on whose unfailing watch we now depend for the peace of the world are built into the machines which monitor the anti-nuclear submarine watch round the world. A short time ago Aaron Latham of *New York* magazine went to Washington to collect material for what he hoped would be the definitive article on American secret intelligence. His conclusion after weeks of digging out the facts was that some of the old-timers could have told him all he wanted to know before he left New York and that 'there is more truth in some spy fiction than there is in books supposedly non-fiction.' He could have added that some fiction read by CIA executives had caused more high blood pressure and panic than any blunders perpetrated by their operatives. To mention two instances: first, Victor Marchetti's *The Rope Dancer,* which precipitated a lengthy and celebrated legal battle with the CIA; secondly, Nicholas Luard's *Robespierre Serial,* which so alarmed Section Q of the CIA and convinced them that here was something far nearer the truth than one was likely to find even in HQ tape-recordings.

This quest for ultra-realism, for accurate mirroring of contemporary trends in espionage and counter-espionage, has become so general on both sides of the Atlantic that it is bound to have some political influence. In the US the revelations of Watergate have provoked a spate of such spy stories and, whereas previously a man like E. Howard Hunt was able to get away with no less than 43 atrociously written specimens of the genre before he was jailed for his part in the 'plumbers' raid', more recent authors of successful and extremely well-written spy stories have been ex-CIA or Secret Service men—Marchetti, Charles McCarry and Wilson McCarthy among them. Their novels, and those of Brian Garfield and James Grady with their investigative approach, have probably done as much as the media to put the spotlight on CIA methods and force the nation as a whole to take a more critical look at the business of 'dirty tricks'. Similarly in Europe there is the gradual development of a highly intelligent new type of spy story that often has a political and even a moral message. Douglas Hurd, Andrew Osmond, Robert Rostand (an American who is almost an enfranchised citizen of the world) and Hubert Monteilhet are all in their different ways highly articulate practitioners of this art: they are didactic without being propagandist or 'factionist'.

The settings for future spy stories will probably switch from Europe to the Far East and Africa, from Jamaica to Seychelles and the Maldives, to Mauritius instead of Haiti. I also have a hunch that the influence of the Chinese Secret Service in all its ramifications will eventually be felt by such writers, though not for some time yet. The Intelligence Services of China have until now been greatly underestimated by the West. This is largely due to the fact that the West has refused to believe that China has an effective Secret Service at all, simply because the Chinese methods of espionage are often based on a combination of esoteric processes and a healthy common-sense allied to highly intelligent analysis of legitimate fact-finding.

This is altogether too complex a combination for Westerners yet to assimilate.

One of the quirks of the spy story at present is a tendency among many authors to worship obscurity for its own sake. The Great God is Technology, the theme that technology baffles brains. Technology is the new bullshit, only far worse than the old spit-and-polish bullshit. But this adoration of obscurity goes much further than that. It has found its way insidiously into the medium of television spy films, where spy story writers can hide behind all manner of nonsense. Nobody tells anybody anything, least of all the reader or viewer. Take, for example, this snippet from a television film, *Dangerous Knowledge*:

> 'What's behind it all? Can you tell me?'
> 'We must find out what he's got. If anything.'
> 'It sounds terribly vague.'
> 'We deal in shadows and whispers.'

As Nancy Banks-Smith commented on this mind-teasing dialogue: 'Not so much hush-hush as a what-eh-what?'

In many respects, when it escapes from the compulsion towards total obfuscation, the spy story may become something more akin to a fascinating intellectual exercise. Just as Edgar Allan Poe first awoke an interest in cryptography in literary circles so the spy story author of the 1980s may give us the 'new look' espionage of mathematically applied astrology techniques, of psychometric readings and analysis, of telepathy and ESP, of the laboratory of the occult and, not least, the application of that forecasting work, *I Ching*. The Chinese have long used *I Ching* as a consultative work in Intelligence when all else failed (Mao Tse-tung himself praised the work); the Germans dabbled in astrology in the Second World War (even using pendulum-swingers to try to track British submarines); while the Russians have for years been working on psychometric readings and the application of extra-sensory perception to Intelligence work. In all this the spy story has drawn nearer to science fiction: in some areas the two types of story may merge, and indeed, in the work of Edmund Cooper this has already happened.

Increasingly, too, the reader of espionage tales of the future must be on his guard against blatant propaganda heavily disguised as spy fiction. The Russians have paved the way with this in recent years, but the Americans have not lagged far behind. *The Penkovsky Papers* are still the subject of much argument as to whether they are fact or fiction, faked by the CIA, as Mr Victor Zorza seems to suggest, or 'a last message and testament from a brave and intelligent man', as Robert Conquest avers.

The list of authors included in this book is, inevitably, a selective one. Some of the writers who in my opinion should have had an entry have been omitted because they have declined to give information about themselves; sometimes their reluctance has been due to a dislike or fear of being dubbed spy fiction authors. In other instances I have still included them, if inevitably provided with scanty material. The number of names originally considered was more than 600, though many of them were short story writers who produced fast and furiously in the inter-war years but have not been heard from since. Some omissions will naturally arouse the wrath of some readers; perhaps rather fewer of the inclusions will also be hotly questioned. What I have tried to do throughout is to cover as wide a range of styles and types both past and present and to stress especially all links between fact and fiction and fiction and fact. Because, unless this link is perceived, the modern spy story loses much of its vitality and purpose. A novel by Nicholas Luard can be regarded as a salutory firing of a warning shot across the bows of the CIA or the KGB. Sometimes an author who has written only one spy story can be of greater interest than another who has written thirty: Michael Innes is one such example. Some young and little known contemporary authors who have not yet written much seem to have things of importance to say, while other tired old scribes past and present who have produced a score or more novels do not seem to warrant a mention. But choice is always difficult: E. Howard Hunt—surprise, surprise!—is in, but because of his CIA/Watergate associations rather than his prose.

The topography and the secret lingo of the spy story are separate and yet inseparable subjects. So, too, is the game of spotting the real-life characters behind such people as Richard Hannay, 'Bulldog' Drummond, Ashenden and James Bond. It is because there really are thirty-nine steps near Broadstairs that Buchan's novel can become an excuse for an afternoon's exploration. Similarly, it is a positive delight of a summer's evening to discover that the improbably named Pett Bottom in Fleming's novels actually exists in East Kent and that one can have a splendid dinner at the Duck Inn, opposite the cottage where James Bond lived as a boy. And the thought of Somerset Maugham having personally directed British Secret Service activities inside Russia in the First World War (with quotations from authenticated documents to prove it) makes Ashenden that much more credible. I have heard on excellent authority that the KGB go through Len Deighton's novels with great diligence and that they spent some time checking on STUCEN and the island mentioned in *Spy Story* where anthrax experiments were carried out in the Second World War (yes, that island actually exists: its name is Gruinard, two miles north of Ross and Cromarty, and it is still banned to the public). It is probably comforting to the really aged romantics of the 1970s to learn that the original 'Bulldog' Drummond is still alive today in the person of Gerard Fairlie.

At the end of the book I have included a glossary of abbreviations, terms, places and jargon used in the twilight world of Intelligence. This has become important for two reasons: first, that increasingly in spy fiction a great many such initials and phrases are picked straight from real life, while others are invented; secondly, the readership of people who are actually in the spy game has risen enormously in the past twenty years. Indeed, any author who can sell to the personnel of his own and rival Secret Services alone can be a bestseller. An American author who writes under the pseudonym of 'Trevanian' creates characters so true to life in the Intelligence world that they frequently make 'in' jokes to tell readers among the professional spooks that they know what it is all about. It is useful today to have a glossary beside one when reading spy fiction and this is being added to every day.

There has always been a sound literary excuse for a 'Spooks' Club (see appendix at the end of book), but it is even more gratifying to learn that there really is such a club and that its members all have coded names. That in itself is almost a good reason for this book. And on that impish and somewhat secretive note I close.

DONALD McCORMICK

A–Z of contributors

Martha Albrand (b. Rostock, Germany, 8 September 1914)

Born Heidi Huberta, Martha Albrand was educated privately under tutors in Germany and later at schools in Switzerland, Italy, France and England. She had a Lutheran upbringing, and this was linked with a strong sense of internationalism. Starting her career as a journalist in Europe, she had her first book published in German at the age of 17, using the pseudonym of 'Katrin Holland'. Later she used another pen-name, 'Christine Lambert', but her best work has undoubtedly been done under the name of Martha Albrand.

She went to the United States in 1937 and, ten years later, was naturalised as an American citizen. Her mystery and crime stories have met with much success. Most were serialised before publication in the now defunct *Saturday Evening Post*, and many of them have been translated into German, Danish, Italian, French, Swedish and even Arabic. Those novels involving espionage plots have included *Nightmare in Copenhagen* (US 1954), which was highly praised, *The Story that Could Not Be Told* (US 1956), *Meet Me Tonight* (US 1960) and *A Door Fell Shut* (US 1966). The last-named is the story of the return of Bronsky, a violinist of renown, to his home town, to give a concert in East Berlin. A CIA agent working there is involved in the defection to the West of Cassan, a Russian, and Bronsky is unexpectedly brought into this East-West intrigue and the escape of the Russian over the Berlin Wall. Martha Albrand has won a number of literary awards for her crime fiction. Her husband is Sydney J. Lamon.

Ted Allbeury (b. Stockport, 24 October 1917)

Theodore Edward Le Bouthillier, Allbeury's father, an officer in the Black Watch Regiment, was killed a few days before the end of the First World War, and Ted Allbeury was brought up by his grand-parents in Birmingham. He started life as a foundry worker, attended evening classes to become a tracer, junior draughtsman and, finally, a jig and tool designer. For good measure he taught himself French and German in his spare time and qualified as a fighter pilot. But when war broke out and he packed in his job to join the RAF, he was barred from entry because he was in a reserved occupation and, with that crass stupidity that only the British seem to possess in their dispensation of justice, he was prosecuted and fined. Without a job and short of funds, Allbeury in desperation answered an advertisement in *The Times* for 'linguists for work with the Army: no possible promotion above lance-corporal'. He went to the back-room of a barber's shop in Trafalgar Square and, after being given a test, was accepted into the Army Intelligence Corps. To avoid complications, the Army put down his occupation as 'labourer' and paid his fine, which shows that Intelligence Services are rather more sensible about legal stupidities than most others. Notwithstanding the advertisement stipulation that there would be no promotion beyond lance-corporal, Allbeury ended the war with the rank of Lieut.-Colonel. He served first in the UK, then in Ethiopia as military liaison officer to the Emperor and finally in Germany at the tail end of the war.

He found it difficult to settle down to civilian life and various sales management jobs followed before he went into advertising and public relations. For two years he ran a pirate radio station, Radio 390, from a fort in the Thames Estuary, playing music and giving his own chats to something like fourteen million listeners. Some acknowledgement of Allbeury's efforts in this direction was made recently when he was appointed a member of the BBC's Advisory Council. His writing career began—quite unexpectedly, he says— as late as 1971 with the publication in England of *A Choice of Enemies*, a spy story that brought praise from a wide range of critics, not least because he not only knew what he was writing about, but how to make it sound convincing. 'My inclinations have been to stick to what I know,' he says. 'Having been in the spy business, I know what it's like and how it all works. Anyone can mug up on the KGB's weapons or the CIA's methods, but only someone who has done it knows what it feels like to arrest a man, to shoot a man, assess a deadly opponent, chase and be chased.' Allbeury has shown how the spy story has progressed not only since Fleming, but since Le Carré and Deighton, too. He gets his mixture right—the correct amounts of excitement, thrills, dialogue, accurate background and know-how. With Deighton the details, the technology are like new toys, paraded for his own amusement. Le Carré becomes too introspective. Fleming's background detail seems almost artificial today against that of Allbeury. That first book was enormously popular on both sides of the Atlantic and the *New York Times* picked it up as one of the ten best thrillers of the year. It was partly autobiographical, if only in minor details. Ted Bailey, the hero, also found himself recruited into Military Intelligence through a barber's shop in Trafalgar Square; the heroine is a Pole named Grazyna, just like Allbeury's present wife. Bailey is practically blackmailed back into Intelligence work twenty-five years after the war. He comes up against a KGB agent he had first met at the end of the war, and finds the spy game just as ruthless as it was then, but played with computers.

This book was followed by *Snowball* (UK 1973), *The Palomino Blonde* (UK 1974), *The Special Collection* (UK 1975) and *The Only Good German* (UK 1976). The theme of the infiltration of communism into Britain is strong in Allbeury's last two books; Lord Chalfont said of *The Special Collection* that 'the whole story has an immense topical significance . . . I hope that people who read it will not regard it entirely as fiction.' At the time of writing two more Allbeury books are on the way to publication—*Moscow Quadrille* and *The Man With the President's Mind*.

Few people who have been in Intelligence have the same flair for writing about it as Allbeury: he gets his facts right, and manages to convey the flavour of the business; the finished product is highly professional. Today he talks of it all with some feeling: 'When you come out, the greatest problem is that you know too much about people because your training has been so good—it has to be, or you wouldn't survive. I still not only know when people are telling lies, I know almost before they do that they are *going* to, and that's terrible. It was a dreadful business to stop doing this in private life. Unconsciously, you dug holes (as you traditionally did in the job) waiting for people to fall into them.' Another interesting comment of Allbeury's is that 'being brought up by and amongst a pack of women gives one the ideal preparation for the life of an Intelligence officer. It is a life where your instinct is often more important than your knowledge. Without having to be effeminate, this is something you can learn from being with women.'

Allbeury lives with his wife and two small daughters at Lamberhurst in Kent and works at the bottom of his garden in what he calls 'my apple shed'. He also writes under the name of 'Richard Butler'.

Margery Allingham (b. 1904; d. Colchester, 30 June 1966)
The daughter of H. J. Allingham, who wrote boys' fiction, Margery Allingham was educated at the Perse High School for Girls,

Cambridge, and the Polytechnic School of Speech Training. She considered the stage for a career, but instead produced a first novel, a pirate story called *Blackerchief Dick* (UK 1921), when she was only seventeen. Six years later she was well on the road to professional success, and had married Philip Youngman Carter, a journalist and illustrator.

Margery Allingham's chief claim to fame was as a skilled teller of detective stories and her celebrated character Albert Campion, 'well-bred and a trifle absent-minded', was immensely popular in the 1930s. Occasionally she would graft an espionage theme on to a detective story, as in *Traitor's Purse* (UK 1941) in which Campion is temporarily attached to the Secret Service in order to uncover a plot to bring down the government by a cunningly conceived artificial inflation. In *Cargo of Eagles* (UK 1968), Campion again links up with Intelligence, to investigate smuggling and extortion in the Essex countryside.

Eric Ambler (b. London, 28 June 1909)

Educated at Colfe's Grammar School, Lewisham, and London University, Eric Ambler worked as an engineer's apprentice and an advertisement copywriter before he published his first novel, *The Dark Frontier* (UK 1936). This was far from being one of his best books, but it marked a revolutionary, disillusioned approach to the spy story, particularly reflected in what one of the characters, Professor Bairstow, had to say: 'It looked as if there would always be wars . . . What else could you expect from a balance of power adjusted in terms of land, of arms, of man-power and of materials: in terms, in other words, of Money? . . . Wars were made by those who had the power to upset the balance, to tamper with international money and money's worth.'

Ambler sounded the death-knell of the Hannays and the 'Bulldog' Drummonds. He had begun to write in a period of intense depression for all thinking people who, in the 1930s, realised the hollowness of the politicians' pretence that the First World War was 'the war to end all wars'. Aggressive forces were on the march all over Europe and in the Balkans, democracy was being spelt out as a dirty word, and the private manufacture of arms was aiding the enemies of democracy rather more than the countries who actually produced the weapons. Ambler struck a note of neutralism in the spy story, sharply and astringently enlightening the reader that in espionage one side was really as bad as the other and that spies and spy-catchers were not only mainly unheroic, but very often of minor significance and unpleasant mien. In short, the agents and spies were not splendid patriots, but hired killers—just as they were in Elizabethan times when they bumped off Kit Marlowe! Ambler was not a prophet in a didactic sense, but his stories of espionage revealed the truth and obliterated the romance. *The Uncommon Danger* (UK 1937) had much the same message as *The Dark Frontier*.

With *Epitaph for a Spy* (UK 1938) Ambler came into his own as a highly skilled, thoughtful, realistic and meticulous writer of spy stories. He had done his homework on the spy story and was determined to modernise and improve the genre. Many years later, in his introduction to *To Catch a Spy* (UK 1964), he revealed that his research into the realms of spy fiction went back to Erskine Childers. More recently, when commenting on a review in the *Times Literary Supplement* which said that all Ambler's earlier books were influenced by the Ashenden ethos, he replied that they were indeed: 'The breakthrough was entirely Mr Maugham's . . . there is, after all, a lot of Simenon and a satisfactory quantity of W. R. Burnett, but only one *Ashenden*.' Perhaps this is one reason why Ambler is a favourite writer of professional Intelligence agents all over the world. While Le Carré is the preferred reading of members of the British SIS and Len Deighton has his devotees in America, Ambler undoubtedly wins adherents in the 'spook' community all over the world. He has the gift of making a commonplace incident seem dramatic and horrifying. What is even more important, Ambler is the most admirable exponent of the probable and the possible as against the improbable and the miraculous coincidence. It is one of the paradoxes of spy fiction that the 'in writers'—i.e. those who have had inside knowledge of 'the game'— tend to write about the improbable rather more than those authors who have never in any way been engaged in Intelligence work. Ambler belongs to the latter category and it is surprisingly but nevertheless recognisably true that he has been far and away the most accurate of all modern spy fiction writers right down to the smallest detail. In all Ambler's books the chain of circumstances is rational and probable, his leading characters are ordinary, cautious people who find themselves caught up in disastrous situations. The detail is faultless, yet Ambler, as far as one knows, was never employed by the Secret Service or any similar organisation.

'I have to be very careful,' he says modestly, 'because I know so little, you see. But perhaps that isn't the same for everybody.' Ambler is also quick to detect errors of accuracy in other works of spy fiction. He points out that 'it does seem rather odd that a man who was in Naval Intelligence, like Fleming, should have got the Golden Horn mixed up with the Bosphorus [*From Russia with Love*]. It doesn't make one entirely confident about Naval Intelligence, does it?'

In *Epitaph for a Spy* Ambler introduced a political element into his work. Even here he was being factual—and singularly prophetic, hinting at the possible emergence of defectors like Philby, someone such as Schimmler who is converted from being a moderate Social Democrat to a Communist. This is echoed again in *Cause for Alarm* (UK 1938) and *The Mask of Dimitrios* (UK 1939), in the latter of which there are objective and not unpleasant portraits of a Greek Communist and a Soviet agent. This would have been unheard of in the Buchan-'Sapper'-Le Queux era: had any author then described a Soviet agent as one who could spare the time to do a good turn to someone who had got into trouble through no fault of his own, he would undoubtedly have been dubbed as a fellow-traveller. But such was Ambler's skill and objectivity, his freedom from any hint of propaganda or prejudice and his talent for telling a lively story, that he was never challenged on this account, but only welcomed as a long-needed antidote to the old school of spy thriller writers.

Ambler also chose a different type of capital city for the setting for his books. Whereas hitherto such stories tended to be set in Paris, Berlin, Vienna and Rome, or the smarter hotels of the Riviera, Ambler chose the seedier, but more topical and infinitely more fascinating cities of Istanbul, Belgrade, Sofia. *The Mask of Dimitrios*, which in many respects is Ambler's masterpiece, opens with the discovery in a mortuary of the dead body of Dimitrios. With consummate craftsmanship, the author uses the lecturer and detective-writer, Latimer, to trace the life story of the mysterious Dimitrios. The minor characters are superbly drawn and full of interest in themselves. When Donald McCormick was researching his biography of Sir Basil Zaharoff, *Pedlar of Death*, he was convinced that Eric Ambler must have based some of *The Mask of Dimitrios* on first-hand knowledge of Zaharoff's early career, when that super-arms-salesman was a brothel tout in Istanbul. But a letter from Ambler revealed that the story of Dimitrios was thought up on a journey by train across Europe shortly before the war and that there was no connection with the Zaharoff saga. This merely

24

exemplifies further the astonishing authenticity of Ambler, which no other spy fiction writer seems able to capture with such regularity and ease.

Journey Into Fear (UK 1940) was his next novel and then in 1941 Ambler was commissioned in the Royal Artillery, serving until the end of the war, when he held the rank of Lieut.-Colonel. In 1943 he served in Italy and from 1944–46 he was Assistant Director of Army Kinematography at the War Office, being awarded the US Bronze Star in 1946 when he was released from the Services. Married twice, Ambler has travelled widely and until comparatively recently lived in California. Today he lives in Switzerland, spending a few months each year in London. Once, doubtless with tongue in cheek, he suggested that an international spy reserve should be created and called the 'E. Phillips Oppenheim Park'. He recommended that the Ile du Lévant, off the Côte d'Azur, should be selected as the ideal location since it abounded in Vauban and Napoleonic fortresses for visiting spies to spy on. Disabled ex-Servicemen would provide a team of dupes for the amateur and escapes by boat to the mainland could be run at scheduled intervals and at dead of night. Female spies in the traditional black satin and 'a small atomic pile' would be further attractions! Knowing how Mr Ambler always seems to get his facts right, doubtless he knew then that half the Ile du Lévant was a secret testing ground for French rockets and the other half was a nudist colony!

After the war when the USSR and the Western Allies turned sour on one another and the 'Cold War' began, Ambler's 'neutral' approach to spy fiction became a little dated. Most of his later books were given different titles in America, for one reason or another: *The Night Comers* (UK 1956) was published in the US as *A State of Siege* and *Dirty Story* (UK 1967) in the rather more obviously gun-toting style of *This Gun for Hire*; even *The Mask of Dimitrios* became *A Coffin for Dimitrios*. Ambler's wartime experience in kinematography encouraged him to explore the world of films and in 1947 he wrote and produced *The October Man*; his various film scenarios have included *The Passionate Friends*, *Gigolo and Gigolette*, *The Cruel Sea* and *Wreck of the Mary Deare*. His own novel *The Light of Day* (UK 1962) was filmed as *Topkapi*.

Despite the fact that some of his earlier work may now seem dated, the quality of Ambler's work still compares well with anything that has been written since. He retains his gentle ironical style and used it to good effect in *The Intercom Conspiracy* (UK 1970), which has been described as 'a conscienceless send-up on the Emperor's Clothes principle of the whole idea of secret intelligence'. The book was presented in dossier-style (*see* Dennis Wheatley) as a collection of purported tape-transcripts, letters, etc. The book opens with this statement: 'It was on May 31 of last year, at Geneva's Cointrin Airport, that the man who called himself Charles Latimer disappeared . . .' The man who called himself Latimer was the hero of *The Mask of Dimitrios*: Eric Ambler had decided to kill him off, despite pleas that he should be revived.

Kingsley Amis (b. London, 16 April 1922)

Kingsley William Amis was educated at the City of London School and St John's College, Oxford. From 1949–61 he was Lecturer in English at University College, Swansea, and in 1958–59 served as Visiting Fellow in Creative Writing at Princeton University. It was during this period that his novel *Lucky Jim* (UK 1954) became a bestseller and a popular film. Then from 1961–63 Amis was Fellow at Peterhouse, Cambridge and in 1967–68 returned to the States as Visiting Professor of English at Vanderbilt University.

While Amis has been at his best as a gentle satirist of the social scene with a nice sense of comedy in his character-drawing, he has shown more than a passing interest in the spy story, notably in his work *Colonel Sun* (UK 1968), written under the pen-name of 'Robert Markham'. Three years earlier, he produced *The James Bond Dossier* (UK 1965), an amusing analysis of the adventures, the foibles and quirks, the ancestry and credentials of Ian Fleming's larger-than-life hero. Clinically, Amis sets the record on Bond right: 'It's inaccurate . . . to describe James Bond as a *spy*,' he writes. 'Vivienne Michel, narrator of *The Spy Who Loved Me*, gave Bond a wrong label out of desire for euphony and simplicity . . . *The Medium-Grade Civil Servant Who Loved Me* would have been more accurate as well as more acceptable. Mr Bond's claims to be considered a *counter-spy*, one who operates against the agents of unfriendly Powers, are rather more substantial.'

Amis is married to Elizabeth Jane Howard, the novelist.

Evelyn Anthony (b. London, 3 July 1928)

Evelyn Anthony says her upbringing was 'decidedly erratic. I was expected to marry, not work, and I did neither until my mid-twenties.' Her father was a naval officer and a brilliant wartime inventor, but his talents were never adequately rewarded by a curmudgeonly Service and Government. She was educated at the Convent of the Sacred Heart, Roehampton, until 1944. Her first short story was published in *Everybody's Weekly* in 1949 and her first historical novel, *Imperial Highness*, appeared in 1953: it was based on the early years of Catherine the Great. Since then she has written twenty-one books in all, one of which, *The Tamarind Seed* (UK 1971), was filmed in 1973. Other spy fiction books include *The Rendezvous* (UK 1966), *The Assassin* (UK 1970), *The Poellenberg Inheritance* (UK 1972), *The Occupying Power* (UK 1973), which won the *Yorkshire Post* Fiction Prize, *The Malaspiga Exit* (UK 1974) and *The Persian Ransom* (UK 1975), the last-named being about a mission to Iran by the chairman of an oil company, which precipitates an unexpected trail of kidnap, blackmail and intrigue. Andrew Hope, writing in the London *Evening Standard* of *The Malaspiga Exit*, said 'The formula of a brave, beautiful and unmarried girl confronting the forces of evil is a well-tested one for story-tellers: Evelyn Anthony adds extra ingredients—a swift narrative, credible emotions, a whiff of sexual passion.'

Anthony insists on authenticity for the locations of her stories: 'The Nazis and the KGB were material for my early plots, but now the settings are more international—oil, terrorism, drugs . . . The central character is usually a woman, but with very strong male support.' She has never worked in Intelligence, although she 'was once asked to do so and refused. I have had friends who worked against the Germans in the war and learnt a lot by listening.' Her favourite spy-story writer is John Le Carré: 'I believe that spy thrillers should stick to the possible and eschew too much fantasy, also brutal and explicit sex. I don't think that is relevant.' She is married to Michael Ward-Thomas, has six children and lives in Ireland.

Gordon Ashe: *see* John Creasey

Francis Beeding
This was the pseudonym of John Leslie Palmer (b. 1885; d. London, 5 August 1944) and Hilary Adam St George Saunders (b. 14 January 1898; d. Nassau, 16 December 1951). Although the major part of

Palmer's work was pseudonymous, he was highly regarded both as a writer and as a literary and dramatic critic under his own name. 'A critic of distinction and discernment', said one obituary, while *The Times* commented that 'by his death the world of English letters has lost a critic of candour and a writer of distinction'. It was perhaps remarkable that two such able writers as Palmer and St George Saunders, with thirteen years' difference in their ages, should be able to form so remarkable a partnership as that of 'Francis Beeding', writing some forty novels under this name. St George Saunders attributed the success of their joint effort to the fact that Palmer was the creator of the characters and the wizard of dialogue, but bored with actual narrative and descriptions, whereas he revelled in this part of their work. During the Second World War Saunders wrote a number of non-fiction books under his own name dealing with various aspects of the British war effort, notably works on the Commandos and the Paratroopers. From 1946–50 he was Librarian of the House of Commons, and he was working on a history of the Bahamas when he died.

Many of the Francis Beeding books were historical novels or of the detective genre, but quite a few were concerned with the Secret Service. Like other novels of this type of the inter-war years, they included the patriotic bias of the period; as a blurb to one of the Beeding books, *The Six Proud Walkers* (UK 1928), put it, 'The hero, his delightful fiancée and his indomitable friend are English; and the villains are a cosmopolitan crew who stick at nothing.' One of the very few spy stories set against the background of the old League of Nations at Geneva came in Beeding's *The Five Flamboys* (UK 1929), doubtless owing much to Saunders' knowledge of both Switzerland and the League HQ. In this book one Angus McGuffie was found murdered after he had started a letter to the Foreign Office which read 'The names of the Five Flamboys are . . .'; he had got no further. As in so many of the Beeding books, the central figure was the urbane and polite Colonel Granby, who set out to track down the Flamboys. Many of the Granby Secret Service stories were set in France, including *The League of Discontent* (UK 1930), *The Three Fishers* (UK 1931), *The Four Armourers* (UK 1931) and *Take it Crooked* (UK 1932). *The One Sane Man* (UK 1934) was one of the best of the Beeding Secret Service stories, which became increasingly topical during the late 'thirties. In *The Black Arrows* (UK 1938) the authors, taking note of the rising tide of fascism in Europe, introduced a new hero, John Couper, and a new villain,

Jiacomo Berutti. The story was set in Venice and told of an attempt to sink a major unit of the British Mediterranean Fleet by a pirate submarine controlled by the Society of the Black Arrows, an extreme fascist organisation led by men who were disappointed because Mussolini was not doing enough to advance their cause.

With the advent of the Second World War the Beeding stories became even more topical. *The Secret Weapon* (UK 1940) concerns a Secret Service quest for the formula of a hush-hush weapon which Hitler is developing. The agent hero goes to Germany, actually meets Hitler and Goering, is involved in the Polish campaign and finally escapes back to England. Later, for some reason not disclosed, but believed to have been due to the sometimes obscure workings of wartime censorship, the title of this book was changed to *Not A Bad Show*.

Captain Geoffrey Martin Bennett: *see* Sea-Lion

Kenneth Benton (b. 4 March 1909)

If ever there was a case of a writer of spy fiction who spent his entire career in the kind of job which would provide him with the background material essential to his first books, it is Kenneth Carter Benton. Educated at Wolverhampton Grammar School and London University, where he obtained a degree in modern languages, he taught and studied languages in Florence and Vienna before joining the Passport Control Office in Vienna as an assistant. There he met his wife, Peggie Pollock, who also worked in the Legation. They had just returned from their honeymoon when, in March 1938, the Nazis marched into Vienna. Shortly afterwards his chief, the Passport Control Officer (PCO was a traditional cover for British espionage), was arrested by the Gestapo and expelled. Later, when witnesses were being interrogated in preparation for an espionage trial, it was decided in London to transfer Benton at forty-eight hours' notice to Riga in Latvia, where he was appointed Vice-Consul in charge of passport control. The following year, when war broke out, he was not allowed to join his Territorial regiment, but 'frozen' in the Foreign Service for the duration. In June 1940, the Russians took Latvia and the Bentons had to remain in Riga for three months to deal with immigration matters. By this time all routes home, except for the Trans-Siberian, had been closed by the

Germans and they had to return to London via Moscow, Vladivostok, Japan and Canada.

In London they were both drafted to the counter-espionage branch of the Intelligence Service and sent to Madrid to take part in an all-out effort to prevent German spies from penetrating the United Kingdom. In 1944 Benton was transferred to Rome as Acting 2nd Secretary. Leaving Rome in 1948, he was posted back there during 1950–53, then back to Madrid (1953–56). This was followed by a spell in the Foreign Office and postings to Lima and Rio de Janeiro, where he was Counsellor of Embassy. He retired from the Diplomatic Service in 1968, having been awarded the CMG two years previously.

Although in his service career he had been engaged almost continuously in writing reports on politics and allied subjects, it was not until 1967, when he visited a goldmine in Minas Gerais, that he thought about writing fiction. His first novel, *Twenty-Fourth Level* (UK 1969), was snapped up almost immediately by a publisher and since then he has produced a number of novels in the spy fiction genre—*Sole Agent* (UK 1970), *Spy in Chancery* (UK 1972), *Craig and the Jaguar* (UK 1973), *Craig and the Tunisian Tangle* (UK 1974) and *Craig and the Midas Touch* (UK 1975). Benton is in the 1970s tradition of matter-of-fact realism in spy fiction. His most recent book, *A Single Monstrous Act* (UK 1976), concerns a coven of violent, left-wing anarchists who plan a series of outrages to pave the way for a revolutionary take-over in Britain. Leading them is Professor Thaxton, whose personality seduces impressionable students and whose sexual prowess ensures him informers inside the ranks of government.

Don Betteridge: *see* Bernard Newman

John Bingham (b. York, 3 November 1908)
Son of the seventh Baron Clanmorris (Ireland), John Michael Ward Bingham succeeded to the title in 1960. After a conventional education at Cheltenham College and spending nearly three years in France and Germany learning languages, he started work on the *Hull Daily Mail*, covering everything 'from flower shows, music and drama to murders and missing trawlers'. He was subsequently transferred to the now defunct *Sunday Dispatch* for which he wrote

general articles and a humorous column, later becoming Picture Editor. His first book was *My Name is Michael Sibley* (UK 1952) and subsequent books have been published in the US, Sweden, Norway, Denmark, France, Holland, Germany, Italy and Japan. A member of the Crime Writers' Association, he has written a number of spy fiction novels, including *Murder Plan Six* (UK 1958), *Night's Black Agent* (UK 1960), *The Double Agent* (UK 1966) and—a new departure in this genre—*God's Defector* (UK 1976). The last-named is about a Catholic priest who, after receiving many secrets in the confessional, defects from the Church in order to aid one government against another in an intrigue involving many important individuals. Not so far fetched a subject as it might seem: the Marxist priests of Guatemala have long since organised their own cosy little network, the COSDEGUA (Confederation of Diocesan Priests of Guatemala) which is Soviet-infiltrated and aims at revolution, while as early as 1952 it was announced that Father Aligheri Tondi, Professor of the Gregorian Academy at the Vatican, had been found to be a Soviet agent 'deliberately planted in the Jesuit Order'.

Alfred Hitchcock has filmed three of Bingham's books, including *Murder Plan Six* (with James Mason) for television. The author is married and has two children; both his wife and one of his children are also writers.

John Blackburn (b. Corbridge-on-Tyne, 26 June 1923)
John Fenwick Blackburn spent his early life in a country vicarage and was educated at Haileybury College and Durham University. During the Second World War he was in the Merchant Navy and in 1952–53 he served with the Control Commission in Berlin and, so he says, 'met several associates of "the Game". The main character, Vanin, in *The Gaunt Woman*, was based on a Russian defector who was kidnapped by the East Germans and driven through the Brandenburger Tor in a box labelled "radio spares".' Blackburn has published twenty-three novels and some short stories, his first being *A Scent of New Mown Hay* (UK 1958), which was on the not un-familiar theme of the mad scientist. His spy novels include *Dead Man Running* (UK 1960), *The Gaunt Woman* (UK 1962) (later filmed by Universal) and *Colonel Bogus* (UK 1967). Most of the locations for Blackburn's books are in Germany, Russia and the United Kingdom. He holds the belief that most professional agents

in the spy game are motivated by blackmail, brainwashing or fanaticism rather than finance. 'During the war,' he says, 'I was once approached by an agent in Portuguese East Africa with a view to selling Merchant Navy code books. The offer was most tempting, but fear rather than patriotism made me refuse.' Blackburn, who is a member of the Crime Writers' Association, is married and lives in London.

Phyllis Bottome (b. Rochester, Kent, 31 May 1884; d. 22 August 1963)
The daughter of the Rev. W. Macdonald Bottome, of New York, and Margaret Leatham, of Yorkshire, Phyllis Bottome's grand-mother was Margaret Bottome, the writer, philanthropist and founder of the King's Daughters' Society of the United States. She was educated privately and from the age of nine to sixteen she lived in the United States. Her first book, *Raw Material*, was published as early as 1905, but it was not until after the First World War that she came into her own as a writer. During that war she was a Belgian relief worker under the Ministry of Munitions. She married Capt. A. E. Forbes Dennis in 1917 and subsequently lived in Austria, France, Italy and Switzerland. Her husband was appointed Intelligence Officer at Marseilles towards the end of the war and after the Armistice became Passport Control Officer in Vienna. For most of her life she moved in what are sometimes tactfully called Intelligence circles and there is a probability that she was to some extent closely involved in 'the game'. Curiously, she made relatively little use of this experience except for one spy novel, *The Lifeline* (UK 1946), and *The Mortal Storm* (UK 1937), probably her best-known and certainly her most successful book, as it exposed the workings of the Nazi régime in Germany. 'If a writer is true to his characters, they will give him his plot,' she wrote. 'Observations must play second fiddle to integrity.' She and her husband gave tuition to Ian Fleming as a youth and encouraged him to write: under her mentor-ship young Fleming wrote an unpublished short story, *Death on Two Occasions*. Phyllis Bottome was interested in psychology and the psycho-analytical system of Dr Alfred Adler, whose biographer she became.

John Braine (b. Bradford, 13 April 1922)

John Gerard Braine was educated at St Bede's Grammar School, Bradford, and became in quick succession a furniture shop assistant, a bookshop assistant, a laboratory assistant and then an assistant in the Bingley Public Library. He served in the Royal Navy in the Second World War and from 1949–51 was Chief Assistant at Bingley Public Library. He had enormous success with his first novel, *Room at the Top* (UK 1957), which netted him more than £10,000 and was filmed the following year. Braine, whose comments on modern life and politics are forthright and uncompromising, is one of a number of authors of his generation who have moved steadily to the right in recent years. In 1975 he demonstrated this by joining General Sir Walter Walker's Civil Assistance organisation, intended to aid Britain in any crisis in which law and order and vital services might have broken down. Needless to say, Braine finds no difficulty in pinning the trouble for Britain's ills on communist infiltration and influence. Perhaps it was no coincidence that in this same year Braine produced *The Pious Agent* (UK 1975). One critic somewhat tartly commented: 'Given Mr Braine's anti-communism and his slightly dotty materialism it was inevitable that sooner or later he should produce a spy story.' In this book he made his hero Xavier, a British counter-espionage killer whose first assignment was to assassinate President Kennedy at the instigation of the CIA. Xavier was well portrayed as a devout Roman Catholic, but somehow seemed to lack conviction as a hero. One has the feeling that this book was a dummy run and that something may yet emerge as a spy story based on projecting Civil Assistance into the near future.

André Léon Brouillard: *see* Pierre Nord

John Buchan (b. Perth, 26 August 1875; d. Montreal, 11 February 1940)

The eldest son of the Rev. John Buchan, of Boughton Green, Peeblesshire, John Buchan was educated at Glasgow University and Brasenose College, Oxford. He had an outstanding career at Oxford, winning the Stanhope Essay Prize in 1897 and the Newdigate Prize the following year. He became a barrister of the Middle Temple in 1901 and from later that year until 1903 was private secretary to the High Commissioner for South Africa, Lord Milner. Thus Buchan became a member of that inner circle of bright young men who were close to Milner and whose political advancement dates from that time. Indeed, perhaps as a result of this influence, Buchan regarded himself as a politician first and a writer second. He was attached to the HQ Staff of the British Army in France from 1916–17, being given the rank of temporary Lieut.-Colonel. When Lloyd George became Prime Minister, Buchan was made Director of Information and this was followed by a spell as Director of Intelligence, a brief interlude in Buchan's career which is masked in some mystery. Nevertheless it was during the First World War that Buchan made the acquaintance of a young Army officer named Edmund Ironside (later to become Field-Marshal Lord Ironside of Archangel) who was then concerned with Intelligence in Russia. Buchan later admitted that it was on Ironside that he modelled the character of Richard Hannay in *The Thirty-nine Steps* (UK 1915).

Hannay was the spy-catcher incomparable of that era, yet one cannot help wondering whether Buchan really discerned his remarkable talent in the young Ironside, or whether this was a case of hindsight—that is to say, whether Buchan, on being pressed by clubland friends to name his original of Hannay, just put forward Ironside as a suitable candidate. For it was after *The Thirty-nine Steps* was published that Ironside entered Intelligence work. This book more than any other paved the way to Buchan's success as a popular novelist. Long before its publication he had dabbled in such subjects as *Scholar-Gipsies* (UK 1896) and *History of Brasenose* (UK 1898). But *The Thirty-nine Steps* struck exactly the right note and, disregarding its more melodramatic episodes, it had all the ingredients of the successful spy story—topicality in the midst of war, an exciting chase in which the spy-catcher is pursued by the spy's agents, and a series of cinematic situations amidst splendid background scenery of moor and mountain which made the book a natural for one of Hitchcock's best films in the 'thirties. And not only in the 'thirties: it was remade in the post-Second World War period, starring Kenneth More. For sheer versatility and non-stop thrills, perhaps no fictional escape can compare with that of Hannay when, almost throughout the story, the hero is on the run. A man is murdered in his apartment and Hannay has to flee because he knows he will be suspected: 'I got out an atlas and looked at a big map of the British Isles. My notion was to get off to some wild district . . . I fixed on Galloway as the best place to go.' Eventually Hannay realises that he is up against a super-spy and his suspicion is confirmed when he finds somebody impersonating the First Sea Lord at a meeting of the Defence Council. At last Hannay, wanted for a murder he did not commit, manages to convince the War Cabinet that a nation's security is threatened. The quest is now for the 'house at the head of the thirty-nine steps': it may interest those who like tracking down such things that such a site exists on the low cliffs not far from Broadstairs. It just goes to show that Buchan, while not troubling himself about melodrama, opted for accuracy of background, whether this was in Galloway or Kent.

The character of Hannay was too good to waste on a single book. Wisely, Buchan the amateur writer became Buchan the professional and Hannay appears again in *Greenmantle* (UK 1916), which some consider to be the best of all the Hannay stories. As a contrast to *The Thirty-nine Steps*, in this book Hannay plays the spy instead of the spy-catcher, though Buchan never even applied this term to one who is 'on our side', such were the conventions of the day. Here Hannay is out to stop the Germans from using an Islamic prophet for their own ends. *Mister Standfast* (UK 1919) was a slight departure from Buchan's normal well-plotted patriotic path in his spy novels in that one of the characters, Lancelot Wake, is a conscientious objector who dies a heroic death while taking a vital message across a river. Just as the conventions of the day were that all heroes were strong, silent Englishmen, so even anyone as abnormal as a conscientious objector was then considered to be, had to be given redeeming features, heroic undertones. But perhaps this comment is unfair to Buchan: after all, he could hardly make a villain out of a conscientious objector and he could not allow Hannay to shoot him like a dog. Curiously, this book marks the transition of Buchan from a Milnerite Tory to a liberal-minded Conservative who, especially in later life, established good relations with people in all political parties and in many countries. Richard Hannay appeared in a number of other Buchan novels, as did Sandy Arbuthnot, his friend, among them *The Three Hostages* (UK 1924), in which Hannay and Arbuthnot tackle a gang of international criminals. By the time *The Courts of the Morning* (UK 1929) appeared Arbuthnot had become Lord Clanroyden and was involved in adventures in a Latin American republic.

Buchan's innate romanticism found its expression in his spy novels in a manner rarely seen in other writers of this genre. *Huntingtower* (UK 1922) is perhaps the best example. This was the story of a middle-aged man who set out in search of Romance with a capital R and found it in a whirl of wild adventure, with the aid of a young man, an imprisoned princess, a group of Bolsheviks and some Boy Scouts from the slums. For many this is one of Buchan's best books, though Nicholas Luard, who resembles Buchan in that both men are story-tellers first and foremost, expresses the view that 'the first half of *A Prince of the Captivity* (UK 1933) remains one of the truest and most spell-binding accounts of an agent working in the field ever written'. This view is important, not merely because it illustrates the story-telling qualities of Buchan, but because it shows how well Buchan's work stands up half a century later. Richard Hannay may seem a less credible figure today, but he is infinitely better than the heroes of 'Sapper', William Le Queux and Oppenheim, and was never such an appalling racialist snob as 'Bulldog' Drummond. Buchan, like Stevenson, Crockett and other Scottish writers, was at his best in describing an escape or a chase and the adventurous quality of his novels, his lively sense of keeping his characters on the move, were not excelled for many years.

In real life, politics counted for more than his books. From 1927–35 he was Conservative MP for the Scottish Universities (this was before the abolition of the University seats) and during this period he became Lord Commissioner of the Church of Scotland (1933–34). In 1939 he was created the first Baron Tweedsmuir of Elsfield, having been made a Companion of Honour three years previously. In the same year he was appointed Governor-General of Canada; in many respects this was a brilliant and unusual choice, for not only were he and his family extremely popular in Canada, on the eve of another world war, but he established the best possible relationship with America's President Roosevelt.

His hobbies were mountaineering, fishing, deer-stalking and exploring the countryside of his beloved Scotland, the terrain in which he sited so many of his adventure episodes. Julian Symons writes that 'Buchan blended invention with material drawn from his own knowledge in [his] tales, which are notable for their sense of scenery and weather rather than their plots.' But Buchan was far superior to most other novelists of the genre in the period in which he lived, and the scenery and the weather made admirable backdrops to the melodrama of the chase.

William Buckley Jr (b. New York, 24 November 1925)
Educated at the Universities of Mexico and Yale. An eloquent Conservative, Buckley is one of the very few articulate right-wing

intellectuals in the United States and easily their most persuasive spokesman. He is totally unpompous and, unlike many American right-wingers, has a delicious sense of humour. He founded the *National Review* in 1955 and has edited it ever since, as well as running a weekly column which is syndicated to 350 US newspapers and maintaining a lively weekly television programme. A devout Catholic and an anglophile, he has done more than anyone to promote a revival of conservative political thinking in America where, under Eisenhower, it had sunk to an abysmal level of inconclusive me-tooism. Though his books have been mainly nonfiction, his first effort in the field of spy fiction—*Saving the Queen* (US 1975)—was surprisingly and untypically sensational in that the most piquant situation in the novel was a Queen of England bedded with a CIA agent. Queen Caroline I ascends the throne of England in the early 1950s at the time when America had the hydrogen bomb and Stalin coveted it. The CIA suspects America's bomb secrets are being leaked all the way to the Kremlin from no less a source than Queen Caroline's court. Buckley's hero, Blackford Oakes, a darkly blond, rich, athletic, popular, good-looking alumnus of Yale, bears more than a passing resemblance to Buckley himself. (Buckley was a CIA agent in Mexico at one time and his boss, Howard Hunt, subsequently achieved fame as a Watergate conspirator.)

Blackford Oakes is given the assignment of going to Windsor Castle to seduce the Queen before a log fire one night when her husband, the Duke, is on one of his tours of Australia. It is almost what might be called the romantic American Tory's wildest adventure in fantasy. However, there can be no hint of disrespect to mar that Toryism: the date of the story is 1951, when there was still a King upon the British throne. Buckley's Queen is a diligent student of the subject of nuclear research. The story tells how America's own efforts in developing the bomb have been damaged by the defections of Fuchs, Burgess and Maclean to Russia. General Eisenhower and CIA chief Allen Dulles suspect that the leak from Britain comes from the Head of State. It is on that night in Windsor Castle when the Queen and the CIA agent are alone that all is revealed: as 'the firelight lit her body with a faint, flickering glow', she casually asks her visitor, with reference to the H-bomb, 'What is the Teller-Freeze By-pass?' This, one assumes, is the moment when the testicles of the CIA agent enter something like a frostbite phase. Writes Buckley: 'Suddenly his fondling of her breasts and haunches was mechanical.' Greater love hath no spy than this.

Eugene Burdick: *see* William J. Lederer

R. Wright Campbell (b. Newark, N.J., 9 June 1927)
R. Wright Campbell completed a three-year course in illustration
at the Pratt Institute in Brooklyn, N.Y., before serving in the US
Army during the Korean War. After basic training he was assigned
to the Anti-Aircraft Brigade, Fort Meade, Maryland. He transferred to the 4th echelon repair unit and spent the last year with
G-2 (General Army Intelligence) at the Pentagon. Campbell
decided to take up writing as a career in 1952 when he arrived in
Hollywood, selling his first major screenplay two years later. *The
Spy who Sat and Waited* (US 1975) was his first novel and into this
book he grafted some highly original elements. His spy, Wilhelm
Oerter, an undistinguished young clerk from a small town in Bavaria,
receives orders to change his identity. He becomes Will Hartz, a
Swiss, and is consigned on a highly speculative basis to the Orkneys,
there to become what is known in the spy trade as 'a sleeper'.

He has twenty years to wait. Meanwhile he becomes owner of
The Sailing Master, a tavern in Orkney conveniently overlooking
the grey waters of Scapa Flow, harbour of the British Home Fleet,
and he marries a local girl and has a son. So successful is his 'cover'
that he sometimes forgets what his ultimate purpose is to be until
his memory is refreshed by some travelling salesman with instructions from Berlin. When 1939 comes the long wait is over. Will
sends back information to Germany concerning the temporary
lifting of submarine protection nets in the Flow, thus leading to
the sinking of HMS *Royal Oak* by torpedoing by a single U-boat.
Will escapes and makes his way back to the Fatherland, numbed
by the knowledge that the people and the country he has betrayed
had become his people and his country. This is a chilling portrait
of one small spy whose whole life is dedicated to his one tiny act of
treachery, with appalling results.

'I wanted to write a book that illuminated the existentialist
quality of modern life,' says Campbell, 'showing life as being quite
absurd and the things we do or are asked to do being even more
absurd. I can think of no character more apt to create hell because
it is his duty than a spy or a government assassin. Oerter's finest
hour is the moment he refuses to enter into the plot against Hitler.'
He found the research into the background for the book the most

pleasurable part. This is not surprising, for behind this piece of fiction is an extraordinary story of fact. On 14 October 1939, the U-47, commanded by Lieut. Gunther Prien, surfaced in Kirk Sound at the northeast entrance to Scapa Flow and, gliding between the block ships, fired three torpedoes at the *Royal Oak*, then swung round and attacked a second time. The ship was sunk with the loss of 24 officers and 809 men. MI5 was blamed by the First Lord of the Admiralty of the time (Churchill). Then in 1942 an article was published in the *Saturday Evening Post* declaring that the mysterious spy who was able to supply the information for Prien's coup was Kapitan Alfred Wehring, a former German naval officer, who had changed his name to Oertel and his identity to that of a Swiss watchmaker, and had been sent to Kirkwall in the Orkney Islands in 1927. This story was repeated by Walter Schellenberg, successor to Admiral Canaris as head of the *Abwehr* (German Secret Service), in his post-war memoirs. It has, however, since been generally demonstrated that the story of Oertel was totally fictitious. Campbell says: 'Allen Dulles was quoted on the occasion of an address being given to a graduating class of CIA agents as being aware of the history of a retired German admiral who had been instrumental in the sinking of the *Royal Oak*. He was known as the Watchmaker of Kirkwall. This voice of authority led to its inclusion in other histories, collections and anthologies. It gained the force of truth. There was no watchmaker of Kirkwall. The only watchmaker there had been born into a family who had been in Orkney for seven generations.'

Campbell takes the view that the affair of Oertel 'was not a tricky German plot, but that of a hungry German writer'. This is substantiated by Ladislas Farago in *The Game of the Foxes*: 'Captain Wehring never existed . . . It was not especially difficult to establish that even Schellenberg's tale, cited as one of the great feats of the German Secret Service, was nothing but a hoax.'

Victor Canning (b. Plymouth, 16 June 1911)
Educated at grammar and technical schools in Plymouth and Oxford, Victor Canning's first real milestone was the year 1934, in which he was married to Phyllis McEwen and had his first book published. This was *Mr Finchley Discovers His England*, an unusual and entertaining travelogue, and it was swiftly followed by other books of similar type, including *Everyman's England* (UK 1936),

described as 'no guide book in the ordinary sense of the word, but the impressions of a young man who has set out to discover the England of ordinary men and women'. During the Second World War Canning served in the Royal Artillery, rising to the rank of Major, and it was only after his war experiences that he branched out into what could be called espionage thrillers, though this versatile author insists that 'I do not write spy fiction as such. I just write stories and I hate labelling them.' *The Golden Salamander* (UK 1947), which was an outstanding success both as a book and a film (1949), paved the way towards the thriller and mystery novel and this was followed by *Panther's Moon* (UK 1948). It was not, however, until *The Forest of Eyes* (UK 1950) that Canning produced a 100 per cent spy story. Robert Hudson, much more like an Ambler hero than a Buchan one, had no hankering for the role of secret agent. He was an engineer and as such went to Yugoslavia. But he soon found himself enmeshed in the Secret Service. In his next book, *Venetian Bird* (UK 1951), Canning combined romantic interest with the story of a down-at-heel English inquiry agent who becomes a hero in spite of himself.

Leslie Charteris (b. 12 May 1907)

This is the pseudonym of Leslie Charles Bowyer Yin, the son of a Chinese father and an English mother, who says that his parents 'dragged me three times round the world before I was 12'. He was educated at Rossall School in England and Cambridge University. While at Cambridge he took such an interest in crime that he 'set out to acquire the best possible education in criminal technique by reading every book on criminology I could lay my hands on'. For some time before settling down to write his own books about crime he undertook such varied chores as travelling across England with a fun fair, tending bar in a Torquay hotel, playing bridge professionally at a London club and working on a rubber plantation. He wrote his first 'Saint' book at the age of twenty-three, *Meet The Tiger* (UK 1930), and since then he has maintained his output steadily over almost half a century. Few popular authors have survived as best-sellers for so long and in Charteris's case that success is almost certainly due to the fact that his own special creation, 'The Saint', has been able to bridge the various generation gaps far better than the 'Bulldog' Drummonds and Richard Hannays—better, indeed, than the James Bonds.

Charteris is not strictly speaking a spy story writer, nor is he a detective story-teller. He is essentially a crime novelist with a character who is a kind of Robin Hood among rogues, an amateur adventure-seeker who tries to put down crime and catch criminals in his own, mostly unorthodox way. Occasionally, which is not surprising considering the length of 'The Saint's' career, the theme is very close to that of a spy story. There was, for example, *The Saint Returns* (UK 1969) in which 'The Saint'—or Simon Templar, to give him his actual name—becomes involved with a girl who claims to be Hitler's daughter. In a second story the globe-trotting Simon takes a stand against the Chinese, who are trying to sow seeds of dissension between Russia and Britain. As there is nothing of the political animal about Templar and he would appear to be totally untrained in the niceties of either Sinology or Sovietology, this last escapade of his seems somewhat unrealistic. Suffice it to say that, however lively television entertainment 'The Saint' stories may make, those that do touch on the world of Intelligence do not begin to compare with the modern mandarins of spy fiction. Either the CIA or DI6 would have taken Simon to the cleaners long ago rather than suffer his meddling in international intrigue. But nothing deters Templar and in *The Saint in Pursuit* (UK 1972) one finds him unravelling the mystery of an American agent who vanished in Lisbon in 1944.

Charteris might well have turned to spy fiction early on if his first novel had not been a failure. This work told how Terry Mannering, disguised as the mysterious masked 'X Esquire', crushed a plot to destroy Britain by distributing lethal cigarettes which did not actually start to kill until ten days after they had been smoked. Charteris thought it was 'an appallingly bad book' and possibly this self-judgement turned him away from espionage themes for some time to come. Despite criticisms of the 'Saint' stories, the sales of these books are phenomenal, with translations in many countries; and the 'Saint', as portrayed by Roger Moore on TV, has a large following. Charteris was naturalised as an American citizen in 1946, has been married four times and lives mostly in Florida.

G. K. Chesterton (b. London, 29 May 1874; d. 14 June 1936)
Gilbert Keith Chesterton's father, Edward, was a member of the well-known Kensington auctioneer and estate agents' business of

Chesterton and his mother, Marie-Louise, was of Franco-Scottish ancestry. From 1887–92 'G.K.C.', as he was later to become universally known, was educated at St Paul's School, London, where at the age of sixteen he showed his talents as a writer by starting a magazine called *The Debater*. Also revealing promise as an artist, young Chesterton went on to the Slade School of Art, at the same time studying English literature at London University. Absent-minded but brilliant, good-natured yet firm of principle, Chesterton was strongly anti-imperialist and liberal-minded. During the Boer War he took a pro-Boer standpoint on the platform and in his writing and between 1900 and 1910 he turned out numerous essays touching on political, philosophical, literary and other topics, crossing swords with Kipling on the right and Shaw on the left and revelling in fierce but friendly debate. His study of *Charles Dickens* (UK 1906) won wide approval from the critics.

One of the greatest masters of prose of his generation, Chesterton, the superb essayist, turned his attention to novel writing and especially to the detective story. His famous creation of Father Brown, the priest-detective, was based on his great friend Father John O'Connor (later Monsignor), parish priest of a church in Bradford, who in 1922 received Chesterton into the Roman Catholic Church. But though the Father Brown of innumerable stories was admitted by Father O'Connor to be something of a likeness—'the flat hat was as I wore it and the large and cheap umbrella was my defence against wearing an overcoat', he later said—there was much of Chesterton himself in the apparently unworldly but none the less shrewd sleuth, with his disconcerting reasoning. There was a romanticism about Chesterton's approach not only to the detective story, but to the spy story as well, a lifting of the genre to a level of what can perhaps be called an esoteric fantasy, which is one of the features of *The Man Who Was Thursday* (UK 1908), described by 'some of the old pros', says Miles Copeland, as 'the best spy book ever written'.

It is interesting to note Chesterton's attitude to this type of story in contrast to those of, say, Oppenheim or Buchan. Not for Chesterton the patriotism of empire, but 'the romance of man'. He put it most neatly when he wrote, 'Every fantastic skyline of chimney-pots seems wildly and derisively signalling the meaning of mystery . . . It is the agent of social justice who is the original and poetic figure, while the burglars and footpads are merely placid old cosmic conservatives, happy in the immemorial respectability of apes and wolves. The romance of the police force is the whole romance of man.'

The Man Who Was Thursday: A Nightmare was unique. When the poet, Syme, is shown into the steel chamber of the Underground Movement, Chesterton makes no pretence at the erudition in weaponry in which modern spy novelists love to show off. He simply writes that 'there were no rifles or pistols in this apartment, but round the walls of it were hung more dubious and dreadful shapes, things that looked like the bulbs of iron plants, or the eggs of iron birds. They were bombs, and the very room itself seemed like the inside of a bomb.' It is all written with a very adroit tongue in the cheek and there is one of the eternal truths of espionage contained even in its early pages. One poet asks the other, 'Why, after taking all this trouble to barricade yourselves in the bowels of the earth, [do] you then parade your whole secret by talking about anarchism to every silly woman in Saffron Park?' 'The answer is simple,' was the reply. 'I told you I was a serious anarchist and you did not believe me. Nor do *they* believe me.' If anyone thinks this is merely an example of the amusing paradoxes which Chesterton loved to weave, he should turn to this passage from Cyril Connolly's *The Missing Diplomats* (UK 1952) concerning a conversation between Donald Maclean of the British Foreign Office and a friend and colleague:

> Maclean: 'What would you do, if I told you I was a Communist agent?'
> 'I don't know.'
> 'Well, wouldn't you report me?'
> 'I don't know. Who to?'
> 'Well I am. Go on, report me.'

And nothing was done. Maclean's openly outrageous anti-Americanism at Embassy parties, his hints of fellow-travelling were simply not believed.

And so in Chesterton's spy story the advice given to Gregory by the President of the Central Anarchist Council as to what disguise he should adopt was: 'You want a safe disguise, do you? You want a dress which will guarantee you harmless, a dress in which no one would ever look for a bomb? Why then, dress up as an *anarchist*, you fool! Nobody will ever expect you to do anything dangerous then.' Gregory took this advice and never regretted it. 'I preached blood and murder to those women day and night, and

43

—by God!—they would let me wheel their perambulators.' It is true that this book is somewhat of a send-up of the spy story, a much more elegant send-up than those of the late 1960s, but so much of it can be related to real-life situations that one can well understand the professional agent laughing his head off when reading it. The President of the Central Anarchist Council is called Sunday and some of his admirers call him 'Bloody Sunday': no doubt Chesterton had in mind that 'Bloody Sunday' of 22 January 1905, when the priest and double-agent, Gapon, crucifix in hand, led the crowds to the Winter Palace in St Petersburgh. There is another delightful Chestertonian item of impishness in the story: a pass-word is that a certain heavy iron door cannot be entered without 'submitting to the humiliation of calling yourself "Mr Joseph Chamberlain" '. And Chesterton, in an era when the double-agent was regarded as a joke in fiction and almost unheard of in fact, except in Czarist Russia, summed up perfectly the kind of modern situation we know so well when two rival agents who have exchanged confidences confront one another. Gregory, having been told by Syme that the latter is a police agent, aims a revolver at him. ' "Don't be such a silly man," he said, with the effeminate dignity of a curate. "Don't you see it's not necessary? Don't you see that we're both in the same boat? . . . We've checkmated each other. I can't tell the police you are an anarchist. You can't tell the anarchists I'm a policeman. I can only watch you, knowing what you are; you can only watch me, knowing what I am. In short, it's a lonely, intellectual duel, my head against yours. I'm a policeman deprived of the help of the police. You, my poor fellow, are an anarchist deprived of the help of that law and organisation which is so essential to anarchy." '

The Man Who Was Thursday anticipates almost every spy story that was ever written. It should still be a model for aspiring writers of espionage fiction, a text-book to prevent them from keeling over too far in the direction of fantasy.

Peter Cheyney (b. London, 1896; d. 1951)
Born Reginald Southouse Cheyney, he had an undistinguished career in his early life, finding little success as a songwriter, bookmaker, journalist or budding politician. It may have been these failures which prompted him to seek compensation in a highly skilled and aggressive recreation such as fencing and, on

the political side, in support of Sir Oswald Mosley's British Union of Fascists. Success came to him suddenly when, aged forty, he created the character of Lemmy Caution in *This Man is Dangerous* (UK 1936). Caution was a 'private eye'; with him Cheyney got right away from the genteel world of country-houseparty detective stories into the sleazier but more normal environment of crime. During the war years Cheyney became compulsive reading for millions and by the end of the war he was topping one and a half million sales a year, with editions of his books regularly published in the US and France.

Cheyney has been decried by the highbrow critics and the dialogue of his characters has been lambasted as spurious. Latterly, no doubt, he was also unfairly damned because of his pro-fascist leanings and his addiction to violence in his stories. In fact Cheyney was an ardent British patriot who carried his patriotism to such extremes that he would challenge to a duel anyone who sneered at Britain or the Royal Family. The violence of the Lemmy Caution and Slim Callaghan (his other private eye) stories was mild compared with Spillane or Fleming. The fact is that the highbrows secretly envied Cheyney for his success. Fleming was not only an avid reader of Cheyney during the war, but studied the latter's books most carefully before creating Bond, who was really an upper middle-class version of Lemmy Caution. Cheyney's work was mainly in the field of detective stories and thrillers, but he made some incursions into spy fiction, notably *Adventures of Julia and two other spy stories* (UK 1954), and the Dark series—*Dark Duet* (UK 1942), *Dark Interlude* (UK 1947), *Dark Wanton* (UK 1948) and *Stars are Dark* (UK 1943). They were exciting, imaginative stories and, if not of a high literary standard, at least struck out in a new direction. Cheyney may have been a poseur, but he breathed fresh life into the thriller and rescued dialogue from its hackneyed, cliché-ridden pedestrianism of the 'thirties. His parents lived in the East End of London; his father helped with a fish-stall at Billingsgate and his mother ran a corset shop in Whitechapel. Yet in *Who's Who* Cheyney's entry read: 'Major Reginald Evelyn Peter Southouse-Cheyney. Father Arthur William Thomas Cheyney, Co. Clare, Ireland. Clubs: Public Schools and Devonshire.'

Erskine Childers (b. London, 25 June 1870; d. Dublin, 24 November 1922)

Son of the pioneer of Pali literature studies in England, Erskine Childers was educated at Haileybury and Trinity College, Cambridge. From 1895–1910 he was a clerk in the House of Commons, though this was temporarily interrupted when in 1900 he was one of the first volunteers accepted for service in the Boer War. He joined the HAC and afterwards was part-author of *The HAC in South Africa*.

In 1903 his book *The Riddle of the Sands* was published, a brilliant and lively narrative of yachting and espionage off the northwest coast of Germany, perhaps the first work of spy fiction other than Fenimore Cooper's to have any pretensions to being literature. This was fiction based on fact, fiction with a set purpose, that of arousing public opinion behind the clamour for building a stronger navy, and motivated by Childers' curious dual patriotism—an intense love for England and Ireland. Its factual basis was the result of Childers' own yachting experiences in the *Vixen* off the coasts of Germany, Holland and elsewhere. Paul Johnson, author and former editor of the *New Statesman*, has said of it, 'What strikes me about this book are both the resemblances and the huge differences, when it is compared to modern spy fiction. The resemblances are in the stress on technical details: Childers describes the philosophy, theory and practice of inshore sailing with loving care . . . the areas he describes, the Baltic coast of Denmark and Schleswig-Holstein, and the low-lying sandy coast between the Elbe and the Ems, he knew intimately. In fact, the geographical structure around which the novel is built is not invented at all; the course taken by the two English heroes could be followed by any skilled yachtsman, and Childers even included maps to help the reader, together with timetables of tides. Writers of modern spy fiction follow this pattern of providing expert technical background, though rarely with the degree of knowledge and skill Childers commanded. Where they differ is in their handling of sex and violence. There is, in fact, a love story in *The Riddle*, but it is presented with such delicacy and reticence that one is scarcely aware of it, and it is never for one moment allowed to interfere with the relentless unfolding of the nautical plot.'

The story concerns two young Englishmen who make a trip to the Frisian Islands and discover the Germans rehearsing plans for an invasion of Britain. Carruthers, a Foreign Office man with foppish mannerisms, is in the best tradition of the English amateur confronted with a difficult and dangerous situation, and his friend, Davies, is the perfect foil. Perhaps some of the best narrative is that concerning the navigation of their seven-ton yacht in a fog through the waters of Memmert Balje. The villain is an Englishman who is working for the Germans, a former British naval lieutenant turned traitor. He calls himself Dollmann—'the vilest creature on God's earth' is Carruthers' denunciation of him in the conventional attitude to all who forsook their native country in that day and age. Childers plays on fear throughout this book, fear of the sea, of the fog, of the Germans and of the unknown: in this sense he creates the propaganda of fear.

The Riddle of the Sands deservedly became famous because, apart from being a remarkably exciting story, it drew attention to German militarism at a time when nobody else had taken up the theme. It was undoubtedly a patriotic gesture on the part of Childers, for his whole career suggests that he was as devoted to protecting England as he was to the cause of Irish nationalism. The book also alerted a somewhat dilatory British Naval Intelligence Division to shortcomings in naval charts. When Capt. Regnart of the NID gave permission to two officers to be sent on a tour of the German sea-coast defences and the Frisian Islands in May 1910, he found that the existing Admiralty charts of this area and Intelligence information generally on the localities were hopelessly out of date and that their only knowledge of the Frisian Islands was obtained from *The Riddle of the Sands*. Yet, if the NID had taken the trouble they would have discovered that all Childers had done was to marry the details of *German* and British charts and incorporate all these in the charts in his book. The two officers who devoted their entire leave to this voluntary spying expedition, Lieut. Brandon, RN, and Capt. Trench, RM, had been inspired by Childers' book. Unluckily, they were both detected and arrested by the Germans, finally being sentenced to a term of imprisonment in Germany. It was shortly after this that the NID was given a drastic overhaul. The two officers were released from prison in May 1913, seventeen months before the expiration of their sentence, being pardoned by the Kaiser on the occasion of King George V's visit to Germany.

Childers joined the Royal Navy in the First World War, taking part in the Cuxhaven Raid in November 1914. For the rest of the war he was Training Officer in the RNAS. He was promoted to

Lieut.-Commander, several times mentioned in dispatches and awarded the DSC. Childers had paid a visit to Boston in 1904 and there he met Mary Alden Osgood, whom he married and brought back to England, where they lived in a house in Chelsea. He described his marriage many years later as being 'the most wonderful and happiest experience of my life'. Increasingly, as he grew older, he devoted his attention to the cause of Irish independence. He had become a convert to Irish home rule and in 1910 and July 1914, he and his wife used their yacht *Asgard* to carry cargoes of arms from the continent to Howth harbour. He justified this on the grounds of Asquith's Home Rule Bill. Unlike many Irishmen, he had not sought to pursue this cause by means of treachery to Britain, especially in wartime, yet he was nevertheless a fanatical supporter of the Irish cause and well to the side of the extremists. In 1919 he settled in Dublin and was the principal secretary to the delegation which negotiated an Irish Treaty with the British Government. Childers vehemently opposed both Arthur Griffiths and Michael Collins, who favoured accepting the Treaty, on the grounds that it did not provide for complete independence. Prophetically, he maintained that to separate Ulster would only prolong bloodshed 'not just for a few years but for a dozen or more generations to come'.

On the establishment of the Irish Free State Government he joined the Republican Army which set itself the task of opposing the new Free State Government, and so became a participant in the civil war between the pro-Treaty and anti-Treaty forces. But his motives were much more humane than those of some of the extremists of the IRA with whom he linked himself as a result of this last stand. Tragedy faced this honourable, patriotic Anglo-Irishman in these last years of his life, when he found himself regarded as a traitor both by the British Government and the Irish Free State Government. On 10 November 1922, Free State soldiers surrounded Glendalough House, his mother's home, where he was living. He was armed, but did not fire, as he feared that some of the womenfolk might be injured. Childers was arrested and court-martialled in Dublin. He refused to recognise the authority of the court that tried him and was condemned to death. Before he was executed at Beggars' Bush Barracks, he shook hands with each member of the firing squad.

Richard Henry Michael Clayton: *see* William Haggard

Francis Clifford (b. Bristol, 1917; d. 25 August 1975)
Francis Clifford worked in the rice trade in the Far East before
the Second World War and then as an industrial journalist for the
steel industry. He started his writing career somewhat late in life,
but his world sales topped the five million mark and he was particularly successful in winning awards on both sides of the Atlantic.
He won the Edgar Allan Poe Special Award of the Mystery Writers
of America for *Amigo, Amigo* (UK 1973) and twice received the
Crime Writers' Association Silver Dagger, for *Act of Mercy* (UK
1959) and *The Grosvenor Square Goodbye* (UK 1974). Outstanding
among his spy stories was *The Naked Runner* (UK 1966), which
opens in Leipzig with Sam Laker, a successful British businessman,
reluctantly agreeing to act as unpaid agent for the West and ends
a few days later with Sam turned into a cold and paranoic killer.
Frank Sinatra bought the film rights, and played the leading role.
  Not all of Clifford's books were spy stories, but *All Men Are
Lonely Now* (UK 1967) was about a Special Branch investigation
into an East German defector's disclosures about a laser-guided
missile. The *Los Angeles Times* described it, perhaps rather too
enthusiastically, as 'the finest espionage novel of the decade'.
Clifford won many friends among the critics and Francis Iles,
writing in the *Guardian*, said that he was 'almost unique in combin-
ing a deeply felt philosophical truth with the real excitement of
the thriller'. *The Blind Side* (UK 1971) was a spy story with a
difference, being a study of two brothers under stress in very
separate situations. One brother was a priest in the starving villages
of Biafra, the other sat at his desk in Naval Intelligence in London,
watching, noting, passing on his only link with trust and affection
to a man he rarely met . . . and then the link between them snapped.
In this work Clifford acquired a mastery of characterisation and he
followed this up in *Amigo, Amigo*, which was, however, more of a
hunt for war criminals in South America than a spy story.

Richard Condon (b. New York, 18 March 1915)
Richard Condon worked as an advertising copy-writer, motion
picture press agent and in various jobs on Broadway before launching out as a novelist at the age of forty-two. Since then he has

written novels, plays, essays, criticism and various non-fiction books, and has been published in twenty languages plus Braille. His first book was *The Oldest Confession* (US 1958) and his first spy novel was the sensational *The Manchurian Candidate* (US 1959), which was not only made into a highly successful film, but was said by many to have provided the inspiration for the assassination of President Kennedy in 1963. This concentrated public attention on the techniques of brain-washing: 'I wrote the novel back from the last scene to the beginning to make sure I included all conveyances to get the book where it should be going,' says Condon.

His most recent spy story has been *The Whisper of the Axe* (US 1976), a book with an ambitious and somewhat complex plot involving a scheme to trigger off 'the Final American Revolution' by unrestrained urban terrorism and the extermination of a third of the nation. It introduced as characters a black woman terrorist and an incestuous brother and sister working for the CIA, secret training camps in China, heroin-running and brain-washing once more. Some authors are name droppers; Condon is a compulsive initials dropper—PLO, AFF, AEC, MATS, ARVN, KEMT, NSC, MACV and NSA are only a few of those he uses. The single fictitious title among these is AFF which stands for 'American Freedom Fighters', a revolutionary guerrilla force 'trained to take away all freedom, life, property and serenity enjoyed by the people, if any'. Condon says that the basis of his viewpoint in his novels has been that 'people are being manipulated, exploited, murdered by their servants, who have convinced these savage, simple-minded populations that they are their masters, and that it hurts the head, if one thinks. People accept servants as masters. My novels are merely entertaining persuasions to get the people to think in other categories.' He has had no association whatever with the world of real-life Intelligence and adds, somewhat whimsically, that 'whenever I need a true acronym I write to Len Deighton or Charles McCarry'. Condon is fascinated and absorbed by the manipulation of the mind and his book *Winter Kills* (US 1974) is about this very kind of manipulation carried out 'by a culture so designed to manipulate . . . There can be no fiction without fact. In the present world of extraordinarily manipulative and industrialised over-communications—electronic, printed, exhorted, pressured in 4,500 messages beating upon each Western citizen daily—it has developed as night into day with its surety that there can be no fact without fiction because the art of prole control is herding their dreams.' That is the somewhat abstract thinking behind the stories; probably most readers would just settle for *The Manchurian Candidate* as a good story.

Cyril Connolly (b. Bath, 10 September 1903; d. 1974)

Essayist, critic, occasional novelist, dilettante and gourmet, Cyril Vernon Connolly, had he lived, would probably have been seriously perturbed to find himself included in a *Who's Who of Spy Fiction*. Educated at Eton and Balliol College, Oxford, Connolly founded *Horizon* in 1939, and edited it until 1950. His first venture into fiction was *The Rock Pool* (1935), a first edition of which is now rare and quite valuable. 'Vitality and imaginative sympathy are among Cyril Connolly's enduring qualities', wrote Peter Quennell in his introduction to Connolly's *The Missing Diplomats* (1952). 'For the young he became a sort of legend—legendary arbiter of *avant-garde* writing . . . it was natural that both Burgess and Maclean should . . . have swum into his sphere of influence.' Their disappearance behind the Iron Curtain fascinated Connolly, but then he was also probably much more secretly dedicated to spy fiction than his fastidious tastes would suggest. It was the mischief behind it all which appealed to Connolly and added to this was an impish desire to deflate reputations. The reason for his inclusion in this book is for his brilliant piece of spoofery in debunking the Fleming cult and all James Bond stood for in his extravaganza, *Bond Strikes Camp*, in *The London Magazine* of April 1963. This was a sparkling and amusing satire on the whole money-spinning business of Bondery, enlightened by some lively and astringent dialogue. In this story 'M' sends for Bond and orders him to disguise himself as a woman in order to trap a visiting KGB general. The general, explains 'M', 'likes drag. That's—er—men dressed up as women.'

Bond, who has not dressed up in 'drag' since he played Katisha in *The Mikado* at his prep. school, sets off to receive the full treatment in disguise—'the fitting of an elaborate chestnut wig . . . the very latest in falsies—foam-rubber, with electronic self-erecting nipples . . . slinky black lace panties . . . black shoes with red stilettos'. When Bond eventually meets the KGB man in this remarkable get-up, the latter asks: 'Who is your best friend?'

'Bond remembered the gambit pawn. "Guy Burgess."'

'The General guffawed. "I'll tell him. He'll be delighted. He doesn't often get a message from such a pretty girl." '

But in the end the General turns out to be none other than 'M' in disguise: 'I'm sorry, James. It was the only way I could get you . . . Don't think I haven't fought against it.'

Bond cuts him short with: ' "Have you got a gun, sir?" M. nodded. Bond looked at his watch. "It's a quarter past two. You may employ what means you prefer, but if I find you are still alive by nine o'clock I shall alert every newspaper here." '

Joseph Conrad (b. nr Mohilow, Poland, 3 December 1857; d. Bishopsbourne, Kent, 3 August 1924)

Teodor Jósef Konrad Korzeniowski was of Polish parentage. His father, a member of a landed family, had translated the works of Shakespeare into Polish, and was an ardent Polish patriot who became involved in the rising against the Russian authorities in 1862. As a result of this he, with his wife and five-year-old son, was exiled to Vologda. The family spent a few years travelling across Russia, often living in conditions of acute discomfort and hardship. After his wife died Korzeniowski senior was allowed to leave Russia and went with his son to live in Austrian Galicia. Young Jósef studied in Cracow before deciding in 1872 that he wished for a career at sea. He went to Marseilles, became a registered seaman with the French Merchant Navy and after eleven years' service held the rank of first mate. During this period he once visited England, arriving first at Lowestoft. In 1886 he became a naturalised British subject, taking the name of Joseph Conrad.

Critics will argue as to whether Conrad would have been a greater writer if he had written in French, which was his first language after Polish. Certainly there are French influences in his prose and his sense of irony is essentially that of many French writers of the last century. Having obtained his ship's master's certificate, he devoted much of his spare time afloat and ashore to writing. Conrad was a man sometimes given to despair and melancholy and he seems to have found it an arduous task to write his first book. He began his first story in 1889, sometimes abandoning work on it for weeks at a time. Years passed by and still the work was unfinished. Twice the manuscript was lost, then found again. At last in 1895 *Almayer's Folly* was published and this was followed by other works based on his sea experiences—*An Outcast of the*

Islands (UK 1896), *The Nigger of the 'Narcissus'* (UK 1897). Success and acknowledgement of his undoubted genius came with *Lord Jim* (UK 1900).

In 1896 he married Jessie, the daughter of a bookseller, and they went off to live in Brittany for a lengthy period. Ill health frequently dogged him, but Conrad persisted with his writing and turned from tales of the sea to his experiences as a boy in Russia for his two ventures into what might fairly be described as spy stories— *The Secret Agent* (UK 1907) and *Under Western Eyes* (UK 1911). Though the background of each owes much to his early years of banishment to Russia and some knowledge of the revolutionary movement in that country, then almost entirely underground, Conrad seems to have acquired a good deal of first-hand information about Russian revolutionaries and anarchists in exile while a seaman. Many of the anarchists maintained links with the Polish community in clubs around London's dockland and between 1900 and the Siege of Sidney Street in 1910 there was considerable activity among the Russian revolutionaries and anarchists in this area. From this viewpoint *The Secret Agent* was topical; indeed, it anticipated the Siege of Sidney Street. Conrad told of an attempted anarchist plot set in the unfashionable environment of Greenwich Park, the details of which bear a good deal of similarity with similar plots and counter-plots between revolutionaries and counter-revolutionaries in the East End of London in that period. This book was dramatised in 1922. In *Under Western Eyes* Conrad becomes the first serious writer to deal effectively with the double-agent. But it could be said that Conrad was writing with burning sincerity and seriousness rather than to entertain: his spies were not characters intended to amuse, but were symbols of what Conrad regarded as the essential evil of revolution. Julian Symons writes that 'in spite of their subject matter, Conrad's books [the two just mentioned] do not seem to me to be spy stories'. He has a point, for he refers to an earlier version of *Under Western Eyes*, called *Razumov*, which 'was much more concerned with the personal problems of the central character. In the published book the conspiracy seems at times to have been grafted on to the original manuscript for the sake of excitement.' Nevertheless Conrad should, I feel, be included as an effective contributor to this genre, because of the accuracy of his background (an unusual characteristic in the days of Oppenheim and Le Queux), and because for the first time the double-agent emerges clearly.

In the First World War Conrad raised funds for refugees from his native Poland and, coincidentally, was one of the few, if not the only author who went to sea in the Royal Navy's 'spy ships'. These were the Q-ships, disguised merchantmen with hidden guns, intended to lure submarines to the surface and their destruction.

Duff Cooper (b. 22 February 1890; d. at sea, 1 January 1954)
The only son of Sir Alfred Cooper and Lady Agnes Duff, sister of the 1st Duke of Fife, Alfred Duff Cooper was educated at Eton and New College, Oxford. He served in the Grenadier Guards in the First World War, being awarded the DSO in 1919, and in the same year married Lady Diana Manners, daughter of the 8th Duke of Rutland. Embarking on a political career, Duff Cooper was first elected to Parliament as Conservative MP for Oldham in 1924, which seat he held until 1929; from 1931–45 he was MP for the St George's Division of Westminster. In 1935–37 he served as Secretary of State for War and in 1937 was appointed First Lord of the Admiralty, but he resigned in 1938 because of the national government's appeasement of Nazi Germany. In 1940 he joined the Churchill administration as Minister of Information, leaving in 1941 to become Chancellor of the Duchy of Lancaster, a post he held until 1943 when he was made representative of HM Government to the French Committee of National Liberation in Algiers. From 1944–47 he was British Ambassador to France.

Duff Cooper's literary career was marked by biographies of Talleyrand (1932) and Haig (1935); then in 1950 he published a surprising novel, *Operation Heartbreak*. To those who were in the know this was a barely disguised fictitious account of 'Operation Mincemeat', the British Naval Intelligence project for fooling the enemy in the Second World War. By means of false messages found on a body (itself a concocted corpse) washed up on the Spanish coast, the Germans were persuaded that the next Allied invasion in the Mediterranean was to be Sardinia rather than Sicily, where it actually took place. The German High Command was successfully deceived. How Duff Cooper got away with this clear breach of the Official Secrets Act has never been revealed: it was probably a question of a nod and a wink rather than any authorised permission. The publication of this book led to certain strong criticisms that the Official Secrets Act had been breached and some muted and half-hearted objections by the NID, not upheld by the government of the day. The Duff Cooper novel led to Ian Colvin, an experienced foreign correspondent, doing some research on his own account. When he discovered that Rommel had admitted he was 'sent in the wrong direction' as a result of a British courier's body being washed up on the coast of Spain and that there was the grave of a mysterious 'Major Martin' in Spain, Colvin wrote a series of articles which paved the way for the ultimate truth of the operation, Lieut.-Commander Ewen Montagu's *The Man Who Never Was* (UK 1953). Duff Cooper was created 1st Viscount Norwich of Aldwick two years before his death.

Edmund Cooper (b. Marple, Cheshire, 30 April 1926)
The son of a village shopkeeper, Edmund Cooper was educated at Manchester Grammar School. 'But,' he says, 'I left at the age of fifteen after a rather serious accident to my right hand. Fortunately, I am left-handed, otherwise I might never have become a professional writer!' After leaving school he worked for some time as a labourer, then as a civil servant and at eighteen joined the Merchant Navy and 'had a taste of war'. His first book was *The Uncertain Midnight* (UK 1958), which had a remarkable success, being published in the US, France, Germany, the Netherlands, Italy, Japan and Brazil, as well as being made into a TV serial which was entered for the Prix Futura in Berlin in 1969.

Cooper does not regard himself as a spy fiction author, but rather more perhaps as a science fiction writer. But there are occasional espionage sub-plots in his novels, of which he has now written fifteen under his own name. One of these can be found in *Son of Kronk* (UK 1970), in which the Chief of MicroWar gives Professor Greylaw a tall order—the designing of an interesting little creature called P939, the best and latest venereal disease that made the aggressive instinct go phut. He was also to invent an antidote to P939, but died before he could do so. This was a remarkably funny story, with horrific undertones of how the Intelligence game can stray into the realms of science fiction. In *Prisoner of Fire* (UK 1974) Cooper did rather more to point the way for the spy story to strike up a liaison, if not exactly a marriage with science fiction, a trend we may eventually see more of. Cooper sets out to show in this book how in the fairly near future science achieves some understanding of the ways in which telepathy, ESP and other puzzling properties of the mind work and the ways in which they can be used. Not for the benefit of the individual, but for the State: for industrial and international espionage, for space communications, for political purposes, for prying into private lives. Vanessa Smith possesses great paranormal powers; she is a prisoner at a special 'school' and her escape from the institute and chance meeting with another fugitive precipitate an exciting adventure. 'I thought of this book primarily as a science fiction story,' says Cooper, 'but the implications of developing such techniques for espionage, or even for simple invasion of privacy, are horrendous. I understand that both the Americans and the Russians have been experimenting with the use of telepathy as a possible means of space communication. I do not know if they have done much work on its development as an Intelligence weapon. I suspect they have. But, to the best of my knowledge, the uses of telepathy as it is now understood are very restricted and undependable. The situation I described in *Prisoner of Fire* postulates developments in paranormal research which have not yet taken place and which, I hope, will never take place. If it is possible to develop telepathy along the lines I suggested, I am afraid the whole of our so-called civilised society will be radically altered.'

James Fenimore Cooper (b. Burlington, N.J., 15 September 1789; d. Cooperstown, N.Y., 14 September 1851)
The son of William Cooper, a prosperous Quaker businessman and the founder of the settlement known as Cooperstown in central New York State. He was educated at a school in Albany, New York, and later at Yale University, from which he was expelled for a youthful escapade. For three years Cooper was a midshipman in the US Navy, mainly serving in patrol vessels on the Great Lakes. It is possible that he may have become interested or even involved in espionage at this time, as a primitive form of intelligence-gathering was carried out along the Great Lakes and there is an historical note of spy work prior to the Battle of Lake Erie in 1812.

In 1811 Cooper resigned his commission and is said to have decided to become an author to prove to his wife that he could write a better book than the English novels which she read. His first real success came with *The Spy* (US 1821), which Julian Symons has described as 'the first spy novel known to me'. This was a book which combined adventure, espionage and romance: its sub-title was *A Tale of the Neutral Ground*. It was far from being the best of Cooper's works, but its setting of the War of Independence made it highly popular. The spy in this instance was, of course, totally different from the fictional spies who followed at the end of the century. He was Harvey Birch, a young English officer who had gone behind the American lines to visit members of his family, discarding his uniform and disguising himself as a pedlar. Though denounced as a traitor by the American Major Dunwoodie, and sentenced to death, Harvey Birch survived in the end.

Cooper's best known work was undoubtedly *The Last of the Mohicans* (US 1826), but he always took a keen interest in naval matters. In 1826 he went to live in Paris, continuing to write, but later becoming US Consul in Lyon. He was an early advocate of the establishment of a Department of Naval Intelligence in the US Navy, the history of which he wrote. But the American Office of Naval Intelligence was not established until 1882. Cooper's latter years were disturbed by fierce controversies over his outspoken criticisms of American government, and he was involved in various lawsuits in which he was the victor.

David John Moore Cornwell: *see* John Le Carré

Stephen Coulter (b. 1914)
Coulter was educated in Britain and France, studying in Paris in the early 'thirties. He began his career as a newspaperman in the British home counties where, he says, 'I was expected to do everything from reporting to making up and sometimes had to drive the delivery vans.' He had travelled widely and in 1937 joined Reuters News Agency as one of their Parliamentary staff correspondents. During the war he served in the Royal Navy and was appointed one of General Eisenhower's staff officers at Supreme Headquarters, assigned to special Intelligence work on France and Scandinavia. His work carried him to Paris immediately after the Liberation and for more than twenty years after the war he was staff correspondent for Kemsley Newspapers, including *The Sunday Times*, in Paris. One of the interesting sidelines on Coulter's career is that, but for his expertise and research, Ian Fleming might never have been able to write the casino scenes in *Casino Royale*.

It was Coulter who provided the background to casino know-how and so saved Fleming from possibly dropping the whole idea. From then on Coulter saw the light and started to write seriously and furiously on his own account. Apart from an admirable study in fiction of the passionate life of Guy de Maupassant, *Damned Shall Be Desire* (UK 1958), he also produced spy fiction under his own name and his pseudonym of 'James Mayo': *Hammerhead* (UK 1964) and *Let Sleeping Girls Lie* (UK 1965) were both Mayo titles; *A Stranger Called the Blues* (UK 1968), *Embassy* (UK 1969) and *An Account to Render* (UK 1970), were all written under his own name.

A Stranger Called the Blues was a story of love and intrigue on the borders of Chinese-controlled Tibet, of which one critic said that the 'background is so good, it gives you prickly heat'. *Embassy* contained a more complicated plot in which a French national is murdered in the United States' Paris Embassy and the Embassy officials try to slip the killer away; handing him over to the French authorities would risk the exposure of a far more important second man, a high-ranking Russian under guard in one of the Embassy rooms. A trip Coulter made to Central America was the basis of *An Account to Render*, a story of a revolutionary movement very similar to that in Guatemala in which four people are deeply involved—Father Hagan, a sick, defeated Catholic priest, Catherine Holland, a young English girl, Major O'Connor Benitez of the police and the US Ambassador.

John Creasey (b. London, 17 September 1908; d. Wiltshire, 9 June 1973)
One of the ablest writers of crime fiction, John Creasey was educated at Fulham Elementary School and Sloane School, Chelsea. After taking various clerical posts, he began writing in 1925. His first book, *Seven Times Seven* (UK 1932), was a racy and amusing story of a gang of crooks. When he died he had written 562 books with worldwide sales of more than 80 million copies in 28 different languages. This phenomenal literary feat was perpetrated by using ten different pen-names, including those of 'J. J. Marric', 'Michael Halliday', 'Gordon Ashe', 'Anthony Morton', 'Norman Deane' and 'Jeremy York'. All his books were written first in longhand on specially ruled paper (on average it took him ten days to complete the first draft) and revised five or six times before going to the

publisher. The actual number of Creasey's characters is almost incalculable, and he used at least ten central figures in different series.

With the approach of the Second World War Creasey devoted more attention to developing the spy novel rather than his straightforward crime and police stories. His 'Department Z' stories, the first of which was *The Death Miser* (UK 1933), had as a common theme espionage in Britain. The Department leader, Gordon Craigie, used a surprising variety of patriotic and intrepid agents whose sole purpose was to guard the nation's interests. Other 'Department Z' tales included *First Came a Murder* (UK 1934), *Carriers of Death* (UK 1937) and *The Peril Ahead* (UK 1946). Creasey's earlier works in this genre had dealt with the pre-war scene and some of them, notably *The Mark of the Crescent* (UK 1935), proved remarkably prophetic. Under the pseudonym of 'Norman Deane' Creasey wrote powerful wartime spy stories in the 1940s, one of which, *Withered Man* (UK 1940), was told through the eyes of a Nazi Secret Service agent, with astonishing realism. In 1938 Creasey lived in the village of Ashe in Hampshire and it was there he took his pen-name of 'Gordon Ashe' and created his character Patrick Dawlish, somewhat in the 'Bulldog' Drummond tradition. When war came Creasey made Dawlish a powerful figure in MI5, but really he should more appropriately have been either MI6 or the SOE, as time and again Dawlish was dropped into occupied Europe, organising resistance against the Nazis. The end of the war sent Dawlish into enforced retirement with his beloved wife, Felicity, rearing pigs and growing apples, but in due course he came back as a kind of unpaid private eye and eventually was appointed a Deputy Assistant Commissioner for Crime at Scotland Yard.

Another spy fiction character of Creasey's was his highly successful Dr Palfrey, the leader of an allied Secret Service whose members owed loyalty to the corporate body of Western Allies, not to any individual nation. In part this was an expression of Creasey's political ideal of 'one world', a theme which he actively pursued after the war. Creasey's political interests and ambitions began to develop about this time and in *The House of the Bears* (UK 1946), *The Flood* (UK 1956) and *The Plague of Silence* (UK 1958) he gave full rein to this. In 1950 Creasey stood as a Liberal Party candidate at Bournemouth and then in 1967 he founded the All Party Alliance in England, a political movement advocating government by the best men from all the parties working together. He fought four by-elections in 1967–68 for APA, once getting fourteen per cent of the votes cast.

Creasey, whose American wife Jeanne wrote historical western novels, had two homes, one in Tucson, Arizona, in desert foothills, and the other near Salisbury, Wiltshire, on land once given to Sir John Botenham by King John. Creasey's astonishing output was fully maintained until his death.

Sanche de Gramont

An American-educated Frenchman living in the former premier spy city of Tangier, Sanche de Gramont is a journalist of international repute and a Pulitzer Prize winner. He has written a number of non-fiction books including *The French: Portrait of a People* (US 1970) and *The Secret War* (US 1962). The latter revealed some fascinating details about the ace Soviet spy, Col. Rudolf Abel. After this agent was arrested in New York FBI agents found in his room 'a block of wood covered with sandpaper—the block came apart, and contained a 250-page booklet with a series of numbers, all in five-digit groups, on each page. It was a cipher pad, an aid to writing coded messages. The tiny booklet . . . contained the key to Abel's personal code, printed in neat columns in black and red . . . A stubby pencil with an eraser that concealed a cavity was also found; inside the cavity were eighteen microfilms . . .' Sanche de Gramont reasoned that almost certainly Abel deliberately left this evidence in order to deceive. His outstanding spy novel was *Lives to Give* (US 1972), a story about loyalties within the French Resistance during the German occupation, and easily one of the most authentic of any on this subject.

Len Deighton (b. London, 1929)

Leonard Cyril Deighton is the son of the chauffeur to the family of Campbell Dodgson, Keeper of Prints and Drawings at the British Museum. During the Second World War the Deightons moved into the Dodgson household in which, says Deighton, he had 'a fascinating glimpse of an Upstairs-Downstairs world of hier-archical struggles among the domestic staff'. He was an astute observer of human life, and the kind of details most of us overlook, even as a boy. 'Writers like me have quite a lot in common with spies,' he says. 'I like to be able to listen to conversations without people turning round to look at me.' As a boy he met his first real-life spy in London. She was the daughter of a White Russian admiral and, when not plotting with fellow-sympathisers with the Nazis, she made hats. One day the police arrested her and she was clapped into jail for fifteen years. Young Deighton's education was considerably disturbed by the war, when many schoolchildren were being evacuated from London. When he left school he began work as a railway clerk before doing his National Service in the RAF. He regards this period as an essential part of his education, for he became a photographer and shared a barrack room with a bookie's runner, a circus artist and an Oxford graduate. Afterwards he obtained an Ex-Serviceman's grant for art training at the St Martin's School of Art, then went on to the Royal College of Art. 'I wouldn't have had the audacity to write a book if I hadn't gone to art school,' says Deighton. 'I think the reason working-class people don't write books is because they are encouraged to believe that only certain people are *permitted* to write books.'

While he was an art student Deighton worked as a waiter in London and it was probably at this time that he developed an interest in cookery, a subject which he later exploited in a diagrammatic strip for *The Observer*. For a while he also worked as an illustrator in New York and as art director of an advertising agency in London. Then, deciding it was time to settle down, Deighton plunged into writing, going to the Dordogne where he started *The Ipcress File* (UK 1962). But the need to earn more money caused him to return to London halfway through the book, and take on some art work. Eventually he went back to France, this time choosing the more remote Isle de Porquerolles, near Toulon, where, with the last ferry leaving in early evening for the mainland, there were no distractions and he finished this first novel. The hero of this story plays a part in the rescue of a bio-chemist who has been abducted to the Lebanon en route to the Soviet Union. There is a fascinating account of affairs in the Soho offices of WOOC(P), a small but important Intelligence Unit, and Deighton gave a new twist to the spy story when, at the end of the book, the chief enemy agent is paid £160,000 to change sides and start up a new little Intelligence Unit.

The Ipcress File was an instant success. 'Better than Fleming', said some critics, though it must be admitted this was more due to their dislike of Fleming than their love of Deighton. The book was serialised in the London *Evening Standard* and the film rights were sold soon afterwards. This book introduced a character who was to serve his author well—Harry Palmer, perhaps the only secret agent of recent times to win fans on the same scale as James Bond. Deighton gave Palmer the right kind of anonymity for the public mood, that of a working-class boy from Burnley suddenly precipitated into a strange new world of intrigue among people out of his class whom he does not trust. Palmer has lasted surprisingly well, though latterly Deighton seems to have lost interest in him.

This book was swiftly followed by *Horse Under Water* (UK 1963), of which one critic wrote that 'the most obviously new thing about Mr Len Deighton's spy stories is the anti-heroic quality of his central character'. Here was an author who was fascinated by war and the gadgetry and hardware that go with modern warfare. He sought authentic background for his second story: 'My hero has to dive to a sunken submarine. So that I could get background stuff the Admiralty gave me access to HMS *Vernon*, the frogman training establishment.' Somebody must have thought he was too interested in these matters, because the Naval Security authorities asked to see the manuscript of *Horse Under Water*. The story dealt with deep-sea diving, drug trafficking and a great deal of the minutiae of the modern spy story—those seemingly irrelevant, rather boring details which occupy much of the time of the average secret agent. Both this book and *Funeral in Berlin* (UK 1964) again marked strongly the reaction away from Fleming; the narrator/anti-hero was politically to the left and mistrustful of the strong, silent upper-class Intelligence chief. But whereas Ambler would have maintained this leftish slant delicately and seriously, Deighton had his tongue in his cheek: his anti-hero kept his gun under a chamber-pot. There was much else that was new about this enterprising newcomer. He delighted in gimmickry, in entertaining his readers with odd items of erudition of a technical kind, such as how to tap a telephone and what RI and D of C codes were, in providing footnotes and appendices such as the spy novel had never had before. It was a refreshing change, though it irritated some because, as another critic said: 'Deighton's prose is elliptical. It needs to be sipped slowly to be appreciated, rather like Yellow Chartreuse.' Indeed, for some he needed to be re-read in order to be understood, for he wallowed in obscurity and ambiguity. He managed to get away with it. People began to warm to the Deighton cult, enjoying coping with the obscurities and built-in puzzle sentences in the same way that a crossword addict loves to tackle increasingly difficult problems. As

Julian Symons aptly put it, 'There is something lyrical about his re-creation of the dangerous and transitory lives of agents . . . Writing of this quality . . . makes Deighton a kind of poet of the spy novel.'

At the same time Deighton adored spoofing his readers and the public generally. Paperback editions of his novels began to give varying potted spoof biographies on the covers. One *Who's Who* of writers solemnly recorded that he was 'son of a Governor of the Windward Islands, educated at Eton and Worcester College, Oxford, President of the Oxford Union' and that his subsequent jobs included being a 'deckhand on a Japanese whaler'. His delight in gadgetry is perhaps one reason why Deighton has no telephone, but only a teleprinter machine on which he can be reached. One doesn't telephone this author, one telexes him. One of his publishers tried a new publicity stunt when they wanted to boost *An Expensive Place to Die* (UK 1967) in America. Deighton faked a set of facsimiles of 'top secret documents' which referred to nuclear weapons and correspondence between the White House and Harold Wilson (then Prime Minister). These were sent to America where the stunt began to get out of hand. Customs officials were apparently fooled and, thinking the documents were genuine, called in the FBI. Later some of the documents were found in a dustbin by a Slav. He realised they were not genuine, but, having a sense of humour, took them to the United Nations HQ and offered them to a Russian. The Russian solemnly explained that he would have to get his senior officer's permission to pay the $100,000 the Slav was asking for the material.

Billion-dollar Brain (UK 1966) was received by the critics with enormous and unusual enthusiasm: 'The best thing he has done, a subtle performance which will delight admirers and should convert those who in the past have found him too complex.' The plot was, like most of Deighton's, as intricate as the Hampton Court Maze, and the story introduced Harvey Newbigin, a buffoon of a double-agent who is shot in the snow outside a Russian train. Also featured was General Midwinter, a John Birch Society-style figure who runs an ultra-right-wing organisation in Texas, has built himself a computer and is out to destroy Russian communism by sending saboteurs into the USSR, spreading viruses and wrecking trains.

This was followed by *Close Up* (UK 1972) and *Spy Story* (UK 1974). By this time there were indications that, as a writer, Deighton was growing away from the spy story, but the last-named reassured his fans. It was about a Soviet rear-admiral who wanted to defect to

Britain in order to have a kidney transplant operation (an odd reason, for he probably would have fared better having it done in Russia). A critic wrote of this that 'Mr Deighton's stories are seldom pellucid-clear and this one is no exception. His current fad is war games, which, to be candid, are more interesting to play than to have described. There is an exciting sequence in a nuclear sub under Arctic ice.' While in Deighton's books there are exciting narratives and skilfully described episodes, the story-line is a very secondary consideration. Technology and all the elements of technology affecting modern espionage are the first and foremost factor in almost all Deighton's stories.

For a while Deighton's fascination for war and war games led him to tackle a twelve-part history of the Second World War, with each volume dealing with a technical development in warfare. He also took six months away from book-writing to do the screenplay of *Oh, What a Lovely War*. *Yesterday's Spy* (UK 1975) made a contrast: it was about the members of a small spy network who had operated against the Nazis in occupied France during the Second World War and examined what they were up to thirty years later. *Twinkle, Twinkle, Little Spy* (UK 1976) saw Deighton firmly back on the conventional espionage theme with what another critic called 'concentric circles of plot and counter-plot'. Again, there was the riddle-me-ree approach in this yarn of a Soviet defector, the laconic dialogue beloved by Deighton fans and the careful scene-setting. This time the story started off in the Sahara Desert, led on to New York and Washington and ended up back in the desert after a spectacular pursuit on Algerian mountain roads. Major Mann and his English side-kick took delivery of the defecting Russian Professor Bekuv in the Sahara and whisked him over to the USA. There the defector, the inevitable electronics expert, was joined by his butch wife. To complicate matters and add a sexual variant, the CIA put in a lesbian agent to seduce Madame Bekuv from her husband. Perhaps Robert Nye, reviewing this book, pin-pointed the main defect in Deighton's work when he wrote that in comparing Deighton with Buchan, 'you begin to see what is lacking in his fiction. It is, putting it simply, a point of view. In the world of Len Deighton the computer is king. That may be true to the superficialities of our culture, but in the long run I doubt whether it can be true even to the superficialities of our espionage systems. You can't escape the possibility of battles between good and evil for ever, especially by retreat into the same areas of limited choice, with a hero whose only declared commitment is to Gauloise cigarettes.'

Deighton, like a number of other British authors in these days of super-taxation, lives in Ireland, near the Mountains of Mourne. And, as a means of communication, he still prefers telex to the telephone, so the computer reigns as much in his private as in his public life.

Charles Dickens (b. nr Portsmouth, 7 February 1812; d. Gad's Hill, Kent, 9 June 1870)

Dickens only ventured outside of England once for the material for one of his novels. This was for *A Tale of Two Cities* (UK 1859), of which G. K. Chesterton wrote that it was Dickens's 'most typical contact with the civic ideals of Europe. All his other tales have been tales of one city . . . Dickens's French Revolution is probably more like the real French Revolution than Carlyle's.' Critics may dispute whether *A Tale of Two Cities* is a spy story in the strictest sense of the word, yet it is undeniable that Dickens positively contributed something to the slow development of the genre. The background of this book is very much that of espionage and counter-espionage, and Dickens's debunking of the high patriotic motives of which spying scoundrels unctuously boast is most skilfully done: '. . . Mr Stryver fitted the prisoner's case on the jury, like a compact suit of clothes; showing them how the patriot, Barsad, was a hired spy and traitor, an unblushing trafficker in blood, and one of the greatest scoundrels upon earth since the accursed Judas—which he certainly did look rather like . . . how the watchful eyes of those forgers and false swearers had rested on the prisoner as a victim, because some family affairs in France, he being of French extraction, did require him making those passages across the Channel . . .'

Sydney Carton's famous last words may today provoke the same cynicism and instinctive mistrust of Dickens's sentimentalism that made Oscar Wilde declare that the death of Little Nell left him speechless with mirth. On the other hand there is a stimulating, *visual* quality about *A Tale* and its exciting, if sometimes melo-dramatic narrative, makes this book appeal to many who do not normally read Dickens. To students of the spy story *A Tale* rewards re-reading today because it throws up parallels with spy fiction of the 1970s. The story, despite its melodrama, is closer to the realistic spy story of today than those of the 1920s. What is also interesting is that it lends itself so well to the medium of the cinema, possibly because at this time Dickens was collaborating closely with Wilkie Collins, whose habit was ceaselessly to dramatise his novels as he thought them up. It is more than likely that Wilkie Collins urged on Dickens not only the setting of Paris as well as London, but the underlying theme of espionage.

Capt. Henry Taprell Dorling: *see* 'Taffrail'

Sir Arthur Conan Doyle (b. Edinburgh, 22 May 1859; d. 7 July 1930)

Grandson of John Doyle, the political caricaturist, and nephew of Richard Doyle, of *Punch*, Arthur Conan Doyle was educated at Stonyhurst Academy and Edinburgh University, where he studied medicine and qualified as a doctor in 1881. Opening a practice at Southsea, Hants, Doyle soon found a need to supplement his income owing to a lack of patients. He made notes for a short story, creating the character of 'Ormond Sacker from Afghanistan' who 'lived at 221B Upper Baker Street with Sherrinford Holmes'. Eventually these two characters were changed into Dr John H. Watson and Sherlock Holmes and in December 1887 they appeared for the first time in Doyle's 'A Study in Scarlet', which was published in *Beeton's Christmas Annual*. The character of Sherlock Holmes was partly based on Dr Joseph Bell, the consulting surgeon at Edinburgh Infirmary, but one could also say that Doyle himself was part Holmes and part Watson. Doyle wanted to create a super-detective who eschewed emotion and relied on logic, a man whose mind soared above the humdrum things of life and who was elevated by his own philosophy. To etch such a man in a form that would appeal to readers Doyle cleverly avoided making Holmes a sanctimonious figure by describing him as prone to occasional fits of depression, a drug addict (albeit a controlled one) and a man who sought consolation and inspiration from pipe-smoking and playing the violin.

Doyle's main work was associated with the detective story, but some of his Sherlock Holmes stories can be called spy tales, most notably *The Bruce Partington Plans* (UK 1908), in which Holmes is brought in to solve a problem which a baffled Secret Service could not cope with. This was the age of rapid technological growth which led to a great deal of industrial espionage; it was from such cases that

66

Doyle and others drew their inspiration for stories about stolen plans, but for commercial spies they substituted the more glamorous 'foreign agent'. Other of his stories have at least a close affinity with spy fiction: in *A Scandal in Bohemia* (UK 1891), for instance, Holmes plays the role of a King's agent rather than a detective in dealing with Irene Adler. Conan Doyle was, however, an inspiration not only to many writers of spy fiction who followed him, but also to such famous figures in real-life espionage as A. E. W. Mason, who admitted that when he posed as a lepidopterist when engaged in espionage in Mexico on behalf of the NID in the First World War, he had got the idea from Doyle's villain Stapleton in *The Hound of the Baskervilles* (UK 1902). It is possible that Sir Robert Baden-Powell's disguise when spying on the gun batteries of a Dalmatian fortress came from the same source.

Maurice Edelman (b. 2 March 1911; d. 14 December 1975)
Of humble Jewish parentage, Maurice Edelman was educated at Cardiff High School and Trinity College, Cambridge. From 1932–41 he was engaged in industry and research in the application of plastic materials to aircraft construction. During the Second World War, largely on the strength of his fluency in various languages (he was an expert both in Russian and French), he was a war correspondent for *Picture Post* in North Africa and France. By 1945 he had become one of the many young intellectuals who had sworn allegiance to the cause of Labour. He was elected MP for Coventry West, a seat he held until 1950, then stood for Coventry North, which he represented until 1974, when the constituency became Coventry North-West and he was again re-elected.

Edelman was very much the individualist socialist. Markedly left-wing on social and domestic issues, he was much more independent than many of his colleagues and sometimes nearer to the Conservative Party on foreign affairs. His early enthusiasm for Soviet Russia changed to hostile criticism of that country's treatment of the Jews in the post-war period. Unlike most Labour MPs, he greatly admired General de Gaulle and it was probably a great error of judgement that the first Wilson administration did not appoint him as Ambassador to France, a post he would have fulfilled with that distinction which only a man of letters can hope to do. He was delegate to the Consultative Assembly of the Council of Europe from 1949–51 and from 1965–70. He did more to improve Anglo-French relations than probably any other British MP and was Vice-President of the Anglo-French Parliamentary Relations Committee and President of the *Alliance Française*. In recognition of all this he was made an Officer of the Legion of Honour in 1960 and received the *Medaille de Paris* in 1972.

His first book, *France: the birth of the Fourth Republic*, was published in 1945 and after that he wrote a number of novels which combined politics and the technique of suspense in a manner which had not been tackled since Trollope. This led quite naturally to the espionage story. *A Dream of Treason* (UK 1954) was a Balchin-like entertainment about a Foreign Office man who, for a devious purpose, is encouraged by higher powers to allow the leakage of certain information only to find that he is to be held personally responsible for his action. Edelman called this 'a diplomatic thriller', adding that he hoped 'it may emerge as a moral thriller as well'. Five years later he produced *A Call on Kuprin* (UK 1959); its storyline, about a scientist who is lured from Cambridge University to Russia, bore a marked resemblance to the defection of Peter Kapitza, the Russian scientist who had been the assistant to Lord Rutherford when the latter split the atom at the Cavendish Laboratory in Cambridge. In Edelman's story a British MP is sent to Russia to try to persuade Kuprin to return. He is compromised in a hotel bedroom controlled by the Soviet Intelligence and in which there is a concealed camera. Only a few years later this exact technique was employed by the KGB against Commander Courtney, MP, with disastrous results for the latter's political career. The case of John Vassal (an Admiralty clerk who had been posted to Moscow), which caused a political scandal in the last years of the Macmillan administration, also bore some resemblance to *A Call on Kuprin*.

The Fratricides (UK 1963) told of the last days of the OAS campaign for *Algerie Française* and of an undercover man who infiltrated the OAS for de Gaulle. Edelman was well liked on all sides of the House of Commons for his charm, his debonair outlook, his ready smile and wit.

Clive Egleton (b. South Harrow, Middlesex, 25 November 1927) Clive Egleton was educated at Haberdashers' Aske's Hampstead School from 1938–44. In 1944 he joined the Army under age, enlisting in the Royal Armoured Corps, and was subsequently commissioned into the South Staffordshire Regiment (later the Staffordshire

Regiment) in September 1946. He was granted a Regular commission and stayed on in the Army until 1975, retiring voluntarily as Lieut.-Colonel. His first book was *A Piece of Resistance* (UK 1970), a realistic, if frightening peep into the future in which Russian forces occupy Britain after destroying Bristol with a nuclear warhead. *Last Post for a Partisan* (UK 1971) and *The Judas Mandate* (UK 1972), completed the trilogy. In the final book the Soviet occupation force in Britain is being depleted because of the Chinese threat to Siberia, yet the Resistance Movement in Britain, now severely split between those who favour stepping up their campaign and those who would prefer to co-operate with the puppet government, is unable to take advantage of the situation.

Outstanding success came to Egleton when he produced *Seven Days to a Killing* (UK 1973), which was filmed the following year as *The Black Windmill*. The story concerned Major John Tarrant, who received a demand for £500,000 in uncut diamonds as ransom for his kidnapped thirteen-year-old son. He had seven days to find these and the life of his son was at stake. But so, too, was the security of his country and while top Intelligence men were prepared to play a dangerous game of bluff, Tarrant was willing to risk everything, including his own life.

The October Plot (UK 1974) was a follow-up to the failed plot to kill Hitler in July 1944. It was the fictitious, but not altogether improbable, story of an operation that could have changed the course of the Second World War and brought it to a conclusion almost a full year earlier. Major-General Gerhardt disappears on the day of the abortive plot to kill Hitler and re-appears in Britain with a plan to assassinate Martin Bormann, the Nazis' deputy leader. Colonel Michael Ashby, head of MI21, links up with Gerhardt to plan Operation Leopard for 14 October 1944—nothing less than a daredevil assassination scheme to be carried out by six carefully chosen men. *Skirmish* (UK 1975) was set in Britain, France and Italy and started off with the Chief of the Department of Subversive Warfare in London happily contemplating the signature of documents, in a 'safe house' nearby, which would give the Department a firm foothold in the Middle East. On the first floor of this house two men are waiting: '. . . It should have been simple, but within the space of seven minutes the whole situation had changed. The two men lay dead . . . McAlister was forced to question his own loyalties and Harper [the Department Chief] learned that no plan survived contact with the enemy.'

Colonel Egleton is well qualified to write spy thrillers such as these remarkably engrossing and intelligent stories. He worked for Intelligence in the Persian Gulf from 1958–59 and was engaged in counter-insurgency operations in Cyprus (1955–56) and East Africa (1964). Much of his material is drawn from first-hand knowledge of serving in India, Hong Kong, Japan, Egypt, Libya, Cyprus, the Persian Gulf, Kenya, Uganda, France and Germany. He has also travelled widely in Europe. 'Throughout the period I was serving in the Army I was fortunate to hold a variety of appointments on the staff dealing with logistics, operations and law and was for a time an instructor at the School of Infantry, specialising in mechanised warfare as well as nuclear and chemical warfare. All the above experiences have been very helpful to me as a writer.'

Gerard Fairlie (b. London, 1899)
Educated at Downside and the Royal Military Academy, Sandhurst, Gerard Fairlie served in the Scots Guards from 1917–24. He was not only very much in the 'Bulldog' Drummond mould, but was actually the model for 'Sapper's' character. Six-foot-two, clipped moustache, gregarious, voicing orthodox patriotic sentiments, Fairlie captained the Army at rugger, boxing and golf and in 1919 won the Army heavyweight boxing championship. 'Sapper' must have recognised his celebrated hero-to-be as soon as they met on a golf course. When Fairlie left the Army he set out to write novels, but also became a journalist and a screen writer and was successful in both fields. In six years he had sixteen novels published. He was one of those versatile Britons of an earlier generation who could not merely succeed as a scriptwriter in the tough world of Hollywood, but at the same time win his laurels as a brilliant golfer and rugger player, a founder member of the Anglo-French Golfing Society and, in the early part of the Second World War, as an inspiring head of a Commando Training School.

Fairlie had a wide circle of friends, but perhaps naturally his closest was 'Sapper' (Lieut.-Colonel McNeile). When McNeile was dying, he and Fairlie discussed the last 'Bulldog' Drummond story plotted by 'Sapper' and finally Fairlie agreed to write the book—*Bulldog Drummond on Dartmoor* (UK 1938). This was the first of a new series of Drummond books, followed up by *Bulldog Drummond At War* (UK 1940) and *Captain Bulldog Drummond* (UK 1945), which re-introduced into Hugh Drummond's life that 'alluring mistress of evil, Irma Peterson'. Fairlie's versions of 'Sapper' stories were more in the nature of thrillers than spy stories and his talent as a scriptwriter enabled him to give a zest to Drummond which McNeile never quite contrived. The truth was that Drummond on screen was usually much better than Drummond in prose.

Fairlie's wartime experiences were as varied as his civilian life. Apart from his post at the Commando Training School, his voice became familiar to millions of French people over the radio and more than once he was dropped in France in a style worthy of 'Bulldog' Drummond. Though not mentioned in the records of SOE, Fairlie saw something of the world of Secret Service with the Maquis inside France. He made the most of these experiences in his book *They Found Each Other* (UK 1946), which told of a Breton, a French aristocrat, and an American-born girl named Micheline, forming a French Resistance unit. 'The book is a novel,' wrote Henry Longhurst, a golfing friend of Fairlie, 'but he weaved his experiences when parachuted into France into the story. It is all true except for two details. I discovered them.' In *Hands Off Bulldog Drummond* (UK 1949) the indestructible Irma Peterson turns up as an ally of the communists: she 'outPaukers Anna Pauker', wrote one critic, comparing her with the Rumanian communist leader. And there was an echo of McNeile in that melodramatic statement of Irma's: 'It is our aim to paralyse the country.' Britain, of course; by strikes, naturally!

Fairlie is now living in retirement in Malta.

Anthony Firth (b. Cheriton, Kent, 4 May 1937)
Anthony Firth is included in this book on the basis of one novel, one of the most promising first spy stories of the past twenty years. It is hoped that he will write another one. He was, in his own words, 'brought up "below stairs" in a succession of grand houses by a formidable Mum' and 'educated by a charming and saintly step-father and, less successfully, by Trinity College, Cambridge, of which I was a senior scholar. I was President of the Union, too.'

His one book was *Tall, Balding, Thirty-five* (UK 1966), which Julian Symons described as 'always stylish and witty', adding that Firth 'manages an exciting story in a mild send-up of the form and a slightly horrific study in psychology. The material is baroque, the manner cool, the whole unmistakably original.' The author himself says that the whole idea of this book began as a parody of the genre:

'It was, if you like, a picture of "the spy to be", the reversed mirror image of all established spy skills and attributes. But it altered rather as one began to write and the book speedily took on a life of its own.'

Firth adds that he might yet return to writing spy stories, but that his career in television has been 'creatively demanding as well as executively active' and that 'a longhand novel is boring hard work'. Those who think this is a mere excuse for idleness should ponder the fact that some of the authors in this book can only function if they use a pencil, even if others can only talk into a dictaphone. Firth's kind of book calls for the self-criticising aid of the pen or pencil that more easily stills the wrong adjective or the unhappy verb, for his prose is that of the perfectionist.

Ian Fleming (b. London, 28 May 1908; d. Kent, 12 August 1964) Ian Lancaster Fleming was the son of Major Valentine Fleming, MP for South Oxfordshire (Conservative) and Evelyn St Croix Fleming. Educated at Eton, Sandhurst and on the continent, Fleming first narrowly failed an examination for the Diplomatic Service and then joined Reuters News Agency. In 1933 he was in Moscow to cover the trial of the six British engineers of the Metropolitan Vickers Electrical Company who had been arrested by the OGPU on charges of spying. Soon afterwards he resigned from Reuters to take a job in merchant banking in the City. Within two years he had moved to the stockbroking firm of Rowe and Pitman where he became a junior partner. During this period he developed a passion for book collecting and shrewdly built up a large range of first editions of books marking what he called 'milestones of human progress . . . or books that have started something'. In due course this collection became worth more than £100,000. In the spring of 1939 he returned to Moscow officially as a correspondent of *The Times*, but unofficially on a brief trip to make a report for the Foreign Office. Then in the early summer of that year, on the advice of Montagu Norman, Governor of the Bank of England, Fleming was chosen to be Personal Assistant to Admiral John Godfrey, the new Director of Naval Intelligence, with the rank of Lieut., RNVR. After Fleming's death Godfrey paid him this tribute: 'I once said that Ian should have been the DNI and I his naval adviser. If he had been ten years older and I ten years younger, this might have had the elements of a workable proposition.'

Fleming organised the No. 30 Assault Unit, which was modelled on the kind of Intelligence assault unit the Germans had used in Crete in 1941. This became known as Fleming's Private Navy, and in beach reconnaissance, in secretly probing enemy territory and bringing back information, it was a great success. Though he supplied many bright ideas for operations during his NID stint and was highly regarded in US Naval circles as well as at the British Admiralty, Fleming received no decorations for his war work. At the end of 1945 he became foreign manager of Kemsley Newspapers, personally selecting a team of foreign correspondents to cover the globe. He held this post until the newspaper group became Thomson Newspapers in 1959. It was then that Fleming wrote his first book, not a spy novel, but a foreign correspondent's guide-book which was issued for the education of his staff. It was a masterly and concise guide, quite unrivalled in its field, and today is a collector's rarity. Fleming, who had seemed to be a confirmed bachelor, married Anne, Lady Rothermere, at the town hall of Port Maria, Jamaica, in 1952, his friend Noël Coward being one of the witnesses. Apart from his London house, Fleming had bought some land and created what he called his 'lotus-eating home' at Oracabessa in Jamaica in 1946. It was here that most of the Bond books were written after his marriage. The character of Bond, the highly sophisticated Secret Service operator, was a combination of a number of people, including Dusko Popov (the British agent code-named Tricycle), Sidney Reilly and Fleming himself. Bond disliked flowers in a room, loved dry martinis and caviare: so did Fleming. But, so Fleming would ruefully tell his friends: 'Bond isn't really as good as Sidney Reilly' (the ace British spy who disappeared in Russia in the late 1920s).

Fleming utilised one of his less fortunate wartime escapades for the gambling scene in his first Bond novel, *Casino Royale* (UK 1953). 'I and my chief, Admiral J. H. Godfrey, were flying to Washington in 1941 for secret talks with the American Office of Naval Intelligence before America came into the war,' wrote Fleming afterwards. 'Our Sunderland touched down at Lisbon for an overnight stop . . . our Intelligence people described how Lisbon and the neighbouring Estoril were crawling with German secret agents. The chief of these and his two assistants, we were told, gambled every night in the casino at Estoril. I immediately suggested to the DNI that he and I should have a look at these people. We went there and there were the three men playing at the high *Chemin de fer* table. The DNI didn't know the game. I explained it to him and then the feverish idea came to me that I would sit down and gamble against these men and defeat them, reducing the funds of the German Secret Service. It was a foolhardy plan . . . I "bancoed" and lost. I "suivied" and lost again and "suivied" a third time and was cleaned out. A humiliating experience.'

That was Fleming's own account of the incident which he claimed inspired *Casino Royale*. But Dusko Popov has another tale to tell about casino life in Lisbon about the same time and this also concerns Fleming. 'I'm told that Ian Fleming said he based his character James Bond to some degree on me and my experiences,' wrote Popov (*Spy-Counter-Spy* (UK 1974)). 'Fleming and I did rub shoulders in Lisbon and he did follow me about. Perhaps he developed what happened that night into a Bond adventure.' Popov, who was a double-agent under the British Double XX operation for controlling spies working for the enemy, had just received $80,000 from the Germans which he was to hand over to Britain's MI6. 'But since the transaction took place in the evening, I was stuck with the money until I could make the necessary contact and arrangements the following day. Probably Ian Fleming got wind of the deal. I noticed Fleming in the lobby, but thought nothing more about it. Then I went to a café for a drink before dinner, and there was Fleming skulking about outside. At dinner he appeared in the same restaurant . . . To have a Naval Intelligence man on my tail at this point was amusing, because I knew it was the money, not me, he was safeguarding. Besides, I was reasonably sure Fleming was operating on his own without instructions. British Intelligence had enough confidence to entrust me with $80,000. The secrets I carried in my head were worth much more. We strolled through the halls of the casino, my shadow and I, observing play at the different tables. A favourite *bête noire* of mine was there, an insignificant-looking but wealthy Lithuanian named Bloch, who attempted to compensate for his tiny stature by arrogant play. . . I don't know what the devil was behind me, perhaps Fleming or the knowledge that he was there, but when Bloch announced "*Banque Ouverte*", I announced "Fifty thousand dollars". I glanced at Fleming. His face turned bile green. Obviously the Lithuanian didn't have that sort of money on him. He squirmed in his chair in embarrassment, "I suppose," I addressed the chief croupier, "that the Casino is backing this man's bet, since you didn't object to his *Banque Ouverte*." ' The croupier said that the casino never backed any player's stake, so Popov swept his cash back into his pocket and commented that he trusted that in future 'such irresponsible play will be prohibited'.

From 1953 until Fleming's death Bond books were produced annually. There seemed to be an increasing preoccupation with violence in the novels, for which he was attacked by some critics. More and more they were touched by sadism, and the deaths of some of his characters were bizarre to say the least: in *Doctor No* (UK 1958) Bond disposes of the communist doctor by smothering him in bird droppings. Anthony Curtis wrote that 'Fleming's famous accuracy of detail was a brilliant journalistic illusion. The loving care for the minutiae with which he described a game of golf, or a meal of soft-shell crabs enabled him to get away with murder in climatic scenes of wild penny-dreadful improbability.' *Live and Let Die* (UK 1954), his second book, introduced a new member of SMERSH, the enemy agency Bond so often found himself working against. Mr Big was the villain and Bond's sufferings were alleviated by the attentions of a girl named Solitaire. Bond's women were seductive, desirable and efficient: they were also the type of women Fleming preferred—'well-scrubbed, . . . clinical, clean and firm'. The novels all made the most of the Cold War period, with Bond operating against the agents of unfriendly powers (invariably the USSR)—men such as *Goldfinger* (UK 1959) and Scaramanga (*The Man With the Golden Gun* (UK 1965)). Fleming went to immense trouble to research the background and details for his books, using some of his foreign correspondents as advisers and making a trip to Japan before writing *You Only Live Twice* (UK 1964). In the latter book the character of Dikko Henderson was based on Richard Hughes, the *Sunday Times* correspondent in the Far East. Fleming took an impish delight in putting real people into the Bond books. His friend, Robert Harling, was roguishly introduced as an itinerant printer, while he had Bond and one of his girl friends travelling as 'Mr and Mrs Bryce' (another friend was Ivar Bryce who wrote *You Only Live Once: Memories of Ian Fleming* (UK 1975)). Tatiana in *From Russia with Love* (UK 1957) was named after Tatiana Preston, who typed the manuscript. *Moonraker* (UK 1955) was followed by *Diamonds Are Forever* (UK 1956), in which Bond is sent to break a 'pipe-line' for the smuggling of diamonds from Sierra Leone via Hatton Garden to New York. This was to some extent based on Fleming's talks with Sir Percy Sillitoe, the former MI5 chief who had been asked to investigate illicit diamond traffic from South Africa.

Other Bond books were *For Your Eyes Only* (UK 1960), *Thunderball* (UK 1961), *The Spy Who Loved Me* (UK 1962), *On Her Majesty's Secret Service* (UK 1963) and *Octopussy and the Living Daylights* (UK 1966). But none of these quite captured the quality of Fleming's first two or three books. In *You Only Live Twice* Bond becomes a victim of amnesia, setting off for Russia under the mistaken impression that he is returning to his fatherland. In *The Man with the Golden Gun*, published posthumously like some of the other later books, Bond is brought back from Russia after having been brain-washed by Colonel Boris of the Soviet Secret Police. This means he is now a dedicated Soviet agent whose first aim in life is to discharge a cyanide pistol into the face of his employer, 'M'. In the end Bond is 're-washed' and a knighthood is offered him (presumably one of the Wilson honours list, judging by the date!). It was Fleming's most melodramatic effort, but certainly not his best: the author had begun to mock his own readers. In between writing Fleming developed a passion for treasure-hunting, not merely in the Caribbean Islands and Seychelles, where he would follow up almost any old pirate's tale and ancient map, but also in England, and this he made the subject of some articles. He drove himself hard in outdoor activities, whether at underwater exploration, skiing or golf. Health warnings he did not heed and it was perhaps fitting that the final heart attack which ended his life came at the Royal St George's Sandwich golf course in Kent. Nobody would know better than Fleming that Bondery was but a phase of his life, albeit a lucrative one. It is as an extraordinarily good Assistant to the DNI that he will ultimately be remembered, or, as Admiral Godfrey, his chief, put it: 'Ian was a war-*winner*.'

Kenneth Follett (b. Cardiff, 5 June 1949)
Educated at Harrow Weald Grammar School, Poole Technical College and University College, London, where he took a degree in philosophy, Kenneth Martin Follett entered journalism via the *South Wales Echo* and the London *Evening News*, then joined Everest Books and eventually became that firm's deputy managing director. His first book, *The Big Needle* (UK 1974), was published under the pseudonym of 'Symon Myles', and was about drug trafficking. This was also published in Germany and the US. His first spy books were *The Shakeout* (UK 1975) and *The Bear Raid* (UK 1976). These are an important contribution to the literature

76

of espionage in that they deal with the largely neglected subject of industrial espionage. 'The spy story has been done by so many authors,' says Follett, 'that it seems difficult to produce anything fresh. My solution was to write about industrial espionage. To the best of my knowledge my character Piers Roper is still the only industrial spy in fiction. Roper is a high-powered marketing executive who takes posts with a series of companies purely to steal their secrets. To move unsuspected in the boardrooms he has to be a member of the upper class, and he is (Eton and Cambridge and an Army commission), but why should such a man betray his background by becoming a snoop? He is withdrawn and inhibited, hopelessly incompetent to deal with any emotion stronger than casual friendship and obsessively fastidious about etiquette, food and clothes. He was the first character of my creation who would not let me do as I liked with the plot: I took this to be a good sign.'

Follett has produced ten novels and one screenplay. He has never had anything to do with Intelligence, but, he adds, 'I do know one low-grade freelance spy who is very helpful.' What is fascinating about Follett's work and the creation of his character, Piers Roper, is the ingenious manner in which he brings the sex element up-to-date. Roper has a tortured romance with a girl. They are in love, but she demands total commitment whereas he, because of his profession, is pathologically self-sufficient. 'To my surprise,' says Follett, 'I discovered that the publishers believe this relationship to be one of the principal attractions of the series.' It is interesting to note that this most recent addition to the spy world in fiction, Roper, likes opera, chess and the later Impressionists, drives a Bentley, invariably dresses in grey, with white shirts and black ties, never eats potatoes, smokes Senior Service without filters and drinks whisky-and-soda without ice, hates pop music and poor food.

Frederick Forsyth (b. Ashford, Kent, 1938)
Forsyth was educated at Tonbridge School and, by the time he left, could speak French, German, Spanish and Russian. He did his National Service in the RAF, becoming a pilot, and then in 1958 entered journalism via the *Eastern Daily Press* first in Norwich and later in King's Lynn. In December 1961 he was offered a job at Reuters in London; the following May he was sent to Paris and from there to East Berlin. It is surprising how Forsyth and Anthony

Grey, the Reuters man detained in China for two years, followed in each other's paths—Norwich, London, East Berlin. Forsyth returned to London in 1965 when he joined the BBC as a radio reporter. He transferred to television and in February 1967 was appointed assistant diplomatic correspondent.

'I enjoyed TV journalism enormously,' he says, 'and then smashed the whole thing to smithereens by quitting the BBC and going off as a freelance to Biafra.' Biafra, however, was a subject upon which Forsyth developed a conscience and something of the spirit of a crusader. There had been a difference of opinion between him and his masters on the subject of the Biafran War when Nigeria systematically set out to put down the Biafrans' revolt. Forsyth was pro-Biafran; many newspapers and even more journalists had taken their cue from the British Government and largely adopted a pro-Nigerian Government slant in their reporting. During his freelance coverage of this war Forsyth wrote a Penguin Special, *The Biafra Story*, which sold 30,000 copies. He left the territory in December 1969, only a few weeks before the war ended. This marked a low period in Forsyth's life; he was waiting for a new job to turn up and he filled in the time by writing *The Day of the Jackal* (UK 1971) in thirty-five days. This novel was rejected by a few publishers before Hutchinson bought it and, of course, the fact that the typescript had been read and approved by André Malraux, the former Minister of Culture to President de Gaulle, helped a lot.

This book, which was an instantaneous success, marked a new development in the spy story. Technically, it really comes into the thriller class, but the background is that of espionage, counterespionage and political assassination. It described meticulously and realistically how the OAS (*Organisation de l'Armée Secrète*) decided to hire a top level professional assassin, an Englishman, to kill de Gaulle and to pay him half a million dollars for doing so. In essence it was a documentary spy thriller, based to a very large extent on fact. All but a few characters were real, although some had their names changed and their descriptions altered to mask the dangers of libel. 'I do not have the kind of imagination to spin a character out of the air,' Forsyth admitted. 'I met the Jackal, although he did not have the smoothness and style of my Jackal. He was simply a professional killer.' Forsyth also had the advantage of knowing the lower ranks of the OAS in France as well as the biographical details of some of their leaders. If ever there was a spy novel based on journalistic experience, this was it. The book was translated into eleven languages and published in twenty-six editions, with estimated sales of a million.

There is still fierce controversy as to how factual this novel actually is. Forsyth himself has declined to say whether the assassination plot he described was real and whether the leak of information through the leadership of the Secret Service he described was also true. But there were a number of attempts to kill de Gaulle during 1963, the year in which *The Jackal* is set. One British mercenary has actually claimed in the bars of Malaga to have been the man on whom Forsyth based the Jackal, at the same time boasting that he was marked down for killing by both the KGB and the French counter-espionage service. Even Harold Macmillan appears in *The Jackal* as 'a sad-eyed bloodhound'.

With his next book, *The Odessa File* (UK 1972), Forsyth gave yet another twist to the spy story. This time he made his spy a reporter—a perfectly legitimate device, and one which makes this no less of a spy story than Dorothy Sayers' Lord Peter Wimsey is less of a detective because he is not in the Police Force. It was again based on Forsyth's own journalistic experiences, this time on the year he spent working in East Berlin, covering East Germany, Hungary and Czechoslovakia. The story concerns Arab plots against Israel, in which the Arabs are assisted by ex-SS men who have banded together in a self-help organisation, Odessa. The whole business is investigated by a young West German freelance reporter, Peter Miller, who is on the trail of a former concentration camp commandant who has gone to live in South America. Miller sets out to penetrate the Odessa organisation, whose ramifications extend deep into German political life as well as to the supply of bubonic warheads to Egypt. For background material of the book Forsyth was allowed to draw on the Roschmann files of the Jewish Agency which has specialised in hunting Nazi war criminals.

Dogs of War appeared in 1974. This again was based on Forsyth's African experiences: it was also the one subject on which Forsyth felt most strongly. 'I get monomaniac about that particular subject. When I think back to all those suffering children, I get angry,' he says. 'The only thing that ever made me fighting mad was watching them die, watching what was done to those people, who after all were simply trying to set up a state outside the aegis of a very brutal and ruthless military dictatorship. To find a British Government, and a socialist government to boot, actively supporting what was after all a military junta and enabling that government to do what it did to the children of Biafra, I find truly and utterly inexcusable. I have neither forgiven, nor forgotten.' In *Dogs of War*, the story of a small African dictatorship called Zangaro, Forsyth allows some of his bitterness to penetrate his description of violence and bloodshed, of mercenaries and gun-running from Europe. Forsyth's future career may lead him away from the spy story unless, if he renews his passion for research and journalism, some other cause appeals strongly enough to him to provide the setting. The iniquities of the tax system in Britain, as applied to the author who suddenly has a spectacular success, have driven him to join the band of British authors in Eire.

Brian Freemantle (b. Southampton, 10 June 1936)

Brian Freemantle is that most unusual of combinations—a British spy story writer who is far better known and more highly praised in the US than in his own country. For some years he was a widely travelled foreign correspondent, experience which he has made full use of in the background to his books. Altogether he has had journalistic assignments in twenty-two countries, including the US, the USSR and Vietnam. He lives in Southampton with his wife and three children and until recently, when he relinquished his post as foreign editor of the *Daily Mail* in order to write full time, used his 80-mile rail commute between his home and his office to work on his books.

This author undoubtedly comes into the category of spy story writers whose work is well researched. Because of this, he has a big following among the professional Intelligence men in the US. Miles Copeland, who was first with the OSS and then the CIA, has paid him the tribute that two of Freemantle's books are 'virtual case histories of the East-West war of dirty tricks'. *Goodbye to An Old Friend* (UK 1973) was hailed by *Publishers' Weekly* as 'a very fine book, meticulously structured, intelligently written and excellent in characterisation'. It was a post-Cold War thriller built around an unprepossessing British Foreign Office man, Adrian Dodds, whose speciality is debriefing VIP defectors from the East. The query posed is why Viktor Pavel, Russia's renowned space scientist, should suddenly defect to the West? Honoured in his own country, adored by his family, why should he throw up all this just to seek asylum in England? The governments of the US and Britain are eager to accept Pavel and they press Dodds to clear the scientist. But Dodds continues to question Pavel, testing and probing in a tense verbal duel, for he suspects something is not quite right. Finally the Prime Minister himself threatens to destroy Dodds's career unless he follows his superiors' advice. Bowing to pressure, Dodds clears Pavel and triggers a climax that is as fascinating in its complexity as it is shattering in its implications.

Face Me When You Walk Away (UK 1974) is a story set in the upper echelons of the Soviet bureaucracy, right up to the Presidium itself. Freemantle makes very clear what is undoubtedly a fact—and probably one of the major factors in the continuing repression in the USSR—that on those levels there is an eternal power struggle with ideological and personal roots that go back to Stalin's day. It is an unusual novel, one of intrigue rather than a thriller. The Swedes are blackmailed into giving the Nobel Prize in literature to a young, emotionally unbalanced Russian. Unlike Solzhenitsyn, he is allowed to leave the country, make his acceptance speech and tour the West. Behind the scenes in Russia there is all manner of manoeuvring around the uses to which this writer is put. 'How accurate is all this?' asked one US critic reviewing the book. 'Nobody can tell, though of course in recent years there have been tantalising bits of information about the dirty work of certain Kremlin operators. What Freemantle writes does not seem exaggerated . . . in any case this is a grim picture of Soviet life today and in the main one that will be endorsed by most impartial observers who have been there.'

Yet by far the most important of Freemantle's books to date is *The Man Who Wanted Tomorrow* (UK 1975). Deep in the heart of the USSR lives Dr Heinrich Köllman, an ex-Nazi vivisectionist 'worse than Mengele'. Köllman is wanted by the Israelis as an arch war criminal and by his ex-comrades as the embezzler of a fortune in concentration camp loot. If the truth were known, he would also be wanted by the Russians, but, as the novel opens, he is camouflaged by plastic surgery and two layers of false identities. Dr Vladimir Kusnov, for that is his new name, is finally run to ground in Berlin after a series of intricate manoeuvres that the author narrates with verve and pace. This last book of Freemantle's attracted considerable attention in the ranks both of the State Department and the CIA, the latter being convinced that the story was based on one of their own cases. For the novel was in effect an extremely accurate and revealing account of the real-life conflict between Israeli Intelligence agencies and the highly secret neo-Nazi movements. In the end the CIA had to admit that this was merely another case of fiction mirroring the truth simply because it was so very well researched. *Charlie Muffin* (UK 1977) is Freemantle's latest.

Sarah Gainham (b. 1 October 1922)

The daughter of Tom Stainer, she took the pen-name of 'Sarah Gainham' from her maternal great-grandmother and, she adds, has 'always wished I had taken a man's name for my pseudonym'. Educated at Newbury High School for Girls, Berkshire, she married Antony Terry, who had served with British Army Intelligence in the Second World War and was then correspondent of Kemsley Newspapers in Vienna. She went out to Vienna in June 1947 and experienced the gradual build-up to the Cold War during the four-power occupation of that city. 'When I arrived in Vienna I was, like nearly all English people at that time, pronouncedly pro-Russian, as well as being young, ignorant and self-opinionated. It was the Russians who cured me in about six weeks.' Sarah Gainham, who also experienced at first-hand the Soviet coup in Hungary in 1956 and was for ten years the Central European correspondent for the *Spectator*, has had an exceptional insight into Central Europe generally since the war and, wisely, she has written about the countries which she knows so well. She started writing books in the mid-'fifties: her first book was *Time Right Deadly* (UK 1956) and this was promptly followed by four spy stories: *Cold Dark Night* (UK 1957), which was about life in Berlin in 1954; *Mythmaker* (UK 1957), a story set in Vienna in 1947, conjuring up the author's own realisation of what the Cold War was all about; *The Stone House* (UK 1959), set in Prague during the grim days of 1948; and *The Silent Hostage* (UK 1960), centred on the Adriatic coast of Yugoslavia. Her best book, and one which became a bestseller, being Book of the Month choice both in Britain and the US was *Night Falls on the City* (UK 1967). She writes with authenticity of detail and background, as one who knows all about the machinations of the Intelligence Services of several countries and has seen the results of some of their gaffes as well as their successes. She admits that her swift change from pro-Russian to anti-Russian views plays a part in her books: 'I had a special feeling for using the thriller as a vehicle for ideas, or rather propaganda. I always used them as anti-Russian propaganda. All the best spy thrillers whose origins are known seem to be based on reality. Certainly my own stories were: they are not really fiction at all, only written *as* fiction.'

Sarah Gainham was married a second time in 1964 to Kenneth Ames, another Central European newspaper correspondent, who died in 1975.

John Gardner (b. nr Newcastle, 1927)

The son of a clergyman, John Gardner was educated at Wantage Grammar School. He volunteered for the Fleet Air Arm for his National Service, but was not accepted. Instead he joined the Royal Marines and served with their Commando section in Hong Kong and elsewhere. After his term of service was completed he went to St John's, Cambridge, and took a degree in theology. Then, deciding to follow in his father's footsteps, he went to a theological college at Oxford and was ordained. Gardner spent five years in holy orders, including a spell as an RAF chaplain, then left the church when he realised that he was an agnostic. In the late 'fifties he turned to journalism, and worked for seven years as theatre critic of a local weekly newspaper at Stratford-on-Avon. He became such an authority on Shakespeare that he was asked to lecture on the Bard in the United States and Russia. This was a traumatic time for Gardner, who was slowly finding the right direction for his talents. 'I was helped by a wonderful doctor,' he said and in a sense his first book, *Spin The Bottle* (UK 1964), was a tribute to that, for it was the autobiographical confessions of a reformed alcoholic.

Like Le Carré, Gardner detested the character of James Bond. (There is little doubt that anti-Bondism actually pumped the necessary adrenalin into the veins of quite a few would-be writers in this period.) While he was proud and happy to be the only full-time drama critic on a weekly newspaper in England, the challenge of a new career as a novelist was accepted with enthusiasm. Though he reacted to the Bond era in much the same way as Le Carré, Gardner evolved his own type of spy story as a kind of send-up of Bondism and the whole game of Intelligence. Where Le Carré evoked gloom and tragedy, Gardner indulged in comedy and laughter. The character of Boysie Oakes was not merely a comic anti-hero, but a positive antidote to Bond. He was introduced for the first time in Gardner's *The Liquidator* (UK 1964): 'The idea came to me in a train,' confessed Gardner. 'Boysie Oakes was based on the idea of a government employing people to murder. The book was written as a joke, but behind it were some of the things I had always wanted to say about this kind of life.' Boysie Oakes, on the wrong side of forty, terrified of violence, suffering from air sickness and afraid of heights, was the antithesis of James Bond. He was, said Gardner, 'the picture of what most of us are like—luxury-loving, lecherous and a mass of neuroses.' In this first of Gardner's spy stories Boysie Oakes is recruited to liquidate British agents who are regarded as security risks. He is not really a born killer, as his superiors believe, but rather a timid character who sub-contracts the killing jobs to a Soho gangster. There are some exciting as well as several comic situations and many good jokes.

The Liquidator was an instant success: it appeared at the psychologically right moment when the reaction to Fleming's work had set in and, probably because of its atmosphere of light-hearted debunking of the spy game, appealed to a wider audience than that of Le Carré. With this book alone and the film which swiftly followed, Gardner hit the jackpot and within a few years became one of the highest paid authors of the books-into-movies school. In 1966 came *Amber Nine* in which Gardner's socialism peeped out in his approach to spy fiction. It was still about Boysie Oakes, who was given the job of liquidating a leftish MP, but passed the assignment on to his Soho gangster. One of the book's memorable characters was Klara Thirel, who ran a sadist's school for spies. Another character in *Amber Nine* voiced something of Gardner's own philosophy when he said: 'Don't you see there are no such things as goodies and baddies any more, only just people standing in the dusk of history?'

Boysie Oakes has survived because it is easy for many people to identify with him and the trend of the 'sixties and 'seventies has been for people to project themselves as ordinary types rather than as heroes. This comic agent is a womaniser but, again unlike Bond, he has a conscience about women. There is a streak of puritanism in him. In *Understrike* (UK 1973) just as he is about to attempt a seduction he draws back because he doesn't think 'it's quite nice'. Though a bumpkin, he has been given a superficially sophisticated training in what to eat and drink and how to tell Bach from Bernstein, and a grounding in Kingsley Amis. He enjoyed what one critic described as 'an elephantine caper' in *Madrigal* (UK 1967) and in *The Airline Pirates* (UK 1970) was put in charge of an air charter company with the appallingly punned title of 'Air Apparent'. Gardner had the experience of seeing enacted in Congo-Brazzaville an attempted coup very similar to the one he described in this book:

'I called the place where the coup took place Etzikas, but in fact it was a bit of Gabon and a bit of Brazzaville,' he said afterwards.

Founder Member (UK 1969) was followed by *Traitor's Exit* (UK 1970), a jaunty, indelicate story about a failing spy fiction author who is bribed to extricate from Moscow (with the assistance of Boysie Oakes, of course) a noteworthy British defector. The party steals a tank and then a helicopter, is befriended by a travelling circus and finally crawls into a minefield in Finland. By 1975 the formula was beginning to show signs of wear. In *Killer for a Song* the perpetually reluctant agent, Boysie Oakes, and his smoothie boss, Mostyn, find themselves in dire trouble. The plot has to do with revenge for a Secret Service killing in Mexico in 1964 and Mostyn gets himself shot dead halfway through the story. It was the last of Gardner's spy fiction to feature Boysie Oakes.

More recently he has turned from the comic spy to more serious work. His *Moriarty* series, dealing with Sherlock Holmes's archenemy, is not without a touch of what he likes to call espionography, for the evil Professor of these books employs a company of 'lurkers' specifically for gaining access to secret Intelligence and criminal information. Now, he sees 'the escalation of security services as a sinister matter'. Other of Gardner's spy fiction books are *Hideaway* (UK 1968), *To Run a Little Faster* (UK 1973), *The Werewolf Trace* (UK 1977) and, in preparation, *The Dancing Dodo*.

There are occasional signs that Gardner would like to escape into other literary pastures, and it is interesting to note that he often heads his chapters with quotations from Brecht, Shakespeare and Shelley. One sometimes has the feeling that he might one day take time off to return to a religious theme or, if not, to a strictly sociological thesis.

Brian Garfield (b. New York City, 26 January 1939)
Brian Francis Wynne Garfield was educated at the University of Arizona. He is that rarity among writers, a devotee of jazz music and a professional musician, and originally started his career as a jazz band member. He has used the pen names of 'Frank Wynne', 'Brian Wynne' and 'Frank O'Brian', though he writes his most important work as Brian Garfield. His books are mostly those of the contemporary thriller narrative type, including *The Arizonans* (US 1961), *The Vanquished* (US 1964), *Sliphammer* (US 1970), and *Relentless* (US 1973), but some of his best books have been of the

spy fiction genre. *Deep Cover* (US 1973) told of a take-over of America's most important missile base by 300 Russians. A master of Soviet Intelligence had worked for twenty years on his plan to teach these 300 men and women to think, act and talk like Americans. So deep was their cover that they themselves did not know which of their colleagues were part of the masquerade. Not only did they surreptitiously take over the base, but, without being unmasked, their influence extended deep into Washington political circles. To combat this unknown factor, which he senses rather than sees, Senator Alan Forrester risks his own career in trying to probe it. *Line of Succession* (US 1974) marked the impressively consistent improvement of this talented author, who is growing in stature all the time. It plunged into the complexities of American politics, with the President-elect being kidnapped and held to ransom by a group of extremists eager to secure the release of important prisoners for which they are prepared to barter the President's life. The book was enlivened by CIA machinations, of which Garfield seems to have made a study, and high-tension thrills.

Writing of *Hopscotch* (US 1974), which he described as 'one of the most compelling thrillers of this season', ex-agent Miles Copeland said: 'This latest book [of Garfield's] features a former CIA official named Miles who is roughly my vintage and physical build, who has lived in Birmingham, Alabama, my home town, who wrote a book that made the CIA's "questors" unhappy, and who decided to annoy them further by enticing them into a "game" of a sort that has given me a certain amount of notoriety.'

Henry Gibbs: *see* Simon Harvester

Philip Gibbs (b. 1 May 1877; d. 10 March 1962)
Educated privately before entering journalism in his 'teens, Sir Philip Gibbs became an editor at Cassell & Company when he was twenty-one and was later made literary editor of the *Daily Mail*. A wide experience in Fleet Street eventually saw him become one of the outstanding reporters of his day, covering such major stories as the Siege of Sidney Street and the trans-Atlantic quest for Dr Crippen. One of his biggest scoops was the exposure of Dr Frederick Cook, who claimed to have discovered the North Pole. During the First World War Gibbs was a war correspondent of distinction, attached

86

to the Bulgarian and later the French and British armies. He was knighted in 1920. The following year he investigated famine conditions in Russia. In 1935 he served on the Royal Commission on the Private Manufacture of Arms. His best known novel was undoubtedly *The Street of Adventure* (UK 1909), about life in Fleet Street, but he wrote an unusual, highly original spy story, *The Ambassador's Wife*, in 1956.

James Grady (b. Montana, 30 April 1949)
A 'bawdy but isolated atmosphere' is the way James Thomas Grady describes the small, Western agricultural town where he was born and spent his early years. He attended the state university of Montana, securing a BA in journalism, having also studied political science and history. 'I intended to be a lawyer, despite the fact that I had been writing ever since I was four (I dictated to my mother), because I knew that writers starve,' he says. However, what he took up was a job with the state's Constitutional Convention as a legislative aide. In the next few years he worked as a labourer, which was how he paid for his education, a juvenile delinquency expert and an impoverished freelance writer until *Six Days of the Condor* was published in 1974. This was the tale of a CIA researcher (employed by an obscure but real branch of that agency) who returns from lunch to find his co-workers have been slaughtered, and who attempts to survive and unravel the mystery. Researcher Ronald Malcolm's job is to read and analyse spy and mystery stories as they are published in order to spot anything that comes close to reality, and thus detect possible leaks of information. A year later this highly successful book was sold as a film to Dino de Laurentis and Stanley Schneider. *Six Days* was followed by *Shadow of the Condor* (US 1975) in which Ronald Malcolm again appeared and was hailed by one critic as 'the most likeable and unlikely CIA agent on record'. In this story the body of an Air Force under-cover agent based in Europe mysteriously turns up at a Montana missile site. The CIA's job is to find out what led the agent there and who killed him. To divert attention from the agency Malcolm is sent to Montana in disguise. What neither the CIA nor Malcolm has counted on is that two, even three, can play that game. Malcolm discovers that all parties are being double-crossed, even by the unusual standards of the world of international espionage.

Grady is himself a born investigator. Since his successful start as a novelist he has been an aide for a United States Senator and is currently working as an investigative reporter for Jack Anderson's nationally syndicated column, writing fiction in his spare time. 'I try to write spy fiction as factually as possible,' he says. 'All my backgrounds are solidly factual. I try to use as much real material as possible, weaving truth through my fiction. I try to paint the world of espionage as it is—largely grey, tinged occasionally with blood, peopled extensively by the type of person most people wouldn't want to invite into their homes. Ronald Malcolm is a very ordinary individual, no superman, who works in the field, propelled by a combination of fascination and revulsion, tinged with a sense of general alienation more than anything else. As a muck-raker I am also a unique type of spy, if you will: I hunt out secrets everywhere from the Pentagon to Congress and the Diplomatic Corps. I handle highly classified, purloined documents. I probe and detect. When I find what I consider wrong-doing, I attack it by shedding light on it through helping Jack Anderson publish. I have to deal with real intelligence officers, military officials, mobsters, prostitutes, crooks, informants, killers and innocent victims.'

Bruce Graeme (b. London, 23 May 1900)
This is the pseudonym of Graham Montague Jeffries. His education was rudely interrupted by the First World War, when he volunteered for the Queen's Westminster Rifles. After demobilisation he became a freelance journalist and travelled several times to the US and France on special assignments. During the early 'twenties he also interested himself in the cinema industry, actually financing, producing and selling a one-reel comedy, as well as doing scriptwriting. His first book was *Blackshirt* (UK 1924), the story of a 'gentleman cracksman'. Though not basically a writer of spy stories, he uses Intelligence work as a background to a number of his crime novels, notably and most outstandingly in *Counter-Spy* (UK 1938), *Holiday for a Spy* (UK 1964), *Much Ado About Something* (UK 1967) and *The D Notice* (UK 1974).

Graham Greene (b. 2 October 1904)
The son of the late Charles Henry Greene, headmaster of Berk-

hampstead School, Graham Greene was one of a trio of brilliant brothers who have distinguished themselves in literature, broadcasting and medicine. Educated at Berkhampstead School, where from all accounts he was on the point of running away on more than one occasion, he went on to Balliol College, Oxford, before starting a career in journalism in Nottingham. In 1926 he joined *The Times* as a sub-editor and it was during this period that his first book was published, *Babbling Brook* (UK 1925). In 1930 he became literary editor of the *Spectator*. *Stamboul Train* (UK 1932) and *Brighton Rock* (UK 1938) helped to make him a popular as well as one of the most consistent and powerful novelists emerging in England over the past fifty years.

It was not until shortly before the war that he introduced an element of the spy story into his work, most notably in *The Confidential Agent* (UK 1939), in which he introduced 'D', the agent of an imaginary Latin government which bore a distinct resemblance to that of the embattled Spanish Republican Government of that era. Greene is not, of course, to be labelled as a spy novelist, but he has used the often interwoven themes of espionage and corruption as a vehicle for his prose. He has also written some of the better books of this genre and Miles Copeland, himself in 'the game' for many years, records that 'the oldest pro [spy] I know told me that if he were dropped on a desert island with just a few books, two of which had to be spy fiction, he would choose Graham Greene's *The Confidential Agent* and *Our Man in Havana*. I asked him why, and he said, "They're good for my soul." He gave me a sly look and added, "Anyone who doesn't get my meaning doesn't know much about my profession." ' Undoubtedly Greene's wartime service in Intelligence provided him with much material for his later spy books, not to mention some of the characters in them. His entry in *Who's Who* states that from 1941–44 he was in a 'department of the Foreign Office', which is a well-known euphemism for Intelligence work, in Greene's case mainly in West Africa. One of his main jobs was to watch the activities of the Vichy French in Freetown. It is noteworthy that the section in which Greene worked was that of the Iberian sub-section of Section V of the SIS, which was controlled by none other than 'Kim' Philby. The authors of *The Philby Conspiracy* write that 'there is a story of earlier Iberian [section] days which sounds very much like the origins of *Our Man in Havana*. The SIS men in Tangier wanted to keep an eye on German submarine movements from Barcelona, and so they hired a Spanish marquis . . . furnished him with money and sent him to the town for a month. The marquis, a man of taste, established himself at an excellent hotel, and, being a homosexual, amused himself copiously with the local boyhood. On the day before the deadline after a number of cables of reminder, he suddenly produced a fat wad of information about submarine sightings in the most circumstantial detail. The SIS dispatched this with great excitement to Naval Intelligence in Britain, where sadly it was found to correspond with no single item of information . . . and to include quantities of U-boats whose numbers were plainly fictional.' But then, as Graham Greene wrote in *Our Man in Havana* (UK 1958), 'Aren't double agents always a bit tricky? You never know whether you are getting the fat or the lean.' In many respects this is the best of all Greene's spy stories, leavened and lightened by its undertones of satire. His inside knowledge of the Intelligence game, his keenly observant eye for the characteristics and quirks that lie beneath the surface of human beings, the dormant, inborn depravity and, not least, the wrestling with conscience, enable Greene to lift the spy story to the realms of literature of merit. Richard Cody calls it 'the mannerist stage' of spy fiction—'the stage of middle-aged, cynical, more or less stateless heroes (often writers by profession) whose inconclusive, semi-documentary adventures in shabby hotels, on slow ships or on uncomfortable continental trains seem to express the malaise of the Europe of the time with an anguish—and a self-consciousness—that the clubland writers never even tried to achieve.'

It would seem that much of Greene's cynicism and keen interest in the weaknesses of the human race spilled over from his writing into his Secret Service work. 'Kim' Philby may have been a traitor, but his own accounts of what went on behind the scenes are factually accurate as far as they go, and he had this to say about Graham Greene, who was brought back to reinforce Section V (the Iberian Section) of MI6 towards the latter part of the Second World War: 'He will forgive me for confessing that I cannot recall any startling achievements of his in West Africa . . . I do remember, however, a meeting held to discuss a proposal of his to use a roving brothel to frustrate the French and two lonely Germans suspected of spying on British shipping in Portuguese Guinea. The proposal was discussed quite seriously and was turned down only because it seemed unlikely to be productive of hard intelligence. Happily, Greene was posted to my section, where I put him in charge of

Portugal . . . his tart comments on incoming correspondence were a daily refreshment' (*My Silent War* (UK 1968)).

Perhaps the most widely known of Greene's books (thanks mainly to the film and its zither music) is *The Third Man* (UK 1950). Though this is not strictly a spy story, its background is almost entirely that of the 'spy city' which Vienna had become just after the war when there was a four-power occupation and each power had a separate zone. Here Greene was stepping into a situation and environment with which he was not unfamiliar. He was searching Vienna in the bleak February of 1948 for a film story for Alexander Korda with only this sentence in his head and on the flap of an envelope in his pocket: 'I had paid my last farewell to Harry [Lime] a week ago when his coffin was lowered into the frozen February ground, so that it was with incredulity that I saw him pass by, without a sign of recognition, among the strangers in the Strand.' In the end, of course, the venue was changed from the Strand, but this was not until Greene had had lunch with an Intelligence officer who told him casually of the 'underground police'. Their job was to patrol the network of sewers that criss-crossed Vienna, carrying not only rats, but agents, unchallenged, from the British to the Russian, French or American sectors. The entrances were through the circular advertisement kiosks that stood unsuspected on the pavements. It is not often that the professional spook is also a writer of great distinction; when this happens it is illuminating to see Greene, the former SIS man, instinctively seeking out those of 'the Brothers' (as the SIS called themselves at one time) who could find him the right scenario for his script and his novel.

The Russians shadowed Greene the whole time he was in Vienna: they had heard all about his links with the SIS and they thought he might be coming to head the Vienna Section of MI6. But they were even more intrigued because they had learned that Greene had once, very briefly, been a communist. A KGB man gregariously chatting up his CIA opposite number in the Casanova nightclub in Vienna told him: 'It's a pity Mr Greene is not staying here for the British. At least he knows what goes on in the sewers here, which is more than the head of the British Secret Service Section in Vienna does.' From that night in 1948 the head of the SIS Austrian Section was effectively blown within twelve months of his posting to that city. Yet it was not until two years later that he was sent elsewhere.

His conversion to Catholicism was the main influence in Greene's life, and, to a great extent, in his books, too. Paradoxically and not untypically, Greene has said that the two authors who most influenced his writing were such disparate figures as John Buchan and François Mauriac. Undoubtedly the Buchan influence is to be seen in *Ministry of Fear* (UK 1943), a melodrama about a Fifth Column in wartime London, and now one of his least remembered works. His travels in Indo-China before the French were driven out of that unhappy land produced material for many articles, including one in the *London Magazine* relating his experiences as an opium smoker, and *The Quiet American* (UK 1955). This was a spy story in striking contrast to the comic melodrama of *Our Man in Havana*. Like W. J. Lederer, Greene is supposed to have modelled his central figure, Alden Pyle, on Colonel Edward Lansdale, USAF, one of the CIA's covert operations agents in Vietnam, though he had had extensive experience in the Philippines in the early 1950s. Maybe Lansdale's friends visualised him as the hero of *The Ugly American*, while his enemies compared him to Greene's anti-hero. But Greene effectively depicts a certain type of idealistic American who, in certain circumstances, can be more dangerous than a straightforward rogue. It was the portrait of a man whose faith in human nature only led to men getting killed. Certainly Lansdale was involved in all manner of sabotage and guerrilla operations against North Vietnam, but he was also a major political manipulator in the background in South Vietnam just as he had indulged in psychological warfare in the Philippines, playing on the superstitions of those who believed in the existence of a particularly virulent vampire. But *The Quiet American*, while having CIA skullduggery as part of its background, was really a plea for commonsense to be used in the Vietnam impasse before too many lives were lost and too many horrors perpetrated on either side. It was a shrewd ex-Intelligence officer's report in the guise of a novel, leaving the reader to draw his own conclusions as to what was likely to happen in Vietnam. Only in this case the ex-Intelligence officer was simply doing his own thing, for himself and nobody else, and expressing it in the only manner he knew.

Francis Greenland (b. London, 29 April 1924)
Francis Laffan Greenland was educated at Westminster School, the School of Oriental and African Studies and Queen's College, Cambridge. He served in the British Army from 1942–49 and was

then in the Civil Service until 1971. Today he lives in Portugal, which has provided him with the background to his first and so far only book, *The Misericordia Drop* (UK 1976), which is about a purloined government document dealing with measures to combat Rhodesian sanction-busting, discovered by chance in an old Portuguese manor house. This is a spy story which deals with what Greenland calls 'the amiable amateurishness of British Intelligence'. Three principal characters are involved: a Director, of the old, élitist, easy-going school; a young economist; and a man-of-action for rough stuff in the field.

Anthony Grey (b. 1938)

Educated at Norwich Grammar School, Grey served for three years in the RAF before taking up journalism. He worked on the *Eastern Daily Press* in the early 'sixties, where he won a travel award for being 'an outstanding journalist of the year'. In 1964 he joined Reuters News Agency. He worked in the Reuter bureau in East Berlin for a while before he was appointed the agency's correspondent in Peking. Then on 21 July 1967, he hit the world's headlines when he was denounced by the Chinese authorities as 'the British spy imperialist journalist' and kept under house arrest and in solitary confinement, presumably in retaliation for the imprisonment in Hong Kong of a New China News Agency reporter. Released in 1969, Grey retired to the Channel Islands to write a book about his ordeal, *Hostage in Peking* (UK 1970). He married a lecturer in German who had kept up correspondence with him during his confinement, and in 1973 joined the BBC World Service in London. He has so far produced one spy story, *The Bulgarian Exclusive* (UK 1976), which is not only set in Bulgaria, but has something of the Bamboo Curtain in it as well.

Andrei Gulyashki

A Bulgarian novelist who responded to the KGB's request for writers to glorify the deeds of Soviet espionage and to improve its own image in the early 'sixties. The object was to popularise secret agents of the Soviet Union as noble heroes who protected the fatherland and it was launched by Vladimir Semichastny, the newly appointed head of the KGB in 1961, when he contributed an article to *Izvestia* on this very subject. Gulyashki then invented an ace Russian spy named Avakum Zakhov whose main mission in life seemed to be to destroy James Bond, 'this supreme example of imperialistic espionage'. It was the Soviet Union's answer to Ian Fleming, whose success actually worried the KGB, some of whose leading lights believed that Britain had scored a major propaganda success in the 'Cold War' by producing James Bond! Gulyashki's book, *Zakhov Mission* (1966), was an instant success and was serialised in *Komsomolskaya Pravda* (the Soviet youth paper) under the title of *Avakum Zakhov versus 07*. (The Bulgarians were unable to get copyright permission to use Bond's name or '007', so they got around this difficulty by deleting one zero from the code name.) The book was translated into English by Maurice Michael and published in the UK in 1968. Avakum Zakhov was, understandably, a much more proletarian figure than Bond; instead of the fastidious culinary tastes of Bond, the Soviet hero gulped down large quantities of cabbage and noodles.

Gilbert Hackforth-Jones (b. Arkley, Herts, 1900)
Gilbert Hackforth-Jones attended the Royal Naval Colleges at Osborne and Dartmouth, served in the Royal Navy, and retired with the rank of Commander. As a writer he started with sea stories and his short stories of naval life are among the best of their kind. He has, however, written a number of spy stories, including *Fish Out of Water* (UK 1954), about a naval officer ashore in wartime and involved in a silent duel with an unknown saboteur; *Security Risk* (UK 1970), a novel with a submarine background; and *Chinese Poison* (UK 1969), set in the Far East in the 1920s. His style, delightful sense of humour and the absolute authenticity of all he writes about, make this author worthy of inclusion here.

William Haggard (b. Croydon, 11 August 1907)
This is the pseudonym of Richard Henry Michael Clayton. Educated at Lancing College and Christ Church, Oxford, he entered the Indian Civil Service and eventually became a judge. During the Second World War he served in the Indian Army, undergoing a course at the Staff College, Quetta. Later he joined the British Civil Service, and for a time was Controller of Enemy Property. Associated with Intelligence work during his career, he retired in 1969.

Haggard could best be described as a writer of suspense novels with political backgrounds or, as he himself modestly refers to his books, 'basically political novels with more action than in the straight novel'. At the same time he has ventured into the fringes of the spy story in a somewhat romantic, Buchanish style, with echoes of the 'thirties in his preoccupation with notions of propriety and correct and civilised behaviour in his Intelligence operators. His earliest book in this genre was *Slow Burner* (UK 1958), in which for the first time appeared Haggard's own special creation, Colonel Russell of the Security Executive, the very quintessence of that *rara avis* of the Intelligence world, the *pukka sahib*. Perhaps Colonel Russell was too pukka for the tastes of the decade, but Buchan would have approved of him. This, however, is not a criticism of Haggard's work, for he created an interesting character who bridged a gap between the 1930s and the 1960s, at least to the extent of having a British Intelligence executive who got along reasonably well with his opposite number in the KGB. *The Arena* (UK 1961) and *The Unquiet Sleep* (UK 1962) were followed by *The Antagonists* (UK 1964), *The Powder Barrel* (UK 1965), *The Hard Sell* (UK 1966) and, more recently, *The Scorpion's Tail* (UK 1975). Latterly Haggard has been moving in a somewhat different direction in his novels and suspense has occasionally been lost in a web of almost esoteric character-weaving.

Michael Halliday: *see* John Creasey

Simon Harvester (b. 1909; d. April 1975)
Simon Harvester was widely known as a writer of espionage stories on both sides of the Atlantic, having in a remarkable way managed to give his books a global appeal. Making his home base on Dartmoor in the English countryside, he travelled far in search of background material and local colour for his novels. He had considerable insight into world politics and anticipated the development of the post-Second World War battle for power in Africa and Asia. In pursuit of knowledge of these areas he visited almost every country in Africa and Asia after the war and, apart from his spy novels, he also wrote under the name of 'Henry Gibbs' a number of straight novels and several works of political analysis, including *Twilight in South Africa* and *Crescent in Shadow*, which foretold of Russian manoeuvres and intrigues in the Middle East.

It was his series of books dealing with Asiatic backgrounds that attracted most interest, beginning with *The Bamboo Screen* (UK 1955). Altogether there were twenty-six of these books which Edmund Crispin in the *Sunday Times* described as Harvester's 'admirable and far-ranging Asia in Turmoil series'. One of Britain's First World War Intelligence experts paid Harvester the tribute of calling his character in this series, Dorian Silk, 'the truest portrait of a secret service agent'. Harvester's last book in the series, *Siberian Road* (UK 1976), was published posthumously. This peered deeply into the future, posing such questions as what was the Russian plan for Siberia in the next world war and how were its vast resources being used, as well as taking a look at 'the Chinese Dimension'. Other of Harvester's spy stories were *A Lantern for Diogenes* (UK 1946), *Sheep May Safely Graze* (UK 1950), *Obols for Charon* (UK 1951), *Vessel May Carry Explosives* (UK 1951), *Cat's Cradle* (UK 1952), *Arrival in Suspicion* (UK 1953), *Spider's Web* (UK 1953), *Delay in Danger* (UK 1954), *Copper Butterfly* (UK 1957), *Golden Fear* (UK 1957), *Yesterday Walkers* (UK 1958), *Unsung Road* (UK 1960), *Silk Road* (UK 1962), *Troika* (UK 1962), *Assassin's Road* (UK 1965), *Treacherous Road* (UK 1966), *Battle Road* (UK 1967), and *Zion Road* (UK 1968). The authenticity of his settings and the topicality of his themes were the chief feature of Harvester's work, some of which almost fictionalised history and was as up-to-date as the current headlines—often, indeed, just ahead of them. The Russians regarded him as serious and compulsory reading for the KGB and when the latter had their No. 1 listening post at Kuala Lumpur, they surprised a local book importer one day by sending a dozen different people to order six copies each of certain Harvester books!

Tim Heald (b. Dorchester, Dorset, 28 January 1944)
After attending the Connaught House School, near Taunton, and Sherborne, Timothy Villiers Heald went to Balliol College, Oxford, where he was awarded the Galpin Scholarship restricted to those born in Dorset, educated in that county and with at least one parent born in Dorset. When he left university he entered journalism, first as an 'Atticus' columnist on the *Sunday Times*, then as a feature writer on the *Daily Express* and, since 1972, as a freelance. His first novel, *Unbecoming Habits* (UK 1973), was set in an Anglican Friary in Oxfordshire where the Friars are investigated by Simon Bognor of the Board of Trade, who discovers that a couple of them have

been smuggling secrets out to Eastern Europe in jars of honey.

'The first book was based on the notes I wrote for a Trevelyan Scholarship while I was at school,' says Heald. 'I stayed in three Anglican religious communities for the project, found my notes years later and felt they should not be wasted. Bognor of the BOT is the continuing character. He was originally called Simon Villiers, but my agent and I agreed this was too 1930'ish, so we went through English place names looking for something slightly absurd. Bognor is not very competent and is constantly turning up in unlikely places —stately homes, newspaper diaries, kennels—which I know first-hand and find easy and enjoyable to write about. Some form of espionage is usually implied in the books.'

Heald has also written *Blue Blood Will Out* (UK 1974), *Deadline* (UK 1975) and *Let Sleeping Dogs Die* (UK 1976). Of his contact with the Intelligence world, he recalls, 'At Oxford I approached the Foreign Office about work and had a strange interview with a man who talked archly about "another branch of the Foreign Office". I consulted my tutor about this and he said he had been similarly approached and had spent a melodramatic few days meeting people in pubs and country houses, but never discovering their names. I did nothing about it. But I have met people who probably are spies or who would like to think they are!'

Paul Henissart (b. New York, 1923)

Paul Henri Henissart was educated at Kenyon College, Ohio, and the Sorbonne, Paris, worked for *Time* magazine for a period and then became a radio and television correspondent, covering the Algerian War and the Sinai campaign. His career as an author first attracted attention with his non-fiction *Wolves in the City* (US 1971), an account of the OAS underground war and the end of French rule in Algeria. *Narrow Exit* (US 1973), his first novel, was set in Tunisia and marked his venture into spy fiction; his second novel, *Winter Quarry* (US 1976), was even better. It was a story about the bizarre games Secret Services play, with human life as the prize. The chief character, Rappaport, was an official of the Hungarian Espionage Agency, which was bluffing both the Russians and the West. Dr Robert Winter, an important American political writer and a double-agent, was murdered in Hamburg to set the starting point for this story in which the scene changes from Hamburg to Vienna to Budapest. So far Henissart has set his books in North

Africa and Central Europe, areas where he has lived. 'It seems to me important in novels about Intelligence work to make the opposition human and believable: one side should not be endowed with all the good qualities and the other made to seem a pastiche of villains.' Numerous characters in his novels have been drawn from real-life counterparts in the Intelligence world, 'without some access to which', adds the author, 'I doubt that I could, or would want to write the sort of books I have written.'

Edward D. Hoch (b. Rochester, N.Y., 22 February 1930)
Hoch studied at the University of Rochester and served in the US Army from 1950–52. He was employed at the Rochester Public Library and with the Hutchins Advertising Company of Rochester before becoming a full-time writer in 1968. Since 1965 he has published thirty-three short stories about Rand, a cipher expert in a mythical British Intelligence branch, entitled the Department of Concealed Communications. All have appeared in Ellery Queen's *Mystery Magazine* and seven of them appeared in a collection, *The Spy & the Thief* (US 1971). Hoch received the Mystery Writers of America Edgar Allen Poe Award for the best mystery short story, *The Oblong Room*, in 1968. Many of his works are thrillers and detective mysteries rather than spy fiction. Among his more notable novels are *The Shattered Raven* (US 1969), *The Transvection Machine* (US 1971) and *The Fellowship of the Hand* (US 1973). These have been published on both sides of the Atlantic, including Germany, France and Japan. A number of his stories have been adapted for television series.

Josephine Hone b. London, 25 February 1937)
An Irish citizen, Joseph Hone is a spy story writer with a serious mission. Educated at Kilkenny College, Kilkenny, Sandford Park School, Dublin, and St Columba's College, Dublin (1951–52), he has had a varied career including working as an assistant in a second-hand bookshop in London, as a teacher at Drogheda Grammar School in Ireland, and with the Egyptian Ministry of Education in Cairo, Heliopolis and Suez, as well as jobs in a publishing firm, radio and television. In 1960 he became co-founder with John Ryan of Envoy Productions, Dublin, and has co-produced a number of plays and musicals at the Theatre Royal, Stratford, East London. His wide experience in radio and television resulted in an appointment

as Radio and Television Officer with the United Nations Secretariat in New York in 1968, and for the next two years he travelled far and wide, making documentary programmes based on trips to Ethiopia, Kenya, Uganda, Tanzania, Malawi, India, Pakistan and the Far East. Out of these experiences came *The Dancing Waiters* (UK 1975).

His first book, however, was *The Private Sector* (UK 1971). This was the first of a trilogy about Marlow, a teacher in Cairo who finds himself becoming a spy for the British. In part this work was a by-product of Hone's experiences in 1957–58 when he was a teacher in Europe. He states that he has not been associated with Intelligence work, but that he has 'worked with and met such people, especially while I was a teacher in Egypt and in New York with the UN'. His character Marlow gets involved in the Six-Day War of 1967 in *The Private Sector*, but it was Hone's second book, *The Sixth Directorate* (UK 1975), which aroused most attention. This book continues Marlow's story after his release from Durham Jail, where he has been sent on a frame-up by his own Department, and it deals with his impersonation of an Englishman, a captured KGB agent living in London, his subsequent adventures as a fall-guy agent in the UN in New York and his eventual encounter with the KGB in Cheltenham. The book took up the theme of those woolly-minded, neo-liberal communists who, repelled by the tyranny of Stalin and his successors, still dream of a 'humane Marxism'; Hone described the development and fate of such a theodocy. The development of the dream was in fact surprisingly spearheaded by a section of the KGB. This may not sound the kind of stuff of which espionage thrillers are usually made, but the book certainly had a message to spell out to International Socialists, Worker Revolutionaries and Young Liberals alike. One critic said 'this book is in essence a spy story . . . it is a solemn, capable, well-written affair, but not, to tell the truth, particularly exciting.' Intelligence professionals, however, find it astutely realistic.

Hone is now at work on the final part of the trilogy, *The Flowers of the Forest*, which takes Marlow from the Cotswolds to Yugoslavia for what the author describes as 'another psychological and action adventure'.

Sydney Horler (b. Essex, 1888; d. 1954)
Sydney Horler was educated at Redcliffe and Colston Schools,

Bristol. He began his professional life in Fleet Street, first on the London *Daily Citizen* and then on the *Daily Mail*. During the last year of the First World War he worked in the propaganda section of Air Intelligence. After the war he joined the editorial staff of George Newnes and was appointed a sub-editor on *John O'London's Weekly*. Later he resigned to write fiction and in all he produced more than 150 novels. A number of these were concerned with espionage, among them *Miss Mystery* (UK 1928), about Diana Fordwych, 'the intimate of Baron Serge Velessoffsky, whom the secret service agents of many countries called "the most dangerous man in Europe" and M. Jacquard, chief of the Monte Carlo Secret Police, called "Mademoiselle Mystery".' Most of his Secret Service stories, set in Cannes, on the Riviera, in Paris and London, were in similar vein—somewhat modelled on Oppenheim, exciting as stories, but highly coloured and artificial. They enjoyed wide popularity in the 'thirties. Other of his spy books were *The Curse of Doone* (UK 1928), *The Secret Service Man* (UK 1930), *The Spy* (UK 1931), *Horror's Head* (UK 1931), *My Lady Dangerous* (UK 1932), *The Traitor* (UK 1936), *Terror on Tiptoe* (UK 1939), *Tiger Standish Steps on It* (UK 1940), *They Thought He Was Dead* (UK 1949), *The High Game* (UK 1950), *These Men and Women* (UK 1951), and *Man Who Used Perfume* (UK 1952).

Harry Hossent (b. London, 12 November 1916)
Harry Hossent believes he was first influenced to write thrillers by his English teacher at Glendale County School, who was Christopher Bush, a well-known detective story writer in his day. After a spell in the film business Hossent joined AP of America and stayed with that agency until he joined the RAF in the Second World War. After the war he had a job with UP, then went into an advertising agency and later became London manager of the Irish News Agency. 'I can't remember the title of my first book,' he says. 'It was a 50,000 word paperback. It was October, I needed some money for Christmas and I saw an advertisement asking for 50,000 word thrillers. So I locked myself in the kitchen and I typed the words "The blonde was very dead". After that it all seemed to work.'

Since then he has enjoyed writing spy stories 'about the seedier parts of Europe'. *Spies Die at Dawn* was first published in 1957, to be followed by *Memory of Treason* (UK 1958), *Spies Have No Friends* (UK 1959), *No End to Fear* (UK 1959), *Run for Your Death*

(UK 1964), *The Spy Who Got Off at Las Vegas* (UK 1969), *Gangster Movies* (UK 1975), and *The Great Spectaculars* (UK 1976). Hossent writes competent, unpretentious spy fiction. The chief character he has developed in his books is the somewhat cynical Max Heald, a Second World War Squadron-Leader seconded to an unnamed department of the SIS (a kind of division of dirty tricks).

Geoffrey Household (b. 3 November 1900)
The son of a barrister-at-law, Geoffrey Edward West Household was educated at Clifton School and Magdalen College, Oxford. He was one of a trio of skilled and highly competent writers who, shortly before the Second World War, sought the format of the spy story as a medium for their ideas. Michael Innes and Eric Ambler were the other two. After leaving Oxford Household lived in various parts of the world, undertaking a variety of jobs. In Bucharest, where he spent eight years, he was confidential secretary to the Bank of Rumania, after which he worked in Spain for some time in the banana trade and as the foreign representative of a firm of printing-ink manufacturers. Arriving in the US in the depths of the depression in the 1930s, he made a living by writing playlets for broadcasting. He married Elisaveta Kopelanoff in New York City in 1930, returned to Europe, visited the Middle East and Latin America and afterwards, just before the Spanish Civil War, lived in a fishing village not far from Malaga.

He settled in England to become a professional writer, but it was not until he wrote *Rogue Male* (UK 1938) that success really came to him. This not only became one of the classical thrillers of all time, but was filmed and broadcast and has recently (1976) been the subject of a new and excellent BBC TV film which showed that the story has lost none of its effectiveness over all these years. *Rogue Male* was about an Englishman, Sir Robert Hunter, who decided to undertake a one-man spy mission to track down and kill a dictator. It was fairly clear that the dictator in question was Adolf Hitler and indeed to present the story effectively in a modern film it is necessary to make this absolutely clear. The story opens with Hunter being trapped by the secret police while watching the terrace of the dictator's hunting lodge through the telescopic sights of his rifle. Captured, tortured and given up for dead by his inquisitors, Hunter escapes back to England after hair-raising adventures that make

Rogue Male as good an escape story as Buchan's *The Thirty-Nine Steps*. But in England, where officialdom and government circles want to have nothing to do with a man who has tried to kill a foreign head of state and failed, he finds himself in equal danger, shunned by some of his own countrymen and still hunted down by agents of his enemies overseas. The scenes in Dorset where Hunter goes to ground in a fox-hole and lives perilously while being sought by the enemy are especially thrilling. Sir Robert Hunter is, as a character, a great improvement on the swaggering 'Bulldog' Drummond-type: in his quiet, but courageous, single-minded way he is merely an Englishman of the upper classes doing what he believes to be right and to hell with the consequences. It is a novel of ideas as well as a superb thriller and the suspense is maintained right up to the end. It is said that General Sir Noel Mason Macfarlane studied this book when working out his own plot to kill Hitler with a telescopic-lensed rifle. The plot never came off, but Macfarlane always swore the Household story was an inspiration for him. The outstanding success of *Rogue Male* has never quite been repeated by Household. His other books include *A Rough Shoot* (UK 1951), *A Time to Kill* (UK 1952), *Fellow Passenger* (UK 1953), *Watcher in the Shadows* (UK 1960) and *Red Anger* (UK 1975). In 1942 he was married for a second time, to Ilona M. J. Zsoldos-Gutman.

John Howlett (b. Leeds, 4 March 1940)
Educated at Tonbridge School and Jesus College, Oxford. John Reginald Howlett is perhaps best known as the co-author of the film, *If*. In *The Christmas Spy* (UK 1975) he introduced a new style of spy, Railway Joe, an agent in his mid-forties employed by an unnamed security organisation under its Parisian controller. Howlett himself sums his character up as 'the sad man of post-war Europe, regressed from the ideals of anti-Nazi resistance to the cynical chess-board manoeuvres of the eternal power game. Wrong man, wrong side, wrong war.' It is what he calls 'the loneliness and the sense of alienation' of the spy game that marks Howlett's approach to the genre. His spy had been left out in the cold since, as a seventeen-year-old-boy of Italian parentage fresh from his English public school, he was seconded to the Italian underground apparently to fight the fascists in Italy. Rootless, tortured, devoid of any lasting personal attachment, except to his gentle, homosexual brother, Railway Joe had been given a new name by the British, who patched

up his war-shattered personality without leaving him any real identity. *The Christmas Spy* is a chilling story which focuses on an assignment begun on a bitterly cold Christmas Eve in a little Swiss village, and carried through right across Europe. In it, the author has added a new quality and dimension to the modern spy novel. Howlett's other work includes film and radio scripts and biographies associated with the cinema.

E. Howard Hunt (b. New York City, 1914)

To include Howard Hunt among such immortals as Conrad, Dickens and Chesterton may seem almost akin to *lèse-majesté* in the world of literature. None the less, bearing in mind the links between fact and fiction, Howard Hunt can hardly be overlooked: he is not so much a milestone as a gallows landmark in the history of the spy story. The son of a New York judge, he served for twenty-one years in the CIA, not only inside the US, but in Paris, Vienna and Latin America. He played a leading role in organising the invasion of Cuba which ended in the Bay of Pigs fiasco. All this experience he used as material for his pot-boiler spy stories, of which he has written forty-three under various pseudonyms. It would be superfluous to cite them all, but his last book, *My Body* (US 1973), was described by Patrick Brogan of the London *Times* as 'a spy thriller of unutterable awfulness'. Its opening sentence runs: 'I was lounging in Hod Gurney's office admiring the burnished panelling and assorted autographed photographs of Supreme Court Justices when Hod cleared his throat, opened a mahogany humidor and offered me a cigar.' Further on he writes of a female character: 'Her eyes were deep and sultry. Coral lips parted to show teeth as white as foam on a sunlit sea. Our glances locked.' All the novels are more or less in this vein and reveal traces of Hunt's unabashed, vehement ultra-right-wing politics.

It was his political beliefs as much as anything else that propelled him into the 'dirty tricks' game. He had no qualms about breaking into the office of Daniel Ellsberg's psychiatrist (Ellsberg was the man who made the Pentagon Papers revelations) solely because he thought Ellsberg might be a Soviet agent. Hunt did not see Reds only under every bed; if he couldn't find them, he had to invent them or dream about them. When he left the CIA in 1970 he was hired by Charles Colson to work in Nixon's White House and the first job he was given was to spy on Senator Edward Kennedy after the Chappaquiddick affair. Hunt also recruited the Cubans for the break-in at the Democratic Party's Watergate HQ in 1972. For his part in this Hunt was one of the seven men originally convicted of the burglary and sentenced to two-and-a-half years' imprisonment. During the various hearings Hunt admitted that he had been involved in a plot to drug Jack Anderson (the columnist hated by the Nixon administration for his revelations of scandals) and discredit him before the country.

Douglas Hurd (b. 8 March 1930)
Eldest son of Lord Hurd, the Hon. Douglas Richard Hurd was educated at Eton, where he was King's Scholar and Newcastle Scholar, and Trinity College, Cambridge. He was president of the Cambridge Union in 1952, and entered the Diplomatic Service in the same year. For four years he served in Peking, thus having an early introduction to Far Eastern politics and imbroglios, which have featured in some of his books. From 1956–60 he worked in the United Kingdom Mission to the United Nations and after that had a three-year stint as Private Secretary to the Under Secretary of State at the Foreign Office. He was stationed in Rome from 1963–66 and then joined the Conservative Party Research Department, eventually becoming private secretary to the then Conservative leader, Edward Heath. During Heath's term of office as Prime Minister Douglas Hurd served as his political secretary. Since 1974 Hurd has been MP for Mid-Oxfordshire.

It was in this post-Foreign Office period that Douglas Hurd branched out as a novelist and in *Who's Who* he describes his principal recreation as 'writing thrillers'. He first produced *The Arrow War* (UK 1967), which was, in fact, history. This was followed by what Hurd himself calls 'political thrillers rather than spy fiction, though I suppose you are right in saying that the two have much in common. The approach is much the same in all five books, i.e. those written with Andrew Osmond and the last two.' The five books are *Send Him Victorious* (UK 1968), *Smile on the Face of the Tiger* (UK 1969) and *Scotch on the Rocks* (UK 1971)—all of which were written in collaboration with Andrew Osmond—and *The Truth Game* (UK 1972) and *Vote to Kill* (UK 1975).

These books have attracted considerable interest and serious study among politicians and foreign affairs specialists and, indeed, British 'spooks' in the Far East who have been shaken out of their complacency by some of Hurd's revelations. But in some respects they are textbooks for indolent and complacent officialdom and the SIS, MI5 and the Foreign Office should make them compulsory reading. One hour with Hurd is probably worth four with Le Carré in a strictly educative sense. Referring to his collaboration with Andrew Osmond, Douglas Hurd says: 'We have tried to start from an ordinary situation with ordinary people, described in detail from past experiences of our own. Then we have added an explosive ingredient which is not absolutely improbable, e.g. a violent outbreak of Scottish nationalism (*Scotch on the Rocks*), a Chinese ultimatum against Hong Kong (*The Smile of the Face of the Tiger*), or, as in the case with my last book, a campaign to get British troops out of Ireland (*Vote to Kill*). The mixture of the ordinary and the extraordinary has to be kept in balance all the way through. As a member of the Foreign Service I met a good many people involved in Intelligence, but I cannot say that they influenced me particularly. I know Hong Kong reasonably well, but it is fascinating not because of the spies—a dull lot—but because of the extraordinary notion of a vast capitalist Chinese city kept steady by a British Governor, Ghurkas, etc. I have no desire at all to attack the British institutions which we describe, though it is often right to laugh at the way they work.'

Michael Innes (b. Edinburgh, 30 September 1906)
This is the pseudonym of John Innes McIntosh Stewart. Innes's father was Director of Education in Edinburgh, and Innes was educated at Edinburgh Academy and Oriel College, Oxford. He has been a lecturer in English at the University of Leeds (1930–35), Jury Professor of English at Adelaide University (1935–45), and lecturer at Queen's University, Belfast (1946–48). In 1949 he was made Student of Christ Church, Oxford, and became Reader in English Literature, Oxford, in 1969. Seven novels and a volume of short stories have been published under his own name, as well as many detective stories and broadcast strips under the pseudonym of 'Michael Innes'. His non-fiction work includes studies of Kipling and Conrad and *Eight Modern Writers* (UK 1963), which appeared as the final volume of the *Oxford History of English Literature*.

It is, however, with his spy fiction that we are mainly concerned here. A man of precise definition, Innes himself says 'as far as I can remember, *The Secret Vanguard* [UK 1940] represents my only attempt at a spy story'. This is undoubtedly the first and the best of his spy stories but, taking a broader definition of the genre, others that seem to qualify for this category are *The Journeying Boy* (UK 1949), *Operation Pax* (UK 1951) and *The Man from the Sea* (UK 1955). Julian Symons says of these books that they are 'closer to Buchan than to Ambler, are too fantastic to be quite convincing, but the spy theme gives Innes's work a fine romantic freedom that is rarely present in his later detective stories.'

The Secret Vanguard is an extremely well-written, original tale in which orders are given in an invented stanza to Swinburne's *Forsaken Garden*. A letter is sent to a newspaper, wondering if it would 'be too much to ask one of your readers to enlighten me on the authorship of these rather trivial lines . . .

> Deep in a garden
> Far to the north
> On a single branch
> The spring crept forth.
> Though the air not warm
> Nor winter fled . . .'

The letter is signed 'Philip Ploss', but by the time any reader could have replied to this request, Philip Ploss, a minor poet, was lying dead in his garden gazebo with a bullet-hole in the middle of his forehead. This book marks Innes's first cautious advance from the purely detective story to spy fiction and it will be noted that he uses the Scotland Yard detective, John Appleby, as the investigator of this mystery. It is a tale filled with literary allusions, and enchantingly leads Appleby from those misquoted lines of Swinburne through an orgy of transvestism in the Scottish Highlands to a missing mathematician, a hornet's nest of foreign spies and a secret formula hidden in a collection of hastily scrawled 'Caravaggios'. This is an absolute classic of the belletristic spy novel, a veritable collector's piece.

Oliver Jacks: *see* Kenneth Royce

Graham Montagu Jeffries: *see* Bruce Graeme

H. R. F. Keating (b. St Leonards-on-Sea, Sussex, 31 October 1926)

Henry Raymond Fitzwilliam Keating was educated at Merchant Taylor's School and Trinity College, Dublin. He has been chief reviewer of crime, espionage and suspense fiction for *The Times* of London from 1967. He has also been prominent in the affairs of the Crime Writers' Association, of which he was chairman from 1970–1971. His first book was *Death and the Visiting Firemen* (UK 1959) and most of his other books have been crime novels. Since 1964 the crime novels have generally featured Inspector Ghote (pronounced Go-tay) of the Bombay CID, who was created by Keating in response to sharp commercial pressure when no American publisher would take his previous books because they were 'too English'. Ghote, though physically different, is in many ways the author expressing his inner fears of always being put upon and his hopes of eventual (though unlikely) triumph, or, at least, this is how Henry Keating himself puts it. The one Ghote book that qualifies as spy fiction is *Inspector Ghote Caught in Meshes* (UK 1967), in which the astute Bombay detective moves temporarily into the realm of espionage when he is seconded to a supposedly undercover Indian Government organisation concerned with national security. What appears on the surface to be a straightforward murder investigation proves to have security implications. The book is primarily concerned with the question of loyalty, a theme which the author saw as most acutely presented by the spy and counter-spy situation; Ghote is deliberately cut off from almost all his customary network of loyalties.

Keating's view of the spy story (which as that of an experienced and discerning critic is important) is that it is 'becoming less technical and more of an ordinary novel, with a strong and welcome story element'. His comments on his recreations are not only subtly humorous, but almost Ghote-like in their esoteric nature. In 1970 he listed his recreation as 'not quite going to India', while in 1976 he declared it to be 'popping round to the post'.

Heidi Huberta Lamon: *see* Martha Albrand

James Leasor (b. Erith, Kent, 20 December 1923)

Thomas James Leasor, educated at the City of London School and

Oriel College, Oxford, served in the British Army in Burma, India and Malaya in the Second World War and became a captain in the Royal Berks. Regiment. At Oxford he edited *The Isis* and then joined the staff of the *Daily Express* in 1948, becoming in turn William Hickey columnist, foreign correspondent and feature writer. His first novel was *Not Such A Bad Day* (UK 1946), but he has also branched out into non-fiction with such works as *Rudolf Hess: the Uninvited Envoy* (UK 1961) and *Singapore: the Battle that Changed the World* (UK 1968). His spy stories include *Passport to Oblivion* (UK 1964), *Spylight* (UK 1966) and *Passport to Peril* (UK 1966). Leasor has also taken a keen interest in films and has been a director of Pagoda Films since 1959.

John Le Carré (b. Poole, Dorset, 19 October 1931)
This is the pseudonym of David John Moore Cornwell. After attending Sherborne School, Berne University and Lincoln College, Oxford, he started his career as a tutor at Eton in 1956, teaching French and German. He then joined the Foreign Office and from 1960–63 was Second Secretary in the British Embassy in Bonn; the following year he served as Consul in Hamburg. Speaking of Eton and the Foreign Office, he once said: 'I found them two institutions so fortified against the outside world that they had no hope of personal contact with the people they were meant to govern.'

It is this early background to Le Carré's career which is most positively related to his fiction. He served in the British Foreign Service in Germany in what was perhaps the tail end of the first phase of the Cold War (the cynic would rightly say that the second phase was *détente*) in the one area in which espionage was indulged in to saturation point. He had first-hand experience of the kind of environment in which George Blake and other double agents operated and of the SIS itself, and it was in this period that he first started to write. *Call for the Dead* (UK 1961) was succeeded by *A Murder of Quality* (UK 1962), but it was his third book, *The Spy Who Came in From the Cold* (UK 1963), which became a best-seller with universal appeal. It also brought style and a literary fastidiousness to the spy novel. Graham Greene said it was 'the best spy story I have ever read', while J. B. Priestley paid the tribute that the book was 'superbly constructed with an atmosphere of chilly hell'. This novel was a reaction to the cult of James Bond, a character whom Le Carré despises: 'the really interesting thing about Bond is that he would be what I call the ideal defector. Because if the money was better, the booze freer and women easier over there in Moscow, he'd be off like a shot. Bond, you see, is the ultimate prostitute.'

Le Carré would seem to be paranoic about Bond, but this is probably why, for the first time since Maugham and Ambler, any author had added a new dimension to the spy story. 'People have always been fascinated in the anatomy of betrayal,' he said, and *The Spy Who Came in From the Cold* won him the Somerset Maugham Award for a work which Maugham himself would undoubtedly have admired. While Eric Ambler had succeeded in making the commonplace incident seem as horrifying and gripping as the earlier melodrama of Oppenheim, Le Carré had given his British agent, Alex Leamas, an authenticity which no previous anti-hero had acquired. This paved the way for the genre of the unheroic spy. In contrast to Bond, Leamas took buses instead of taxis and his love affair was not with a glamorous sexpot, but with a lonely, underpaid librarian. Le Carré enhanced his reputation with his disciplined, clinical prose and the realism of his dialogue. *The Spy* was the story of a frustrated British agent (Leamas) who decided, after his sub-agents in East Germany had been liquidated, to go behind the Iron Curtain to destroy the mastermind who had directed these killings and ruined a segment of the British Intelligence network. Soon he realised that his own people had framed him in order to frame Fiedler, an East German. Leamas's whole world seemed to have gone mad in an orgy of double-crossing and phoney defectors. Ultimately he was brutally discarded by his own Secret Service and he slithered deeper into drinking and destitution and eventually to death.

No doubt the Le Carré school of spy fiction was not only an understandable reaction away from the antics of James Bond and the snobbism and branded names-dropping of the Fleming books, but it was also a salutary antidote to previous spy fiction, a much more accurate interpretation of the complex intrigues of the rival Secret Services during the Cold War. It certainly seemed so to the Russians who, having discovered that Le Carré was the pen-name of a man who had been in the British Foreign Service in Germany, asserted in their *Literary Gazette* that the author had himself been a British Intelligence agent. It was a statement that was never denied, though it caused Le Carré to reveal his true identity, blandly replying that he 'stole the plot from secret files back in 1948 . . . I was an enterprising spy, aged sixteen. But there were extenuating circum-stances. I'm also the son of Groucho Marx and Mata Hari!'

The Looking-Glass War (UK 1968) was in much the same mould and again explored the intrigues of Intelligence Services. It began with the death of a courier who had been sent to Finland to collect films taken by a commercial pilot who had ostensibly flown off course while over East Germany. Orders are given for planting an agent in this territory where, it is suspected, a new type of rocket site is being set up. Le Carré is at his best describing the plans for this operation, the recruitment of the agent, his training and briefing and the cynical, inhuman professionalism of the executive planners. Here is espionage in a team which lacks all *esprit de corps*, but which can cold-bloodedly plan the disavowal of an agent once it becomes clear that his slow transmission on single frequencies on an obsolete radio makes his capture inevitable.

Le Carré's association with the Foreign Office still calls for a certain amount of discretion. 'I clear the names of the fictional agents through the Office just in case I should accidentally blunder on a name. I did once, and they got me to change it.' The pen-name was, of course, chosen because he was still in the Foreign Service while writing his early books. But *A Small Town in Germany* (UK 1968) was published after Le Carré had left the Foreign Service to settle in Cornwall, and he daringly set the scene in the very offices in which David Cornwell had worked—the British Embassy in Bonn. In this novel an unsatisfactory, unpromotable Second Secretary in Chancery, Leo Harting, has disappeared and apparently defected along with a trolley, a typewriter, a tea-making machine, an electric fan and a green file. The reader is at once plunged into the world of student riots, neo-Fascism and a nervous British Embassy staff. Le Carré seems to have a very serious message; the reader is, in fact, being invited to reflect on whether there is a lesson to be learned in Britain from what might happen in the near future in Federal Germany. It was an ambiguous message which made one ponder whether Le Carré was anti-German. When asked this by one interviewer, he replied with that kind of diplomatic evasion so typical of the Foreign Office: 'There is a curious ambivalence in the English, a constant cycle of attraction and repulsion.'

His incisive mind and uncanny gift for character-reading made him an admirable choice for the writing of an introduction to *The Philby Conspiracy*, by Bruce Page, David Leitch and Philip Knightley (UK 1968). This was a succinct commentary on the whole story of 'Kim' Philby's career in the British Secret Service and his subsequent departure for the Soviet Union, whose cause he had all along espoused. Anyone who has read the Le Carré novels and wishes to ascertain how accurate an observer and commentator he is on the true life Intelligence set-up should turn to this Introduction. Within a few paragraphs Le Carré got to the essential underlying question to the whole affair: who was the mysterious, all-powerful man behind it all, the man who had recruited not only Philby, but Burgess and Maclean as well? 'Was he our countryman? He recruited only gentlemen. Was he himself a gentleman? He recruited only from Cambridge: was he a Cambridge man? All three recruits would travel far on the reputations of their families alone: was he, too, a man of social influence? . . . And did he pick only winners whoever he was?' But every line of this Introduction is good value: it is packed with fascinating theories. Referring to the notorious allegations by Rolf Hochhuth and others that Winston Churchill ordered the killing of the Polish general Sikorski, whose plane crashed at Gibraltar on take-off on 4 July 1943, Le Carré astutely points out: 'At that time Kim Philby was in charge of SIS counter-intelligence operations in the Iberian Peninsula. If Sikorski *was* assassinated, is it conceivable that Philby planned the operation on behalf of his Russian masters, and that the assassin whom he hired believed he was working for the British?'

In *Tinker, Tailor, Soldier Spy* (UK 1975) Le Carré re-introduced George Smiley, an agent who had a small part in both *The Spy* and *The Looking-Glass War*, but now had the main role. The story concerned finding 'the mole', deciding which of four men was the double-agent at the centre of British Intelligence. Miles Copeland, a shrewd commentator on the world of Intelligence (in which, on the American side, he has served), says that Le Carré is the favourite writer of British 'spooks': 'They like the way he captures the mood of their world, its internal rivalries and the personal problems that get tangled up with their professional lives.' It is his direct approach to reality, devoid of the tinsel, that is Le Carré's chief appeal. This was a relief from an indigestible abundance of the snobbish minutiae of the Fleming stories—the Oxford marmalade, the 'plain gold Patek Phillipe watch with a black leather strap'. What Le Carré achieved was to throw a large question mark over the whole business of espionage and at the same time to give a certain quality of integrity both to the writing and the message of his books. And the message, especially in *The Looking-Glass War*, is that those in the espionage game are so constantly pretending to be characters 'outside of themselves', that they live their deceits and inevitably make a career of betraying people. The note of doom and pessimism comes as a salutary douche of cold water after the high life and vodkaktinis of James Bond, yet, to be objective, one cannot but ponder the possibility that Le Carré has over-reacted, that he is a kind of Solzhenitsyn in reverse.

William J. Lederer (b. New York City, 1912)
William James Lederer attended the De Witt High School in New York, and went on to the US Naval Academy and Harvard. He served with the US Navy from 1930–58, finishing up with the rank of Captain. For a time he was Far Eastern reporter for *Reader's Digest*. Apart from various solo works, he is perhaps best known for *The Ugly American* (US 1958), which he wrote in collaboration with Eugene Burdick. The hero of this work is believed to have been based on that remarkable CIA covert operations agent, Air Force Colonel Edward Lansdale, whose exploits in the Philippines in the 1950s and later in Vietnam, were so publicised that he was made the model for the heroes of at least two books. He was said to have chosen the 'lucky' election colours for the rival candidates in Vietnam, ensuring that Ngo Dinh Diem had red—reputedly a lucky colour all over Asia.

William Le Queux (b. London, 2 July 1864; d. 13 October 1927)
William Tufnell Le Queux was the eldest son of William Le Queux of Chateauroux, Indre, France. His early life seems to have been spent travelling with his parents, having a somewhat haphazard private education in London, at Pegli, near Genoa and in France. During these travels he accumulated a vast amount of information of all kinds, especially concerning military history and current affairs and he was an observant youth never afraid to ask questions. For a while he studied art in Paris and lived in the Latin Quarter, but wanderlust caused him to abandon a career in painting and sketching and to tour France and Germany on foot. On the strength of his travels he became a journalist and was a roving correspondent until in 1891 he was appointed foreign editor of London's *Globe* newspaper. This post was given to him on the strength of a series of articles he had written for *The Times* about the revolutionary

movement in Russia. It was on his trip that he thought up the idea for his first book, *Guilty Bonds* (UK 1890), which was actually banned in Russia. The theme of the book was political intrigue. In 1893 Le Queux resigned his editorship to spend all his time writing books, of which he produced more than a hundred during his lifetime. His writing was intermingled with a good deal of travel and journalism: in the early part of the century he visited Algeria, Morocco and the Sahara Desert; in 1907 he travelled in Albania, Macedonia, Montenegro, Serbia and Turkey; the following year he made a trip to the Arctic and in 1909 he was in the Sudan. During the Balkan War he was a correspondent of the London *Daily Mail*.

Le Queux's lively imagination as a novelist was somewhat of a handicap to him as a journalist and, when it comes to sober fact, he was not always a reliable witness and was much given to extravagant embellishment of a situation—sometimes presenting downright fiction as fact. For this reason it is not easy to assess all that he himself wrote about his activities. He was at one time Consul in London of the tiny republic of San Marino and he claimed to be a 'Commander of the Orders of St Sava of Serbia, Danilo of Montenegro, the Crown of Italy and the San Marino Order'. In *Who's Who* he stated that he had 'intimate knowledge of the secret service of continental powers' and that he was 'consulted by the Government on such matters'. Presumably he meant the British Government. Certainly he was involved in Secret Service work both before and during the First World War, but one suspects that Le Queux did the volunteering and the authorities were quite often conned by him. For example, he declared that the Kerensky Government in Russia handed over to him in confidence a great quantity of documents found in a safe in the cellar of Rasputin's house after the death of the strange *moujik* who had intrigued his way into the Court of the Czar. Out of this material, which has never been independently vouched for, Le Queux produced *Rasputin the Rascal Monk* and *Things I Know* (both 1923). It is well known that pre-1914 agents of the British Secret Service were badly paid: either they had to be patriotic gentlemen of independent means or crooks who made their own 'perks' and financed themselves by means of dubious tricks. Le Queux, who always fantasised himself as a patriotic English gentleman, insisted that his spy stories were written to pay his expenses as a freelance member of the British Secret Service! This is not as improbable as it sounds.

Certainly Le Queux was one of the earliest writers of spy fiction proper and he set the pattern for the genre for the best part of a quarter of a century. Something less than a third of the books he wrote were spy fiction, but they made a greater impact than those of Oppenheim in the latter part of the nineteenth and early part of the twentieth century. Though his warnings of the unpreparedness of Britain to face a continental invasion had none of the literary quality of Erskine Childers, his sheer sensationalism and journalistic sense for the topical made his novels potent propaganda. Le Queux reached a huge readership and his adherents were numerous and vocal. Curiously enough they included that fastidious aesthete, A. J. Balfour, then leader of the Conservative Party: when asked once what he could possibly see in Le Queux's works, he replied, 'They are worth several thousand votes for the Conservative Party'.

Le Queux's first novel concerning military threats to Britain was *The Great War in England in 1897* (UK 1894), in which he described a Russo-French plot for the invasion of England. *A Secret Service* (UK 1896) had as its background the anti-Jewish pogroms in Russia; its chief character was a Jewish nihilist. Three years later he produced *England's Peril* (UK 1899). Le Queux, though of French origin, was not then concerned with helping to improve Anglo-French relations: he was fanatically the foreigner who had become more British than the British. Edward VII had not yet come to the throne and the *Entente Cordiale* was not to be established for five years, so, as in Napoleonic days, France was still seen by the masses as 'the enemy just across the Channel'. Thus Le Queux was conforming to popular opinion when he wrote of Lord Casterton's sudden death being caused by an explosive cigar given to him by his wife, who turns out to be having a love affair with Gaston la Touche, head of the French Secret Service. Casterton had been haranguing the House of Lords about Britain's military weakness and the French had decided he must be silenced. But Le Queux's further travels in Europe and North Africa, as well as the Middle East, convinced him that the real threat to Britain's security came from Germany and he then set out to pin-point that country as the potential enemy in his spy novels, using them as a powerful propaganda instrument. *The Invasion of 1910* (UK 1905) was the first of his anti-German novels and this was swiftly followed the same year by *The Mystery of a Motor-Car*, in which a country doctor is called upon to attend the victim of a motor-car accident only to find himself involved in a German plot.

Le Queux forged an alliance with a number of senior British Army officers who took much the same view as himself on the subject of Germany's growing preparations for war. Chief among these was Field-Marshal Lord Roberts, who had become a campaigner for conscription. Lord Roberts collaborated with Le Queux, notably in *The Great War* (UK 1908), in which he foretold the 1914–18 holocaust, and again in *Spies of the Kaiser* (UK 1909), in the preface of which he told how England was 'in grave danger of invasion by Germany at a date not far distant' and went on to hint at thousands of German agents living in Britain and worming vital secrets out of shipyards, arsenals, factories and individuals. When war actually came Le Queux continued the same theme in such books as *No. 70 Berlin* (UK 1915), *The Mystery of the Green Ray* (UK 1915), *The Unbound Book* (UK 1916) and many others. He tended to make his plots increasingly preposterous, though some of the background detail was authentic. In a sense he was a war casualty from a literary point of view, for he became so obsessed with the war that this robbed his writing of any objectivity or detachment. The blurb for *The Mystery of the Green Ray* will give some idea of his plots at the time: '. . . of today's war—how the lover solved the mystery of the Highland loch, recovered his girl's sight for her, captured for the British NID the wonderful installation of the Green Ray, upset the devilish and deep-laid schemes of as cunning a pair of spies as ever Mr Le Queux's fertile brain invented.' After the war came *Cipher Six* (UK 1919), said to have been based on 'actual events which occurred in the West End of London during the peace negotiations in the autumn of 1918. Mr William Le Queux was engaged in assisting the police to unravel one of the most extraordinary mysteries of the past decade, and in this book he places before the public the facts, with the actors in the thrilling drama duly disguised.'

Le Queux himself had a great sense of melodrama and was well aware of the values of self-publicity. He boasted that, when war broke out, he carried a loaded revolver around with him wherever he went, as his life was constantly threatened by 'enemies of the State'. A major defect was, however, that when he ventured into non-fiction he could not resist inventing dramatic situations in order to lend colour to his work. He lectured extensively in later life on 'spies and spying' and became a keen wireless fan, being a member of the Institute of Radio Engineers and President of the Wireless Experimental Association. Latterly he lived in Switzerland where he was an enthusiastic skier as well as an experimenter in wireless telephony. Many of his later books had a Swiss background, notably *Hidden Hands* (UK 1925), the blurb of which is a fascinating specimen of one of his spy stories: 'Seton Darville, elderly novelist and secret service agent, can make love "for business reasons" with excellent and thrillingly successful results. But between him and Edris Temperley it is a different matter altogether. She loves him— but she is young and so is Carl Weiss, ex-spy, and Darville is not. He nearly loses her, and she nearly loses both him and her unworthy Swiss lover, but comes to her senses in the nick of time.'

Tom Lilley (b. London, 25 September 1924)
A relatively new author, Thomas William Lilley's education was, he says, 'interrupted by war and more noticeably by the Battle of Britain. I joined the RAF at the age of eighteen and furthered my education in Bomber Command.' In 1948 he joined HM Overseas Civil Service and saw service in Malaya during the Emergency, Singapore, British North Borneo, Hong Kong and Brunei. After twenty years' service he retired as Deputy Head of the Special Branch (Police) in Sabah, most of his service having been spent in this Branch, first-hand knowledge of which provided the background to his first two novels.

The first of these was *The Projects Section* (UK 1970). Some critics carped that the book was 'not very vivid' and that 'clichés were plentiful', but Lilley is well worth inclusion among contemporary authors of spy fiction if only because he presents some aspects of the Malayan jungle war between British and Chinese that history has not recorded. The story is an account of the extraordinary measures taken by Special Branch to eliminate the leaders of the Communist insurrection in Malaya. Traps are set based on research and appraisal of the personal characteristics and behaviour of the individuals concerned. Carter of the Special Branch, hero of the story, gets to know his enemies and exploits their weaknesses. His own weakness, a beautiful Malayan mistress, is almost his undoing. While the book does not explore the morality of violence in depth, it does demonstrate vividly the effect on personality of continued association with violence. Henry Keating wrote in the London *Times* of this book that Lilley wanted to show what the Malayan War was really like and that 'this truth was as beastly as it is possible to conceive. The Communists are shown flaying alive British soldiers and snipping to death with scissors suspected traitors. The British are shown doctoring food in discovered enemy dumps and allowing the innocent to be killed to preserve security. Perhaps without proof that is no longer obtainable, the indictment cannot be told as fact. But it cannot either be told as fiction . . . But fiction can bring out one answer: a well-conceived novel can tell not how foul certain people were, but how appalling in similar general circumstances man can be to man.'

Lilley himself sees his books rather differently: 'I seek to show the impossibility of effectively fighting terrorism and remaining within the law.' The answer is the same whether in the jungle or Northern Ireland. His second book was *The 'K' Section* (UK 1972), this time about police activity behind the scenes in a British South-East Asian colony in danger of being taken over by the Communists. Lilley's hero Carter is now head of K Section and grappling with Russian intrigues and Chinese Tongs with equal adaptability. A desperate Russian reaction to the Special Branch success produces a tremendous catastrophe—a planned explosion on the cathedral steps after a State wedding, wiping out some royal guests and all the leading administrators. 'Incidentally,' writes Lilley, 'in chapter 20 of *The 'K' Section* I spell out Communist technique on how to start a riot out of a lawful demo in precisely the way that the Red Lion Square riot in London took place—over two years later.'

Lilley now lives in Japan.

Robert Littell (b. US, 1939)
Robert Littell, who has been a general editor for *Newsweek*, stationed in Eastern Europe and the USSR, now lives in France. On the basis of his experience behind the Iron Curtain he wrote his first spy novel, *The Defection of A. J. Lewinter* (US 1973), which was about a politically bland American scientist who suddenly defected to Russia. The complications that arose when neither side could gauge the value of the prize to be won or lost was the crux of this deft and ironic story. 'One of the best Cold War thrillers for years', declared the *New York Times*, while Clifford Irving, languishing in an American jail, wrote: 'I hope you'll pass along my thanks to Littell for writing a book that let me knock off two beautiful evenings in this otherwise dreary joint.' The book won him the Crime Writers' Association Gold Dagger for the best crime novel of 1973. His next book was *Sweet Reason* (US 1974), based on his own three years'

experience aboard an American warship—not quite a spy story, but telling of an elderly American destroyer patrolling an alien coast and the mysterious tactics of one unknown figure, Sweet Reason, whose messages urging Uncle Sam's Navy to lay down their arms are pinned to bulkheads and wrapped up in serviette rings.

Nicholas Luard (b. 26 June 1937)

Nicholas Lambert Luard spent his early childhood in Iran, partly in the capital and partly in the Kashgai tribal areas in the northern desert. He was educated privately in Britain and later at Winchester, the Sorbonne University in Paris, Cambridge University and the University of Pennsylvania. Having enlisted in the Coldstream Guards at the age of eighteen, he was commissioned, detached from royal guard duties and then trained as a NATO long-range patrol commander with a special sabotage and forward Intelligence unit. He was assigned to this unit on the strength of his linguistic talents (he is not only fluent in German, French and Spanish, but specialises in local dialects) and his athletic record (member of the Rhine Army athletic championship team and ranked as a welter-weight boxer). Known at Cambridge as 'the King of Satire', Luard was a contemporary of that band of brilliant young men, including Dr Jonathan Miller and Peter Cook, and in the early 'sixties was in the vanguard of the satire movement which was sweeping the West End of London, finally reaching the general public through the television programme 'TW3'. Luard was part-founder and part-owner of *Private Eye* magazine and also launched the highly popular home of satire in Soho, the Establishment Club. In 1963 he married Elizabeth Longmore, daughter of the British Minister in Mexico. The following year, together with Dominick Elwes, he wrote an amusing spoof handbook for conmen, *Refer to Drawer*. He is a dauntless traveller and one of his more recent journeys has been a double crossing of the Kalahari Desert.

It should not have surprised anyone when Luard suddenly blossomed forth as a spy fiction author, for it was *Private Eye*, on 9 August 1963, that first broke the secrecy, until then inviolate, concerning the head of the British Secret Service. The *Eye* accurately suggested that Sir Dick Goldsmith White was the boss. MI5 officials threw up their hands in horror; senior civil servants spoke of prosecution and copies of the paper were seized and taken to the Ministry of Defence for inspection. No action was taken and *Private Eye* survived. The truth was that this was the year of the Profumo Scandal, which had closely followed the Vassall Scandal and the British government's muddled handling of such breaches of security as the Blake affair and the defection of MI6's former pin-up boy, 'Kim' Philby. How could the government prosecute *Private Eye* when it had failed to act in the face of much bigger and really dangerous scandals?

Luard's first book was *The Warm and Golden War* (UK 1967), a subtle and sophisticated political novel about a multi-millionaire who hired mercenaries to open up a segment of the Austro-Hungarian frontier to let through 1,000 refugees to the West. The book was based on the author's experiences on the border during the 1956 Hungarian revolution. Luard's other spy stories have been *The Robespierre Serial* (UK 1975), *Travelling Horseman* (UK 1975), *The Orion Line* (UK 1976) and *The Dirty Area* (UK 1977). The general settings of his books tend to be in areas of 'conflict' which Luard knows well. *The Orion Line*'s climax takes place on another troubled border—that between France and Spain where the Catalan and Basque Separatists are operating. *The Dirty Area* is set in the mouth of the Mediterranean where tensions, intrigue and violence have been constant factors for centuries. *The Robespierre Serial* caused almost as big a panic in Section Q of the CIA as the *Private Eye* revelation did among MI5 twelve years earlier. In this novel Luard told a convincing espionage story about an Arab grandee who, having meddled in too many intrigues, sought refuge in the West when he was in danger of assassination. He settled in Spain where a British agent, unaware that his own Ministry had organised a pretended assassination in order to frighten the CIA, took over the assassin's role in earnest and almost succeeded, despite the efforts of his superiors to stop him. This was the *pièce de résistance* of Luard's spy thrillers and the merest hint that he was going to write yet another bombshell of fiction sent Q Section into another huddle: there was even an attempt to get an advance look at the typescript on the grounds that a German publishing firm was interested in translation rights! *Travelling Horseman* was about the inner core of the PLO's Black September terrorist arm, which, wrote one critic, 'Luard appears to have penetrated . . . a true documentation'. Nevertheless it was fiction, but the CIA—or at least some of its executives—are still convinced that Luard obtained his plot and many of the details from one of their indiscreet operators. One thing is certain: Luard will be compulsory reading for CIA departmental chiefs and most 'spooks', American, British and Russian, for some time to come. Luard's own comment on the CIA reaction to *The Robespierre Serial* was: 'They knew that I had high-grade sources in the Agency and they also knew my prime interest was in writing books about field operations. A popular and widely-held misconception—which the Agency assiduously promotes—is that the CIA is primarily worried about leaks concerning its technological espionage equipment, "ElInt" in their jargon. In fact leaks about ElInt developments—satellite surveillance to planted bugs—worry them very little. They are well known to the other side and they don't damage the Agency's image. But what does worry the CIA are revelations and stories about field operations. Field operations involve individuals. They're fast, unpredictable, often messy and if exposed potentially explosive in their consequences. *The Robespierre Serial* dealt with a field operation that went wrong. That was why the Agency's response to the book was so extreme. I was delighted! They bought more copies (for study, evaluation and, if necessary, repudiation) than any other single purchaser in America!'

Luard's interest in the espionage game probably goes back to childhood. He grew up in Teheran in the Second World War when the city was a hive of intrigue. His step-father was a much decorated SOE agent. 'If I had to single out one theme that I'm particularly attracted to—and explore in my books—it would be that of the "man alone". The agent, the operative, who gets cut off from his superiors and his logistical base, and has to act on his own. This of course means that I'm concerned with field operations rather than analytical-evaluative espionage. I do use the same fictional (i.e. disguised) general organisation in several books and also several of the same "background" characters. But the central figure, the protagonist, changes from book to book. This reflects real life field operations. A man suited for a certain operation in France won't necessarily be suited for quite a different operation in, say, Tangier.'

Charles McCarry (b. US, 1929)

Charles McCarry started life as a newspaperman, became a speechwriter for President Eisenhower, saw something of the inside world of politics, decided he had had enough and wanted to escape Washington and write a novel. Instead he joined the CIA! The manner in which he tells how this happened is a model of gentle irony, leavened with a subtle wit and perhaps an element of ambiguity. 'I'd sold five short stories in a row. It was 1957 and I wanted to write the great American novel in Majorca. So I called Allen Dulles's office and asked if we could do a deal. Someone called me back and told me to meet a Mr Smith at Room 506 of the Statler Hotel, Washington. I arrived and knocked. No answer. But a guy outside Room 504 was trying to fit a key into his lock. Suddenly it clicked. He said, "This goddam door won't open," and I said, "Have you tried Room 506, Mr Smith?" and that's how I joined the CIA. That little interlude reassured me quite a lot. Even the CIA is human.' McCarry then spent the next decade travelling around Africa and Asia, getting away from Washington all right, but not doing what he had intended and having to keep a marriage on an even keel while able to tell his wife only part of the truth.

After Watergate and Vietnam and a great deal of soul-searching and cynicism, a host of 'deep cover' CIA agents chose to blow their cover and make their revelations in something that seemed like a religious orgy of virtuous, public self-confession of sins. Not so McCarry, though almost everyone thought he had followed in their path. His book, *The Tears of Autumn* (US 1975), had government and CIA officials alike hopping around like scalded cats wondering what new revelations were going to emerge. The book caused a stir because its story was built on an explanation of the first Kennedy assassination, which not unnaturally irked those officials whose main purpose in life seems to have been trying to stop the case from being reopened. *The Tears of Autumn* relates how the CIA engineered the murder of President Ngo Dinh Diem of Vietnam and how, three weeks later, Diem's right-wing allies sent their agents to shoot Kennedy in revenge. Paul Christopher, an intellectual, once a poet, a member of the most secret Intelligence agency of the US, undertakes a one-man investigation to uncover an assassination conspiracy which combines oriental fatalism with the ruthlessness of the Mafia. The search for the truth becomes a kind of crusade, waged by Christopher against his own employers as well as the enemies of his country. This was not merely a sensational book cashing in on a seemingly insatiable American appetite for learning nasty things about themselves and their political way of life; it was superbly written, knowledgeable and of undoubted literary merit. *The New Yorker* called it 'the best thriller of the year' and it was praised in Britain as being 'a valuable contribution to contemporary literature'. This was not altogether surprising, for even so perceptive a critic as Eric Ambler had said of McCarry's first novel, *The Miernik Dossier* (US 1974), that it was 'the most intelligent and enthralling piece of work I have read for a very long time. The level of reality it achieves is high indeed; it is superbly constructed, wholly convincing and displays insights that are distinctly refreshing.'

Perhaps McCarry's resounding success as a swiftly established writer of literary merit has put a damper on the activities of those in US security agencies who would like to slap him down, this middle-aged character with the soft voice and the thick glasses. Though their first reaction was one of horror, they have had to admit that McCarry's only crusade is to sell his novels, not to abuse the CIA, of which he talks with some affection. 'The CIA', he says, 'deals with things as they are and doesn't make moral judgements' and in reply to criticisms of the CIA he states that countries with some freedoms are better than those without any freedoms. As to the story about the Kennedy assassination, all he says is: 'Maybe the Vietnamese did kill Kennedy. But they sure didn't tell me.'

Wilson McCarthy (b. Washington, D.C., 1930)
A man who has had a varied career in different parts of the world, Wilson McCarthy served as an infantryman with the US forces in the Korean War and later worked for Presidents Kennedy and Johnson in various capacities. At one time he directed the Presidential Advance and he has had wide experience of Secret Service operations and techniques, all of which has given him the know-how and background for some exciting and well-constructed spy stories. After leaving the White House McCarthy joined MGM as their European representative, primarily as a trouble-shooter. He then returned to the US as an executive with the company before moving into the production area of the business to make films. Leaving MGM to join Warner Brothers as a producer, he next formed his own company in the animation field before moving to Britain, where he lived for three years prior to going to Ontario in 1974.

Outstanding among McCarthy's spy thrillers are *The Fourth Man* (US 1972) and *The Detail* (US 1974). The former told how the President of the US is threatened with assassination. The Mafia, rightist organisations and individual psychopaths (a formidable combination!) are conspiring, each for their own motives, to rid American political life of what they see as a radical scourge. The

American Secret Service is aware of the threat to its institutions, but seemingly powerless to prevent it. McCarthy is extraordinarily skilful in dealing with this theme and making it seem plausible and somehow frighteningly natural. His novel plunges the reader into an ambiguous world of double-crossing and deceptions and, behind it all, there is still a nagging doubt: could it really have happened in the Kennedy era? *The Detail* is again concerned with the US Secret Service's responsibility for protecting the President, but with emphasis this time on another role—that of safeguarding the US currency. Peter Maas, author of *The Valachi Papers*, wrote of the book that it made '*The French Connection* look like a Sunday School outing'. What is especially interesting about this fictional thriller is the authentic picture it draws of the US Secret Service—how it is much smaller than the FBI, but has powers extending far beyond its size, powers which are not easily understood outside the country. The action shifts from Los Angeles airport to Washington, London and Palm Springs, with Scotland Yard and the British Customs involved.

Philip McCutchan (b. Cambridge, 13 October 1920)
An unusual feature of a number of authors of spy thrillers is that they started life either in the Army or at Sandhurst and then switched to the Navy. Like Fleming, Erskine Childers and others, Philip Donald McCutchan followed this path. Educated at St Helen's College, Southsea, Hants, and the Royal Military Academy, Sandhurst, he served in the Royal Navy in the Second World War as a lieutenant, RNVR. For three years afterwards he sailed in Orient liners on the Australian run and then, for a time, was an assistant master at a preparatory school. He began writing in 1956 and his best-known books are probably those in the popular Commander Shaw series. He has occasionally used the pen name of 'Duncan McNeil', especially for his James Ogilvie novels about Victorian soldiering on India's North-West frontier. His spy stories include *Gibraltar Road* (UK 1960), *Redcap* (UK 1961), *Bluebolt One* (UK 1962), *Man From Moscow* (UK 1963), *Moscow Coach* (UK 1964), *Poulter's Passage* (UK 1967) and more recently, *A Very Big Bang* (UK 1975) and *Blood Run East* (UK 1976). *Call From Simon Shard* (UK 1974) introduced Simon Shard of the Security Service, who is answerable to the Foreign Office, a character who also appeared in *A Very Big Bang* and *Blood Run East*. The 'Big Bang'

story centred on a plot for a major explosion in the London Underground Railway system. In *Blood Run East*, Simon Shard is given the task of seeing Katie Farrell, the Belfast bomber, removed from the country, but he loses her and word comes of a threat to blow up the Chemical Defence Establishment at Porton Down. McCutchan is a past chairman of the Crime Writers' Association.

John Dann MacDonald (b. US, 1916)

For MacDonald, writing stories was rather like doing the football pools for many years. Great concentration, an enormous output, but absolutely no success. He himself reckons that he wrote 800,000 words in four months, but couldn't sell any of it, and that kind of output is enough to make any professional author jealous. But he kept on writing and today he has finally established himself not only as a successful writer, but a spy story-teller greatly admired by the Intelligence fraternity. Since those abortive 800,000 words, he calculates that he has now had published some tens of millions of words. MacDonald served with the US Army in Ceylon in the Second World War, and was demobilised as a Lieut.-Colonel in 1945. Not all his books are spy stories, but his private eye creation, Travis McGee, a girl-fancying sleuth who lives on a boat, is sometimes mixed up in the game. MacDonald has published fifteen books in all and it is worth noting that every title has the name of a colour worked into it somehow—*A Purple Place for Dying* (US 1964), *The Girl in the Plain Brown Wrapper* (US 1968), *Dress Her in Indigo* (US 1969), *The Lond Lavender Look* (US 1970), *A Tan and Sandy Silence* (US 1971) and *The Scarlet Ruse* (US 1973).

William Rutledge McGarry: *see* James P. Smythe

Helen MacInnes (b. 7 October 1907)

Helen Clark MacInnes was educated at the Hermitage School, Helensburgh, Glasgow University and University College, London. In 1932 she married Gilbert Highet who, since 1950, has been Professor of Latin at Columbia University, New York. She started writing books in the early 'forties with such works as *Above Suspicion* (UK 1941), and *Assignment in Brittany* (UK 1942), quickly acquiring a reputation for novels of adventure and suspense, tending increasingly towards the well-constructed spy story with such later books as *Pray for a Brave Heart* (US 1955), *Venetian Affair* (US 1963) and *The Double Image* (US 1966). She has been described as 'the Queen of Spy Writers' (*Sunday Express*) and she certainly shows a special talent for what one critic calls her 'satin-smooth novels of international intrigue'. In 1961 three of her earliest books were re-issued under the title *Assignment: Suspense* with an introduction posing three questions which the author said she had often been asked about her novels: what is true? how much is invented? did you yourself experience any of those situations? Her reply was that in her novels the 'physical backgrounds are as factual as I can make them', that the characters and plots were invented and that it was a misconception that novelists write only from experiences.

Her novels generally cover one of three areas: some deal with the Second World War; others, such as *The Salzburg Connection* (US 1968), seem to take a peep back at certain secrets and trends in that war which are still relevant today; and still others embrace the theme of plots from without to weaken and ultimately overthrow the Western World. She has travelled widely since the war and used these experiences in settings for her books, notably in *North From Rome* (US 1958), *Decision at Delphi* (US 1960), *The Venetian Affair* and *Message from Malaga* (US 1972). Helen McInnes has that penchant of female spy and suspense story writers of using a brilliant and distinguished amateur as her hero and chief agent. And her heroes, while undergoing all manner of trials, invariably emerge unscathed, which in a modern spy story gives a certain unreality to the episodes if repeated too often. At the same time this technique is linked with the interpolation of moral messages into her work. But, these foibles apart, such stories as *I and My True Love* (US 1953), *The Salzburg Connection* (one of her best books) and *Agent in Place* (US 1976) manage to keep the reader in a state of animated suspense. The last-named book starts off with a wounded Russian agent being killed by a colleague to stop him talking, from which point, one critic writes, 'we move into a world of double-cross and intrigue, with a secret NATO memorandum as the prize for the winner . . . and right at the end, in sunny Menton, none of your torrid sex, but simple old true love.' Only Helen MacInnes, it would seem, can today bring Romance into the environment of 'safe' houses, secret codes and sleeping agents activated.

Marthe McKenna (b. Roulers, Belgium, *c.* 1893; d. 1969)

Most traces of the history of Marthe McKenna have vanished, or remain unrecorded, but she was in some respects the perfect example of the spy who turned to spy fiction. Born Marthe Cnockaert, she grew up in Belgium and saw her native country overrun by the German armies in 1914–15. She became a spy in the service of the British and at one time, while carrying on her entirely voluntary efforts in espionage, she was also a nurse at the German military hospital in Roulers. How she enticed secrets out of German senior officers while still preserving her virtue, though often precariously, she told in two non-fiction books, *I Was a Spy* (UK 1933) and *Spies I Knew* (UK 1934). Relating how churches were rendezvous places for spies in Flanders, she wrote 'no celebration of divine service took place without a Secret Service agent being present'. Eventually Marthe Cnockaert was caught, court-martialled and condemned to death. Fortunately execution of the sentence was delayed but when armistice came in 1918, she was still in prison.

Mentioned in a dispatch by Field-Marshal Earl Haig 'for gallant and distinguished services in the field', she was awarded a citation on 8 November 1918. Sir Winston Churchill wrote a foreword to *I Was a Spy*, and in his comments on her work said: 'Behind the German lines many people followed the honourable profession of a spy.' He later praised her as 'brave, wise, virtuous and patriotic'. After the war Marthe Cnockaert married a young British officer, Jack McKenna. Following the success of her first two non-fiction books, she launched into spy fiction. Her novels included *A Spy Was Born* (UK 1935), *My Master Spy* (UK 1936), *Drums Never Beat* (UK 1936), *Lancer Spy* (UK 1937), *Set a Spy* (UK 1937) and *Double Spy* (UK 1938). As spy stories concerning the First World War began to lose interest, she turned her attention to books dealing with the threat of the Nazis and, of course, the Second World War when that broke. Her later books were *Hunt the Spy* (UK 1939), *Spying Blind* (UK 1939), *Spy in Khaki* (UK 1941), *Arms and the Spy* (UK 1942), *Nightfighter Spy* (UK 1943), *Watch Across the Channel* (UK 1944), *Three Spies for Glory* (UK 1950) and *What's Past is Prologue* (UK 1951).

Compton Mackenzie (b. W. Hartlepool, 17 January 1883; d. 1973)

Born Edward Montagu Compton, he was educated at St Paul's School and Magdalen College, Oxford. He originally studied law, and even flirted with the idea of acting as a profession. His first publication was a book of poems (1907) and his first successful novel was *The Passionate Elopement* (UK 1911), followed by such best-sellers as *Carnival* (UK 1912) and *Sinister Street* (UK 1913–14). Early on in life (1900–01) he was a 2nd Lieut. in the 1st Herts. Regiment and when the First World War began he joined the Royal Marines, achieving the rank of Captain and serving with the Royal Naval Detachment in the Dardanelles Expedition, 1915. Invalided during the same year, he was appointed Military Control Officer in Athens in 1916 and later Director of the Aegean Intelligence Service, Syria. During this period Mackenzie was mixed up in a good deal of cloak-and-dagger activities of a type which aroused among both enemies and neutral parties strong criticism of the British Secret Service. Compton Mackenzie described something of the Secret Service machinations in Greece in that war in his book *Athenian Memories* (UK 1931). He was appointed head of the Anglo–French police in Athens, accepting this post with considerable enthusiasm for he had very definite ideas about what British policy should be in the Balkans and was anxious to see a Greek crusade against both Turks and Germans. As a result some grossly inaccurate and wildly extravagant stories were told about him in Athens. He was even alleged to have made an attempt on King Constantine's life and to have tried to surround the palace with fire so that there should be no possible escape for the inmates.

Mackenzie was always in trouble. As he describes in *Aegean Memories* (UK 1940), on one occasion Capt. Sir Mansfield Cumming, head of the British Secret Service, told him that it had been reported that while visiting Maxim's in Paris Mackenzie had 'talked with the greatest indiscretion of diplomatic secrets'. In fact, Mackenzie had never been to Maxim's, and the alleged indiscreet talk could only possibly refer to a dinner party given in the British Embassy. The story was part of a Foreign Office campaign to discredit certain Secret Service agents. Capt. Sir Mansfield Cumming was known in the Secret Service as 'C' and it was by this initial that Mackenzie denoted him in *Aegean Memories*. What brought Mackenzie into deep trouble was his *Greek Memories* (UK 1932; withdrawn and re-issued 1940). In this he told about a colleague of his in British Intelligence who devised a plan for blowing up a certain bridge near Constantinople. This officer was so tediously attentive to detail that he obtained samples of various types of coal used in that part of Turkey in order to choose a few pieces, to be forwarded to England, to serve as models for the casings of the bombs. Mackenzie was charged under the Official Secrets Act, brought to trial at the Old Bailey in 1933 and fined £100. It was a ridiculous charge and a ludicrous sentence in the land which had a reputation for justice: in the inter-war years the calibre of an ageing judiciary was more thrombotic than sympathetic. Some British judges in that period were little better than *bent* puppets—not quite such an extravagant adjective as it seems—or geriatric adjudicators, more mindful of governmental approval or disapproval than was ever the case in the surprisingly more enlightened Victorian era. Possibly the best judiciary material had been killed off in the First World War. These quotations from the trial may suffice to show that this is not such a tendentious statement as it may seem: in *Greece in My Life* (UK 1960) Mackenzie described how the prosecutor, Sir Thomas Inskip, condemned him because he had 'revealed the mysterious consonant by which the Chief of the Secret Service was known'. 'But, Mr Attorney,' inquired the judge with a rare touch of commonsense, 'if C is such a dangerous consonant, why is it still being used nearly fifteen years after the war?' 'That I couldn't say, m'lud.' 'No, I shouldn't think you could. The consonant should surely have been changed by now.' One would imagine that any normal judge today would have found the charge unproved. But Mackenzie got his own back at both MI5 and MI6 when he wrote his spoof novel on the British Secret Service, *Water on the Brain* (UK 1933). This could not be banned because it was fictional!

The hero of this spy novel was a hen-pecked, retired Army major named Arthur Blenkinsop, recruited into the Secret Service under the cover of a banana importer. In the preface to a new edition of the book, published two decades later, Mackenzie wrote that at the time of publication his novel must have seemed 'a fantastic Marx Brothers affair', but that during the Second World War 'many more people discovered that those responsible for Secret Intelligence do, in very fact as often as not, behave like characters created by the Marx Brothers.' It is a tribute to Mackenzie's sense of realism and his satire that, halfway through the war, when the Americans were building their own Intelligence Services, they used *Water on the Brain* as a text-book for their trainees. Blenkinsop in *Water on the Brain* makes the mistake of referring to his chief, N, by his real name, Colonel Nutting. He apologises quickly and is told: 'I know you won't do it again. Of course, in one way, it doesn't matter in my room at the War Office. But it's against the principles of the Secret Service. You do it once in private, and then before you know where you are you'll go and do it in the middle of Piccadilly. After all, the whole point of the Secret Service is that it should be secret.' 'Quite, quite, sir, I'm very sorry.' 'Of course, I wouldn't go so far as to say that the secrecy was *more* important than the service, but it's every bit *as* important. Well, it stands to reason that if the Secret Service was no longer secret, it would cease to be the Secret Service. After all, we're not Cabinet Ministers. We can't afford to talk.'

There was also a certain amount of satire directed against MI5 in Mackenzie's wartime humorous novel, *Whisky Galore* (UK 1947). In the Second World War Mackenzie was a Captain in the Home Guard and he was also invited by the Indian Government to visit all the battlefields of the Indian Army during that war. From 1931–1934 he was Rector of Glasgow University and in 1952 he was knighted.

Alistair Maclean (b. Scotland, 1923)

Alistair Maclean served in the Second World War as a torpedo rating in the Royal Navy, much of the time on Russian convoy routes. It was from these experiences that he drew heavily for his novels about the sea. He tells how on one occasion he was ordered to fire three torpedoes at an Italian ship: all missed their mark. 'I was roundly cursed at first, then it was discovered there was a mechanical defect. But I felt greatly relieved later when we learned that this was a hospital ship which wasn't flying the right flag. I couldn't have lived with the knowledge that I had sunk a hospital ship.' After the war Maclean went to Glasgow University and then became a teacher at a junior secondary school in Rutherglen, Glasgow. In 1955 he had an instant success with his first book, *HMS 'Ulysses'*, which made him a fortune, to be followed by the equally successful *Guns of Navarone* (UK 1957).

Some have assessed Maclean's earnings at around £250,000 a year from his books, film scripts and other activities (at one time he owned at least two hotels, including Jamaica Inn in Cornwall). But success has not made this author big-headed: 'I'm not a born writer,' he insists, 'and I don't enjoy writing. I wrote each book in thirty-five days flat—just to get the darned thing finished.' It was first as a writer on the sea and naval life and then as a thriller writer that Maclean made his name. He sees almost every book as a film script before he starts to write it and his real talent is that he tells a story with speed, economy and attention to detail. He allows nothing to hold up the action: one reason why there is no sex in Maclean's novels is, he says, because it slows down the narrative and hinders the action. He has ventured into spy fiction, his first of this genre being *The Last Frontier* (UK 1959), about an unlikely agent who blunders across the Hungarian frontier with 'one Belgian automatic and silencer, one rubberised torch' and one flick knife, the blade of which 'gleams evilly'. There are oddities of expression like this which creep into Maclean's prose and dialogue; another example, sounding almost like a parody of Ian Fleming, is 'the Chateauneuf had the ambrosia whacked to the wide'. Maclean has also written under the pseudonym of 'Ian Stuart', notably *The Dark Crusader* (UK 1961), in which a tough but none too bright secret agent is sent on a mission which lands him on a Polynesian island where a new rocket is waiting to be tested. Rather more complicated was *Ice Station Zebra* (UK 1963, under his own name) in which a British Secret Service team sets off in an American submarine ostensibly to rescue the survivors of a British meteorological post in the Arctic which has been gutted by fire. In fact their quest is to recover a capsule from outer space containing a long-range, top-secret reconnaissance camera and its films—before the Russians get there. This is good, strong melodramatic stuff for the silver screen, but makes improbable reading. Indeed, most of Maclean's books read like film scenarios, which is undoubtedly his intention. *Where Eagles Dare* (UK 1967) told of seven men and a girl who were parachuted into wartime Germany, their objective being a mountain-top schloss in which an American general is held captive by the Gestapo. This was a tale of double-agentry with a grand finale aboard a cable-car.

Maclean's ties with Britain are not strong—'the place is flat on its bottom', he is reported to have declared—and he is now a Swiss citizen, married for the second time to a Frenchwoman. Perhaps because he is his own sternest critic he has continued to be one of the most successful novelists of the past quarter century. His most recent book on an espionage theme was *Circus* (UK 1975), which was all about the greatest high-wire artist in the world attempting on behalf of the CIA to climb into an impenetrable Iron Curtain fortress to steal the secrets of 'anti-matter' and abduct the mad scientist who had discovered how to control it.

Victor Marchetti

Victor Marchetti is best known for his non-fiction work, *The CIA and the Cult of Intelligence* (US 1974), which was described as 'the bombshell bestseller that blows the cover of the CIA' and became the subject of a prolonged legal battle between authors (John D. Marks was the co-author), publishers and the CIA. By federal court order the authors were required to submit the manuscript of the book to the CIA for review prior to publication. Under the terms of the court ruling, the CIA ordered the deletion of 339 passages of varying length. Later these deletions were reduced to 168 items. Marchetti wrote that the CIA had 'secured an unwarranted and outrageous permanent injunction against me, requiring that any- thing I write or say, *factual, fictional or otherwise*, on the subject of intelligence must first be censored by the CIA.'

The background to this request undoubtedly lies to some extent in the publication of Marchetti's novel, *The Rope Dancer* (US 1971), of which one critic, writing in 1975, said 'this terrifying piece of fiction has more truth in it than his best-selling non-fiction CIA exposé.' And so, apparently, thought the CIA. *The Rope Dancer* did not attract anything remotely like the sales of his later non-fiction books (though it aroused wide interest after the publication of *The Cult*), but it certainly alarmed the CIA. It was a novel all about that Agency, though Marchetti called it the NIA, and in effect was an exploration of the inner workings of a spy's mind. The plot con- cerned a highly placed American who suddenly went over to the Russians and revealed a good deal about the administrative workings of the CIA. There were snide comments on a certain President with a Texas accent for whom the author had little liking (almost certainly written with Lyndon Johnson in mind). The CIA executives believed the novel went far too near the truth for comfort and that shackles should be put on Marchetti in future—thus the court ruling three years later over *The CIA and the Cult of Intelligence*.

Marchetti's introduction to the world of Intelligence came in 1952 when he was serving in the US Army in Germany. He was sent to the European Command's 'special school' at Oberammergau to study Russian and the techniques of Intelligence. For a period he was on special duties on the East German borders; then he returned to the US to attend college, specialising in Soviet studies and history and eventually joining the CIA in 1955. He became a Soviet specialist, mostly on military affairs, and from 1966–69 was a staff officer in the Office of the Director of the CIA. His highest position in the Agency was as executive assistant to Admiral Rufus Taylor, who was Deputy Director of Central Intelligence from 1966–69.

It would seem that Marchetti became increasingly critical of CIA tactics while still in that organisation. In an article in *The Nation* magazine entitled *The CIA: The President's Loyal Tool*, he once wrote: 'The CIA is basically concerned with interfering in the affairs of foreign countries', and in a foreword to his book on the CIA he stated: 'Disenchanted and disagreeing with many of the Agency's policies and practices, and for that matter, with those of the Intelligence community and the US Government. I resigned from the CIA in late 1969.' He felt unable to speak out publicly: 'I therefore sought to put forth my thoughts—perhaps more accurately my feelings—in fictional form. I wrote a novel, *The Rope Dancer*, in which I tried to describe for the reader what life was actually like in a secret agency such as the CIA, and what the differences were between myth and reality in this overly romanticised profession.'

Robert Markham: *see* Kingsley Amis

J. J. Marric: *see* John Creasey

A. E. W. Mason (b. London, 7 May 1865; d. 22 November 1948) Alfred Edward Woodley Mason attended Dulwich College before going on to Trinity, Oxford, where he won an exhibition in classics in 1887. Mason had a distinguished career, both academically and socially, being an outstanding speaker at the Oxford Union and a member of the University Dramatic Society. His experience with the latter made him take up acting as a career and for some years he toured the provinces. Though he played in the first production of Shaw's *Arms and the Man*, Mason found it difficult to obtain parts in the West End.

Both Oscar Wilde and Sir Arthur Quiller-Couch encouraged him to take up writing rather than continue acting and in 1895 he had his first novel published, *A Romance of Wastdale*. This was followed immediately afterwards by *The Courtship of Morrice Buckler* (UK

1896), of which a contemporary critic said: 'This puts Mr Mason in the front rank of cloak and dagger writers.' For a while after this he turned his attention to the historical novel and eventually found fame with his still popular romance, *The Four Feathers* (UK 1902). As a writer, Mason was more skilled both in narrative and characterisation than Oppenheim or Le Queux and he proved equally successful with his detective stories, of which the Inspector Hanaud series was easily the best. Substantial earnings from his books enabled Mason to satisfy his zest for travel and almost schoolboyish love of adventure. He explored the interior of Morocco at a time when it was still somewhat dangerous, sailed in quest of small uninhabited islands in the Mediterranean and did much Alpine climbing. For good measure he was also Liberal MP for Coventry from 1906–10. Tall, a dominating extrovert who usually wore an eyeglass, and a lively raconteur in great demand at dinner parties and country house weekend parties, Mason was as popular in Bohemian circles as in clubland or with members of the Services. From 1914–18 he served in the Royal Marines, reaching the rank of Major, but his principal war service was as a highly enterprising secret agent of the NID. Mason thoroughly enjoyed the kind of dangerous adventures which he invented for his own heroes: Admiral Sir Reginald Hall, chief of the NID, called him 'my star turn'. His biographer, Roger Lancelyn Green, gives a detailed account of some of his activities as a secret agent, but Admiral Sir William James commented that although Mason 'used his experiences for several of his novels, the true story of his adventures in Spain, Morocco and Mexico was still unpublished when he died thirty years later. It would have been a prince of thrillers.'

Mason sailed a yacht around the Spanish and Moroccan ports during the war, obtaining much useful information about German ships and submarines which made use of Spanish facilities by surreptitiously re-fueling in Spanish ports. In the early part of 1915 Lyautey, the French commander in Morocco, was busily engaged trying to put down a rebellion among the tribes engineered by the Germans. Mason went to Morocco to report on the best methods of preventing the revolt spreading. Admiral James stated that Mason 'sent in a long report of what he found . . . and recommended that the best way to destroy the German influence was to discover and cut off the channel by which their money was flowing into Morocco. This he proceeded to do himself.' But perhaps Mason's most important Secret Service mission was one about which few details are available. Mason's biographer says that it is referred to in Mason's notes as 'Anthrax through Spain'. A report had reached the British Secret Service that the Germans were aiming to spread an anthrax epidemic on the Western Front among the Allies. Two methods were to be used: first, to inject anthrax germs into mules, and secondly, to infect shaving-brushes which were to be imported for the French Army via Spain and South America. Mason managed to intercept a cargo of shaving brushes, but there is no information on what happened to the mules.

Later in the war, in Mexico, Mason emulated Sir Robert Baden-Powell's ruse of posing as a lepidopterist when spying. Whether Sir Robert had borrowed the idea from Conan Doyle's villain, Stapleton, in *The Hound of the Baskervilles*, is perhaps doubtful, but Mason afterwards admitted that he had got the idea from the book. Using this disguise, he discovered that German wireless officers from ships interned in the harbour at Vera Cruz were using the wireless station at Ixtapalapa every night. Mason wrote that at that time he had working under him 'three Mexicans of worth; the first had been a prominent officer of President Madero's private police, the second had been chief of President Huerta's police, and the third was a young fellow with a great charm of manner who held one of the highest positions as a burglar in Mexico.' With the help of this trio he planned and brought off the mission of putting the wireless station out of action.

There seems little doubt that Mason performed more important Intelligence missions than these, and that his influence in the Secret Service was considerable even after the war. It is said that he was 'entirely responsible for winning over as a spy for the British the head of a powerful smuggling ring operating in Southern Spain. This was Juan March, who lived in Majorca and became one of the most influential men in Spain and a millionaire.' Mason was offered a knighthood, but declined the honour, commenting that as he had no family (he never married) there was not much point to it. *The Summons* (UK 1920) was a romance with undertones of espionage, involving the exploits of Spanish spies, while something of his Moroccan adventures emerges in *The Winding Stair* (UK 1922). Latterly, however, he turned back to his detective stories.

F. Van Wyck Mason (b. Boston, Mass., 11 November 1901)
Educated at Berkshire School, Sheffield, and Harvard, Mason had

planned to take up a diplomatic career, but his father's sudden death forced him to abandon these ambitions and go into business. He started his own importing firm, buying rugs, antique books and other items on trips to Europe and North Africa. In the First World War he was a 2nd Lieut. with the Allied Expeditionary Force in France from 1918–19 and in the Second World War he served as a General Staff Corps Officer and chief historian in the civil and military government section. He was made a Colonel and he numbers among his honours the *Croix de Guerre*.

Mason has written under the pseudonyms of 'Geoffrey Coffin', 'Frank W. Mason', and 'Ward Weaver'. Possessed of a lively and objective mind, with a penchant for diligent research, he has drawn heavily on his travels for background for his novels, some of which are set in unexpected areas of the world. For his novels of international intrigue and espionage he has created the character of Col. North, a cosmopolitan sleuth, as well as 'the Captain' and 'the Major'. One of his earlier spy stories was *The Branded Spy Murders* (US 1932), followed by *Two Tickets for Tangier* (US 1936) and *Military Intelligence—8* (US 1941), which contained *The Washington Legation Murders* (1935), *The Hong Kong Airbase Murders* (1937) and *The Singapore Exile Murders* (1939). Other books include *Saigon Singer* (US 1948), *Himalayan Assignment* (US 1953), *Secret Mission to Bangkok* (US 1961), *Trouble in Burma* (US 1963), and *Zanzibar Intrigue* (US 1964).

J. C. Masterman (b. 12 January 1891)
Born John Cecil Masterman and educated at Royal Naval Colleges, Osborne and Dartmouth, he started life as a midshipman, but soon turned to his natural environment, the academic world, when in 1909 he won a scholarship to Worcester College, Oxford. He achieved a lectureship at Christ Church shortly before the First World War, during which he was interned in Germany for four years. In the immediate post-war years he found a welcome relief from his long incarceration by representing England at hockey and lawn tennis. His years between the two wars were mostly taken up by his academic life at Oxford University (he was Censor of Christ Church from 1920–26), but he found time to write two fictional works which in some ways anticipated the future path of his career. They were *An Oxford Tragedy* (UK 1933) and *Fate Cannot Harm Me* (UK 1935). Of the former, Professor Norman Holmes Pearson, of Yale

University, who served with the American Office of Strategic Services in London, wrote that it 'may even have played a part in drafting him for the "XX" Committee whose task it was to pass on and manage the complex manipulation of double agents' in the Second World War.

Masterman's task in this second war was rather more exciting than that he describes in *Who's Who* as 'Major (Local) and specially employed'. It was, in fact, concerned with the manipulation of enemy agents to which Pearson refers. Or, as Masterman himself succinctly expressed it in his official report to the Director-General of the Security Service in 1945, 'by means of the double-cross system we actively ran and controlled the German espionage system in this country'. The double-cross system was a remarkable apparatus of deception whereby both those who were pro-Allies and posing as German agents and real German agents captured in Britain were induced to serve the Allied cause by supplying to Germany information devised and manipulated by British Intelligence. Afterwards Masterman turned this report into a history of the whole affair in *The Double-cross System in the War of 1939–45* (UK 1972). 'As time passed,' wrote Masterman, 'it occurred to me and to others that there might well be a case for publication . . . it was also right to give credit for a successful operation to those who deserved it . . . this I took to be important because the general opinion of the Secret Service was low [at that time, 1971] . . . Failures are exaggerated, successes never mentioned.'

After the war Masterman, who was knighted in 1959, became chairman of various bodies including a Committee on the Political Activities of Civil Servants, the Army Education Advisory Board and a member of the BBC General Advisory Council, as well as being Vice-Chancellor of Oxford University from 1957–58. In 1957 he published another novel which told a story very similar to that of the double-cross system and of life in war-time Lisbon—'a kind of international clearing-ground, a busy ant-heap of spies and agents'. This was *The Case of the Four Friends*, which in its sub-title Masterman described as 'a diversion in predetection'. He portrayed a centre where 'secrets and information—true and false, but mainly false—were bought and sold'. Masterman's autobiography, *On the Chariot Wheel*, was published in 1975.

W. Somerset Maugham (b. Paris, 25 January 1874; d. St-Jean Cap Ferrat, 16 December 1965)

Novelist, short-story writer and playwright, William Somerset Maugham was born in the British Embassy in Paris, the son of Robert Ormond Maugham, a solicitor employed by the Embassy, and Edith Maugham. He spent his early life in France. After the death of his father he was sent to live in England, about which he later wrote that 'the accident of my birth in France, which enabled me to learn French and English simultaneously . . . instilled into me two modes of life, two liberties, two points of view, [and] has prevented me from ever identifying myself completely with the instincts and prejudices of one people or the other.' His mother died when he was eight years old, and this proved to be a shock from which he never fully recovered: his bedside bureau even in later life contained three pictures of her. Brought up by a clergyman uncle at Whitstable in Kent, Maugham was educated at King's School, Canterbury, where he seems to have been singularly unhappy, possibly due to his stammer and short stature. His first taste of real liberty came at the age of seventeen when he spent a year in Heidelberg and decided to go in for medicine. Five years of medical studies wearied him and he yearned to become a professional writer. When *Liza of Lambeth* was published in 1897 he saw his way out of medicine. He went to Spain to write, but it was many years before he really established himself in his new profession.

In 1907 the London Court Theatre produced his play *Lady Frederick* and in the following year *Mrs Dot*, *Jack Straw* and *The Explorer* were played at the Comedy, Vaudeville and Lyric respectively. Maugham had arrived. Soon he was to become probably the highest paid writer in history. His financial success enabled him to buy the Villa Mauresque in St-Jean Cap Ferrat, where he entertained lavishly people in all walks of life. He travelled widely in the Far East and the Pacific Islands, trekked through Burma, visited Indian yogis and shrines, sampled the Bohemian life in Paris. In 1916 he married Syrie Wellcome (née Barnardo). It was not a happy marriage, but it produced a daughter, Liza, named after the heroine of his first book.

During the First World War Maugham joined a Red Cross unit in France as a dresser, ambulance driver and interpreter. After a short while he was transferred to the Secret Intelligence Service and spent a year in Geneva as a secret agent. Finally, in 1917, he was sent to Russia with the task of supporting the Provisional Government against the Bolsheviks, who planned to make a separate peace with Germany. In his book *The Summing Up* (UK 1938), Maugham claimed that the Russian revolution might have been prevented if he had arrived six months earlier. There is ample evidence in the Private Papers of Sir William Wiseman in the E. M. House Collection, Yale University Library, that Maugham played a considerable role in the espionage in Russia in 1917. Wiseman was head of the British Secret Service organisation in the US during the war. His papers contain letters and lengthy reports by Maugham in which he names the chief German agent in Russia, analyses the political situation and makes various suggestions. The outcome of all this experience was what Eric Ambler has described as 'the first fictional work on the subject [the life of the secret agent] by a writer of stature with first-hand knowledge of what he is writing about.' The title of Maugham's first book on espionage was *Ashenden: or, The British Agent* (UK 1928): it was not only based on first-hand experience of the world of espionage, but it was the first exposure of what espionage really meant—not romantic melodrama, but long periods of boredom, fear, human weakness, callousness and deceit. Ashenden was in a way the first of the anti-heroes, though nothing like as unpleasant as the latter-day anti-heroes. The book is really a collection of short stories, beginning in Geneva and ending in Petrograd during the revolution. The agent Ashenden, who is the central, linking figure of all the stories, is in some ways a self-portrait of Maugham himself. Ashenden was not a brilliant performer of courageous deeds: he worried about missing trains and had an attack of nerves when a fellow agent was about to murder a Greek spy. Maugham gave one clue in his book as to the real identity of Ashenden. The latter's superior officer asked him where he had been living 'all these years'. 'At 36 Chesterfield Street, Mayfair,' was the reply. This was Maugham's own address before the war. An interesting revelation in the Wiseman Papers is that Maugham's cover name was 'Somerville'. He used this as Ashenden's code-name in the novel.

The realism of *Ashenden* contrasted markedly with the heroics and melodrama, the high-life of Oppenheim and Le Queux: 'Ashenden's official existence was as orderly and monotonous as a City clerk's. He saw his spies at stated intervals and paid them their wages; when he could get hold of a new one he engaged him, gave him his instructions and sent him off to Germany; he waited for the information that came through and dispatched it; he went into France once a week to confer with his colleague over the frontier and to receive his orders from London; he visited the market-place on market-day to get any messages the old butter-woman had brought him from the other side of the lake; he kept his eyes and ears open; and he wrote long reports which he was convinced no one read till having inadvertently slipped a jest into one of them he received a sharp rebuke for his levity.' This piece of descriptive fiction is worth comparing with Alexander Foote's experiences as a real-life Soviet agent in Geneva in the Second World War as told in *Handbook for Spies* (UK 1949): the parallel between fiction and fact is almost incredible.

There was a typical Maugham twist to the end of one Ashenden story: it is discovered that an agent has killed the wrong man in error. Referring to this, the *Times Literary Supplement* prissily stated: 'Never before or since has it been so categorically demonstrated that counter-intelligence work consists often of morally indefensible jobs not to be undertaken by the squeamish or the conscience-stricken.' Perhaps after *Ashenden* any other ventures by Maugham into spy fiction would have been an anti-climax. He was a wise enough writer to realise he had laid a new milestone in the history of this genre and that was enough. Late in life Maugham was made a Companion of Honour, but it cannot be said that his latter years were altogether happy. Domestic rifts clouded and poisoned the atmosphere and this was revealed by a notorious series of articles entitled *Looking Back*, which Maugham had serialised in the US and UK in 1962. These contained the 'vengeful outpourings of an old man approaching senility', wrote one critic, and they were marred by a vicious attack on his wife.

James Mayo: *see* Stephen Coulter

Hubert Monteilhet (b. Paris, 1928)
Educated at the Sorbonne, Hubert Monteilhet brings to bear a special quality in his spy fiction—a touch of the *matoufan* or mischievousness, of which de Maupassant wrote, a subtle hint of *les dégringolades*. Most of his books are concerned with crime and mystery, some with espionage, and he is holder of the Inner Sanctum Mystery Award and the *Grand Prix de Littérature Policière*.

His first book was *The Praying Mantises* (France 1961), followed by *Return From the Ashes* (France 1961), *The Road to Hell* (France 1963), *The Prisoner of Love* (UK 1965), *Cupid's Executioners* (UK 1966) and *The Cupedevil* (UK 1967). His works are published in France, the US and the UK.

Of all his spy stories *The Cupedevil* is in many ways unique and its originality sets it apart from the run of the mill tales of espionage. The novel seems to reveal a peep at the mind of an author who, during the years of the war, was himself an adolescent living in a strange, unreal world. The Cupedevil was a catalystic evil genius named Arnaud. He started out as a normal adolescent until he became the pawn in his own game and the games of others. The name of the game was Diane. Arnaud loved her, but didn't get her; Jacques didn't love her, but got her. Count Daspect wasn't sure, but he never refused a gift. The Maquis didn't even know they, too, were involved with the game of Diane. And there was a French officer who actually invented the game. All rather mysterious until the story is gradually unwrapped and then it becomes stylish entertainment—a comi-tragedy of studied depravity.

Monteilhet, who lives in Tunisia, lists as his recreation a subject which will surprise anyone who has read his spy novels: it is theology.

Anthony Morten: *see* John Creasey

Bernard Newman (b. Ibstock, Leics., 8 May 1897; d. 19 February 1968)
Bernard Newman was a grand-nephew of George Eliot, a matter in which he took particular pride. He served with the BEF in France from 1915–19 and, the story goes, because he was unable to stay on a horse the Army gave him a bicycle. And it was cycling which became Newman's great passion ever afterwards: he made innumerable tours by this means, always on bicycles he called 'George', until after his sixtieth birthday.

He entered the Civil Service in 1920 and at one time he was in danger of being dismissed because the Foreign Office objected to a book of his, *Danger Spots of Europe* (UK 1938). This was a period when the Foreign Office was determined to appease the European dictators and to stifle any criticism of them. Mussolini, furious at what Newman had written about Italy, tried to get him sacked, but without success, for the British authorities relented and allowed the book to appear while Newman was still 'a civil servant'.

Newman started writing what were almost conventional thrillers, like *Death of a Harlot* (UK 1934), while at the same time touching on the theme of military strategy—*The Cavalry Went Through* (UK 1930). The latter book was a thoughtful study in fictional form of what might have happened and what could have been done, in the 1914–18 war, if the higher command had shown more imagination and originality to break the trench warfare deadlock. Such a distinguished military authority as Sir Basil Liddell Hart wrote that Newman's 'detailed ideas were so good . . . and had such a clear bearing on the future, that I put it on successive lists of recommended reading for military students . . . For me it is, in retrospect, a matter of regret that he did not pursue his studies and writings on tactics and strategy, for which he had shown such remarkable gifts.'

The backgrounds to Newman's books, which, after these early ones, were mainly about spies in fact and fiction, were always well researched. He collected the necessary details on his cycling tours around Europe. He made espionage very much his special subject and from 1934 onwards he was in great demand as a lecturer on spies and spying and on European affairs. One of his great virtues was that, outside his fiction, he kept very much to the known facts, plus a few tit-bits that he claimed to have discovered. It was *Spy* (UK 1935) which made Newman's name and brought him into the limelight of controversy. This was a subtle psychological study of Ludendorff's nervous collapse in September 1918, and Liddell Hart wrote after Newman's death that 'it was based on my account of that episode, along with a maxim of mine that the mind of the enemy commander is the basic target in war, and it purported to relate how a British officer had infiltrated into Ludendorff's staff and played demoralisingly on his mind. As it cited my maxim and conveyed that I had uttered it in the narrator's presence, the publishers submitted the proofs of the book to me . . . Many of the reviewers tended to regard the book as factual rather than fictional.' The book had a wide success and the press generally thought it was the genuine confession of a secret agent until its author admitted with some glee that he had made it all up. The whole affair was a marvellous leg-pull, but not until one or two inquiring newspapers had discovered that the author's claims could not be entirely substantiated.

Thereafter spy stories poured from the pen of Bernard Newman.

Altogether he wrote 128 of them, as well as a number of travel books. He was one of the first to realise the threat from the Nazis and the Fascists and *German Spy* and *Mussolini Murder* (both UK 1936) were followed by *Secret Servant* and *Woman Spy* (both UK 1937), *Death under Gibraltar* (UK 1938) and *Maginot Line Murder* and *Death to the Spy* (both UK 1939). Generally speaking, Newman concentrated on espionage in Europe, which he knew so intimately. He caught the new mood of authenticity and topicality in spy fiction. With the approach of the Second World War, Newman kept an eye open on his travels for any signs of new developments in German arms production. Quite by chance, he was the first man to make a report on the V2 rocket when, in 1938, he came across some installations built on reinforced concrete and surrounded by barbed wire on the Baltic coast at Peenemunde. A friendly hotel-keeper told him that the place was being used for experiments with a new type of rocket. But the British Secret Service foolishly ignored his report.

When war broke out Newman was engaged as a lecturer first with the British Expeditionary Force and then, in 1942, as a staff lecturer with the Ministry of Information. Of course, few lecturers had such a wealth of experience on which to draw and he made as effective use of this in his talks as in his novels. He had travelled in more than sixty countries and among his adventures were those of becoming a strong man in a Polish circus, living with Balkan gypsies, being banned from Italy by Mussolini and being chased by an elephant. In 1940 he was very nearly captured while talking to French troops in the Maginot Line.

Spy Catchers (UK 1945) was a collection of short stories and is still one of the best books written around the subject of counter-espionage. Newman was especially good when dealing with the use of radio for code messages, and the story, 'Spy by Music', dealt with musical codes. There was a suspicion that the Germans were making use of these in their broadcasts. A team of experts started to study them and discovered that a musical alphabet was being used, with one or more letters allotted to the minim. Nobody was better at producing fascinating stories around codes and ciphers than Newman, who always went to immense trouble and in this instance actually worked out his own musical code and reproduced it in the book. Another of his books, *Second Front—First Spy* (UK 1944), told how to read invisible writing. Occasionally there was a querulous note from a critic: Howard Spring, for example, grumbled that women characters were Newman's 'weak point: most of them are too lush'.

After the Second World War Newman cycled behind the Iron Curtain on a number of occasions and went as far afield (without a bicycle) as India, Pakistan and the United States. He wrote many articles summing up the political situation in countries he had visited. In 1954 he was made a *Chevalier* of the *Légion d'Honneur*. Perhaps the lecture which gave him most cause for pride was one on 'Spies in Fact and Fiction' to the Royal Society of Arts. His later spy books included *The Red Spider Web* (UK 1947) and, under the pen-name of Don Betteridge, *Not Single Spies* (UK 1951), *Spy and Counter-spy* (UK 1953), *Case of the Berlin Spy* (UK 1954) and *Spies Left!* (UK 1956). He was married twice, in 1923 and again in 1966 to Mrs Helen Johnstone, the founder of a lecture society to encourage good citizenship. He regarded her, he said, as possessing all the qualities that he laid down, in a 1946 lecture, for a good wife.

Christopher Nicole: *see* Andrew York

Pierre Nord
This is the pseudonym of André Léon Brouillard, a French writer who has produced two notable spy thrillers, *Double Crime on the Maginot Line* (France 1967) and *The Thirteenth Suicide* (France 1970). The latter was made into a successful film, by Henri Verneuil, entitled *Le Serpent* (1972). It was about a defector, Vlassor, from the USSR to the US who revealed to the CIA a list of spies operating in Western Europe for the Kremlin. The suspense derived from whether Vlassov could be an agent of the KGB, for he made allegations of treason among high personages in both France and Germany. There is an echo of both the case of Colonel Abel and the Topaz Affair of the 'sixties in this book.

'Pierre Nord' has written other espionage books, and eight of his novels have been adapted for the French cinema, including *Deuxième Bureau contre Kommandantur, Intelligences avec l'Ennemi, La Bigorne* and *Caporal de France*. He lives at Monte Carlo where he has been working on his trilogy on the activies of the French Secret Services concerning Hitler.

E. Phillips Oppenheim (b. London, 20 October 1866; d. Guernsey, 3 February 1946)

Son of a leather manufacturer, young Oppenheim was educated at Wyggeston Grammar School, Leicester, where he won the history prize, but had 'shocking reports for his maths'. He left school at the age of sixteen to help his father who at that time was in financial difficulties. One must assume that Oppenheim was quite efficient in business, as he stayed in the leather trade until middle life and he seems to have improved the family firm early on, as in 1887 his parents were able to finance the publication of his first novel, *Expiation*. On the strength of this Oppenheim was able to secure a contract to write six serial stories for the *Sheffield Weekly Telegraph*. He had a quick, fertile and imaginative mind and the additional asset of being a voracious reader of newspapers, which he avidly combed for ideas. In 1891 he married Elsie Clara Hopkins, of Easthampton, Massachusetts, whose parents also came from Leicester. This marriage gave Oppenheim a transatlantic outlook and his books soon became popular in both the United States and Europe.

He was fascinated by the world of secret diplomacy and set out not merely to explore it but to use it as a background for his fiction. In 1898 *The Mysterious Mr Sabin* was published. Oppenheim described this as 'the first of my long series of stories dealing with that shadowy and mysterious world of diplomacy . . . So long as the world lasts, its secret international history will continue to engage the full activities of the diplomatist.' He was a prolific writer— altogether he turned out 115 novels and 39 books of short stories— but never a polished one. His stories were the Edwardian version of spy fiction, a mixture of romance, adventure, espionage, secret diplomacy and high life intermingled with criminal activities and gambling in the world's greatest cities, Budapest and Vienna being two of his favourite settings early on. Eventually he gravitated towards the gay cities and resorts of which he wrote and thus added some first-hand local colour to his work. Monte Carlo then became a favourite setting for his spy stories, notably *Mr Grex of Monte Carlo* (UK 1915). He loved the good things of life and had a zest for exploring the capitals of Europe.

Like William Le Queux and Erskine Childers, though to a lesser extent, he became one of a small band of writers deeply concerned about what in the early 1900s was known as 'the German menace'. This was a theme which he introduced into some of his novels, despite the fact that it lost him his popularity as an author in Germany in the years just before 1914. Oppenheim, whose love of golf had made him take a cottage on the Norfolk coast, close to a course that overlooked the sea, decided that this part of England was singularly vulnerable to a determined attempt at invasion, despite the protection of the Royal Navy. He passed on his views and detailed observations on undefended wide stretches of flat, lonely East Anglian coast to the Admiralty, but there is no evidence that anyone paid heed to this. His more lasting contribution was to become one of the outstanding authors of what Eric Ambler calls the 'early cloak-and-dagger stereotypes—the black-velveted seductress, the British Secret Service numbskull hero, the omnipotent spymaster'.

His heroes and heroines appealed to the snobbery of the average reader of those days: the men were from Eton and the Guards, the women from Embassy parties and elegant country house gatherings. In the First World War Oppenheim was employed escorting journalists of neutral countries on tour of the battlefront in France, and it was during this period that he wrote the best of his novels of espionage, *The Kingdom of the Blind* (UK 1917). It was a story full of lively adventures, including submarine attacks and Zeppelin raids and purported to reveal something of the methods of Secret Service operators. He followed this up with *The Pawns Count* (UK 1918), another German spy tale which opens, like so many of Oppenheim's narratives, in a fashionable London restaurant where John Lutchester, of the British Secret Service, Oscar Fischer, a German American, and a beautiful New York girl, Pamela Van Teyl, are keenly interested in securing the formula of a new and wonderful explosive.

There was a slight variation in theme in *Mr Lessingham Goes Home* (UK 1919) in which an observation car attached to a Zeppelin drops a passenger in civilian clothes near an English North Sea coastal town. The hatless Hamar Lessingham enters the home of Sir Henry Cranston: he is, of course, a German spy. *The Strange Case of Mr Jocelyn Thew* (UK 1919) tried to imbue a little realism into the novel by purporting to tell the true history of how the secret documents of Count Bernstorff, the German Ambassador to the US in the early part of the war, were smuggled out of America. Oppenheim made a subtle change in this story: he created one of the very first villain-heroes. By this time, of course, the war was over!

Oppenheim, in common with Le Queux and other spy story writers of his age, relied on coincidences favouring the hero to an extent which would not be tolerated by today's much more sophisticated readers. In his book *The Double Traitor* (UK 1918) a supposedly ace German spy, Selingman, briefs one of his agents in a railway carriage, despite the fact that there is an Englishman sitting in the same compartment: 'That's all right, he's just told me he doesn't speak German.' One couldn't get away with that kind of sloppiness today, but worse follows: a slip of paper falls out of Selingman's wallet and into the Englishman's hand without the German noticing. On it is a list of German agents. For any ordinary citizen, let alone a secret agent, this is the kind of Walter Mitty dream of a lifetime. And in Oppenheim's time it was acceptable.

It was after this war that Oppenheim began to earn enormous sums from his books; many of his works were serialised in the US in journals like *Colliers* and the *Saturday Evening Post*. *The Great Impersonation* (UK 1920) and *The Devil's Paw* (UK 1921) were also stories of espionage, though in the latter title the heroine was a beautiful Russian woman and the plot involved Secret Service designs on her lover's life. His later books were not of the same quality as the earlier stories and in *The Great Prince Shan* (UK 1922) Oppenheim seemed to be imitating Sax Rohmer's Fu Manchu and his obsession with the 'Yellow Menace', which for a while in the 'twenties took the place of what had been the 'German Menace'. Eventually an Oppenheim *Secret Service Omnibus* was published and it comprised *Miss Brown of XYO* (UK 1927), a British SS story, *The Wrath to Come* (UK 1925), an American SS story, *Matorni's Vineyard* (UK 1929), about the Italian SS, *The Great Impersonation* (UK 1920) (German) and *Gabriel Savara* (UK 1923) (Russian). *The Spy Paramount* (UK 1935) marked the end of his era as a spy fiction writer. He dictated nearly all his books often leaving it to the bevy of pretty young secretaries who surrounded him to 'tidy up' the finished draft. His wealth enabled him to live on the Riviera for most of his later years and he sought something of the life about which he wrote when he went yachting, wined and dined in nightclubs and visited casinos. These activities served as a kind of artificial substitute for the high society life after which he hankered. In 1940 Oppenheim had to leave the home he had made for himself on the Riviera, as the Germans were driving across France. He had another home at Le Vauquiedor in Guernsey, but this was seized by the Nazis when they invaded the Channel Islands and used as a HQ for the Luftwaffe. He returned to Guernsey on its liberation in 1945, but died the following year.

Baroness Orczy (b. Tarna-Örs, Hungary, 23 September 1865; d. Monte Carlo, 12 November 1947)

Born Emma Magdalena Rosalina Marie Josepha Barbara Orczy, she was the daughter of Baron Felix Orczy, head of an ancient land-owning family, and the Countess Wars. The family lived in Buda-pest and Brussels, where Emma was a pupil in a convent school, and then in Paris before settling in London when she was fifteen. Emma studied at the West London School of Art and Heatherleys and was sufficiently successful as an artist to have three pictures hung at the Academy. It was here she met Montagu Barstow, the artist son of a clergyman, whom she married in 1894. Baroness Orczy (the name under which she wrote) first concentrated on chil-dren's stories, but it was a spy story that brought her greatest fame and recognition, though some critics might jib at its being included in this book. This was *The Scarlet Pimpernel* (UK 1905). The manuscript of this work was rejected by at least twelve publishers but, doggedly determined to succeed, Emma and her husband turned it into a play which was accepted for production with Fred Terry and Julia Neilson in the leading parts. This was presented in Nottingham in 1903 and was an instant success, after which the novel was published. The story was not only an exciting romance set during the French Revolution, but introduced as its chief character the seemingly indolent and affected fop, Sir Percy Blakeney, who, beneath his mask of frivolity and idleness, was a brave and efficient secret agent who rescued aristocrats from the guillotine under the noses of the revolutionaries.

So successful was the Scarlet Pimpernel (the code-name under which Sir Percy went) that Emma Orczy re-introduced him in *I Will Repay* (UK 1906), *Eldorado* (UK 1913) and *Sir Percy Hits Back* (UK 1927), all of which were published in an omnibus volume in 1933, together with the original story. There was always a love story worked into all the Baroness Orczy's espionage tales, which may have irritated those who liked their spy fiction 'straight', but Sir Percy, with his quick-changing, baffling disguises—as pipe-smoking old woman, charcoal-burner, Republican officer, or what have you—remained a firm favourite for many years. Not all the Pimpernel stories could be classified as spy fiction, however, and it was with historical romances that this author was mostly concerned. After the First World War Orczy and her husband went to live in Monte Carlo and it was from there that she wrote her most positive espionage book—*A Spy of Napoleon* (UK 1934). This was a story of the days of the Third Napoleon and told how Gerard, sentenced to death for treason, was spirited away by Papa Toulon of the Secret Service to marry one of his most efficient spies.

Andrew Osmond (b. Barnoldby, Lincs., 16 March 1938)
Andrew Philip Kingsford Osmond was educated at Harrow and Oxford University. He did his National Service with the Gurkhas Regiment in Malaya and was described later by William Rushton in one of the latter's instant quips as 'a born leader of little yellow men'. In 1961 he was one of the founding proprietors of *Private Eye*, but after eighteen months he sold out his interest to Nicholas Luard and joined the Foreign Office, 'not as a spy, though they did ask me', he says. He served in France, West Africa, London and Rome— 'hated it and got out, as did Douglas Hurd with whom I'd written half of *Send Him Victorious* (UK 1968). Collins accepted the day I reached England, broke and jobless.' In the interim Osmond became the co-author with Hurd of two other political novels with espionage undertones—*Smile on the Face of the Tiger* (UK 1969) and *Scotch on the Rocks* (UK 1971).

'I then ran out of money and ideas and returned to the *Eye* for four years as its managing director,' says Osmond. Then in 1972 he wrote what he called 'a little pot-boiler', *Harris in Wonderland*, with Richard Ingrams, editor of *Private Eye*, under the pen-name of 'Philip Reid': 'The Americans bought . . . and the Hungarians!' His first solo work of the spy species was *Saladin* (UK 1975). This was a story woven around the murdering of the eleven Israeli athletes by the Black September gang on 5 September 1972, telling how this brutal event marked a turning point in the Arab-Israeli conflict and how escalating violence seemed to make a fourth Middle East War almost inevitable. A small group of Israelis and Palestinians strove against the odds to bring about a settlement, their aim being to create a Palestinian state acceptable to both sides. Their leader was Anis Kubayin, code-name Saladin, and their chief instrument was Stephen Roscoe, an ex-British Army officer, retaining all the lethal skills he learned in his years in the Special Air Service.

The group's objective was to cause a major act of sabotage and so to capture the world headlines and create a political initiative. Fact and fiction were neatly woven together in this book and Osmond used the framework of a spy story to deliver a political message— a battle-cry for peace. The book was a considerable success and nine countries bought the rights.

Osmond believes the spy fiction genre both 'ought and will grow up a bit'. He would rather have his work labelled didactic (my adjective, not his) than be called 'fiction', and 'in either case the actual story and plot are everything. It's likely to have a political idea at its core; I've always enjoyed the novel at the service of ideas.'

John Leslie Palmer: *see* Francis Beeding

John Pearson (b. Carshalton, Surrey, 1930)
Educated at King's College, Wimbledon, and Peterhouse, Cambridge, where he gained a double first in history. Pearson was working as a television scriptwriter at the BBC when Ian Fleming offered him a job as his assistant in writing the Atticus column of the *Sunday Times*. At the age of thirty-two he gave up journalism to write books and one of these was his *The Life of Ian Fleming, Creator of James Bond* (UK 1966). The character of James Bond fascinated a number of writers after Fleming's death. Kingsley Amis produced *The James Bond Dossier* in 1966, which was an analysis of the character of Bond, his morals and his methods. Pearson went one better than this in 1973 when he published *James Bond: the authorised biography of 007*. This was what he himself termed 'a fictional biography', though it gallantly tried to maintain the spoof that Bond was a real person. It dealt at some length with Bond's childhood, his expulsion from Fettes for hanky-panky with a housekeeper, his enlistment in the Secret Service at the age of seventeen (they must have been hard up for personnel in those pre-war days!), and for good measure gave him as a secretary 'the delightful Miss Una Trueblood' (compiler's note: I can confirm she exists as she once worked for me!). Fleming himself is made to pop in and out of the story and at the book's end Bond, who has been recovering from hepatitis in Bermuda, is sent off on yet another mission, this time to Australia, which is somewhat of an anti-climax. It was perhaps a pity that Pearson did not conduct some

research behind the Iron Curtain on the subject of Bond. For Russian Intelligence took the Bond stories seriously, regarding them as deliberate anti-Soviet propaganda and commissioned a Bulgarian writer, A. Gulyashki, to write a book in which the Communist hero defeated Bond.

Chapman Pincher (b. Ambala, India, 29 March 1914)
Educated at Darlington Grammar School and King's College, London, Henry Chapman Pincher was a Carter Medalist in 1934 and took a BSc degree with honours in botany and zoology. From 1936–40 he served in the Royal Armoured Corps and then became a staff officer in the Rocket Division of the Ministry of Supply, a post he held until 1946. He is best known as Defence, Science and Medical Editor of the *Daily Express* and in this capacity he has over the past thirty years brought off many news scoops, not least in the field of defence and security. His early books touched on such subjects as *A Study of Fishes* (UK 1947) and *Into the Atomic Age* (UK 1947) and his first novel was *Not With a Bang* (UK 1965). His first spy fiction, *The Penthouse Conspirators* (UK 1970), was followed by *The Skeleton at the Villa Wolkonsky* (UK 1975) and his spy thriller *The Eye of the Tornado* (UK 1976), an exciting action-packed tale about an IRA plot to hijack Polaris missiles. Having made it clear that the fantasy hijack could become reality, Pincher then reveals that the IRA have merely been used by another power and that the hijack is a step towards a massive coup designed to crush democratic Britain. This calls for a Cabinet Minister who is a traitor and Pincher makes this feasible, too. Probably no other Fleet Street reporter in recent years has had such excellent contacts in the twilight world of defence and Intelligence, and none understands better the workings of current security arrangements in Britain and elsewhere. Pincher was the centre of a storm concerning the British Government's D notice system of disguised censorship in 1967 because he disclosed in the *Daily Express* that British Security men were scrutinising commercial cables being sent from the UK by private individuals and businessmen. Harold Wilson, then Prime Minister, worked himself into a somewhat hypocritical frenzy (in opposition he had sneered at the D notice system) and denounced the *Express* and Pincher for violating the system. But he had to admit the practice of cable-reading had been going on since 1927 and named a committee to investigate the Pincher article.

Wilson was hoist by his own petard: the committee eventually pronounced that there had been no violation of any D notice. Enraged at this set-back, Wilson published an extraordinary white paper which disavowed the committee's findings and insisted that there had been a breach of two specific D notices. Even more ridiculously, Wilson claimed that national security had been threatened. All this was done under cover of House of Commons privilege, too often the last resort of angry men who like to vent their spleen without risking legal action being taken against them. It was, however, a moral victory for Chapman Pincher and the press almost unanimously condemned Wilson. Not surprisingly Pincher includes among his recreations 'ferreting in Whitehall and bolting politicians'.

Edgar Allen Poe (b. Boston, Mass., 1809; d. 1879)
Apart from his genius as a poet of great imagination and sensitivity and a writer of mystery and horror stories, Edgar Allen Poe was at one and the same time the father of the detective story and the spy tale. Purists may repudiate his entitlement to be included in this volume, yet the fact remains that he undoubtedly influenced many subsequent writers of stories of espionage and that his supreme detective, C. Auguste Dupin, was in some respects more spy, or unofficial secret agent, than detective. In no work is this shown so clearly as in *The Purloined Letter* (US 1845), for the tale contains all the ingredients of the classic spy story. A top-secret document is stolen from the royal apartments, and the authorities strongly suspect that the culprit is a Minister, too important and influential to be arrested without positive proof. The secret police search the hotel apartment in which the Minister lives night after night without success. It is then that Dupin is called in to investigate the whole affair and discreetly to locate the missing document, just as, in similar circumstances in real life today, an agent of MI5 or the French counter-espionage would be asked to solve such a case.

Dupin sets out to analyse the Minister's processes of thought in order to work out exactly how he would have hidden the document. The Minister is a scholar, a mathematician and a poet. When the Prefect of Police says he is prepared to pay 50,000 francs to anyone who would aid him in the matter, Dupin replies: 'In that case you may as well fill me up a cheque for the amount mentioned. When you have signed it, I will hand you the letter.' Dupin then produces the missing document and explains that the Minister expected the police to ransack his apartment and search it thoroughly. But he has counted on their not expecting the letter would be left in a prominent place where they could hardly fail to miss it. In such a place Dupin looked—'at length my eyes, in going the circuit of the room, fell upon a trumpery filigree card-rack of pasteboard, that hung dangling by a dirty blue ribbon, from a little brass knob just beneath the middle of the mantelpiece. In this rack, which had three or four compartments, were five or six visiting cards and a solitary letter.' It was, of course, the solitary letter which the police had failed to notice.

But it is when one comes to examine the origins of Dupin that the links between this first, tenuous and almost unintended spy story and a metamorphosis in the world of the real life secret agent of the day become apparent. Dupin was far removed from the average police inspector in the America of the 1840s: this is probably why Poe made him into an amateur detective. In *The Murders of the Rue Morgue* (US 1841), in which Dupin is first introduced, he is described as 'This young gentleman . . . of an excellent—indeed of an illustrious family, but by a variety of untoward events had been reduced to such poverty that the energy of his character succumbed beneath it', not an unusual portrait of somebody who has become a secret agent. Poe's biographer, William Bittner, wrote that the poet wanted to project 'a character possessing his intelligence enlarged to the exclusion of emotion. This creature of pure intellect he named C. Auguste Dupin, borrowing from the first instalment of Vidocq.'

The Vidocq referred to was Eugène François Vidocq, born in Arras in 1775, and the author of *Mèmoires* (France 1828). This work was published in four volumes and later was sold overseas and translated into English, notably in serial form in *Burton's Magazine*. It was here that Poe must have read of this remarkable character who started life as a criminal and, after a number of escapades, was caught and sentenced to eight years' imprisonment with galley slaves at Brest. After a time he escaped and surprisingly offered his services to the secret police in Paris. In his new role Vidocq showed gifts of organisation and improvisation, brilliantly welding together a team of ex-convicts and reformed thieves into a powerful network of police spies. But the Prefect of Police, M. Delavau, who was very much under the influence of his priest, showed increasing distaste for using an ex-convict and an even greater dislike of Vidocq's methods. A conspiracy was mounted against Vidocq, inspired, so it is said, by the priest, and in 1832 he was forced to resign. Yet, ironically, the hypocritical M. Delavau chose in his place another ex-convict, Coco-Lacour, who merely carried on Vidocq's methods. After he resigned Vidocq opened up in Paris a bureau for the recovery of stolen goods.

In this period such detective work as there was in America was done mainly by private agencies and in England Scotland Yard and a Criminal Investigation Department had not been thought of. The nearest approach to a detective was the somewhat disreputable chief agent of the secret police in Paris, a man who was much more like a combination of spymaster and spycatcher. It is this fact which gives a sound excuse for including Poe as the father of the modern spy story. In another direction, and in an oblique way, Poe also gave some impetus to the future shape of some spy stories by his interest in cryptography. In an article in a Philadelphia weekly magazine in 1840 Poe, who had then been studying cryptography for some time, opined that there was no such thing as an unsolvable cipher and offered to solve any such message sent to him. He received about 100 ciphers and solved all but one—and that one he denounced as a fake intended to deceive him. Out of his interest in this subject came *The Gold Bug* (US 1843) which, though not a spy story, is still one of the best stories yet written about ciphers and codes. Poe prompted great interest in cryptography in both literary and Intelligence circles. Jules Verne introduced cryptograms and their solution as features of some of his own stories and Balzac, writing furiously to make money, found the trick of putting ciphers into fiction so popular that he included a three-page cryptogram in *La Physiologie du Mariage*. It is also interesting that Major Kasiski, a Prussian staff officer, was inspired by reading Poe to produce the first comprehensive modern book on cryptography in 1863. It was Kasiski who revolutionised the German cipher systems.

Thus, with Poe, real life inspired fiction and some of his fiction inspired real-life developments in Intelligence. For from 1850 onwards the Intelligence game became very much the war of the cryptographers, a period when each major military power included courses in cryptography in its training programme. Perhaps, too, there was a warning for those in the spy game in Poe's opening comments when introducing Dupin: 'The higher powers of the reflective intellect are more decidedly and more usefully tasked by the unostentatious game of draughts than by all the elaborate frivolity of chess. In the latter, where the pieces have different and bizarre motions, with various and variable values, what is only complex is mistaken (a not unusual error) for what is profound. The attention is here called powerfully into play . . . the possible moves being not only manifold but involute, the chances of . . . oversights are multiplied . . . In draughts, on the contrary, where the moves are unique and have but little variation, the probabilities of inadvertence are diminished, and the mere attention being left comparatively unemployed, what advantages are obtained by either party are obtained by superior acumen.'

Joe Poyer (b. Michigan, 1939)

Educated at the Michigan State University, where he obtained a BA degree in communication arts, Joe Poyer has come to the fore in spy fiction within the last few years with three novels—*North Cape* (US 1970), *The Balkan Assignment* (US 1971) and *The Chinese Agenda* (US 1972). The last-named is one of the few modern novels to touch on the subject of espionage in China. Poyer told in this book the story of a secret mission that began in conditions of the utmost danger and ended in wholesale slaughter. The story takes place on the Sino-Soviet border, in the Tien Shan Mountains, a high range of treacherous, snow-capped peaks. Twelve-thousand feet high in that range is a pass leading into the interior of the Tien Shan and deep inside that terrain is a secret installation that threatens the peace of the world. To probe this secret a joint American-Soviet intelligence team is sent on what appears to be a suicidal mission. Six men cross the border into China, but only one comes back.

Joe Poyer has been praised by a number of critics for carefully researched spy fiction. He is at present the manager of Project Operations for a pharmaceutical company in California.

Anthony Price (b. Hertfordshire, 16 August 1928)

Anthony Price was educated at King's School, Canterbury, and Merton College, Oxford. After being commissioned during his National Service (1947–49) he entered journalism and is today editor of the *Oxford Times*. His special interests are archaeology and military history, both of which are reflected in the detailed backgrounds to his novels. He won the Crime Writers' Association Silver Dagger for his first novel, *The Labyrinth Makers* (UK 1970), and the Gold Dagger for his more recent *Paths to Glory* (UK 1974). His first book was on the theme of the loss of the Schliemann Treasure and the Stalin purges. Other books have been *The Alamut Ambush* (UK 1971), *Colonel Butler's Wolf* (UK 1972), *October Men* (UK 1973), *Our Man in Camelot* (UK 1975) and *War Game* (UK 1976). *The October Men* was one of his most effective books, but his spy novel, *Our Man in Camelot*, was highly praised. This was about David Audley, a super-cool, super-intellectual top British agent who appears in all Price's books, but, says the author 'not necessarily as the leading character: his colleagues share that role more or less in turn, or even the CIA can supply a hero.' In the Camelot story Audley was spending his holiday writing about an obscure medieval knight. Mosby, a CIA agent with rather more likeable qualities than British authors usually attribute to those of his type, has been sent to con Audley into finding the site of the sixth-century Battle of Badon, which Americans think is part of some devious KGB plot. Mosby, posing as an amateur historian, soon finds himself deeply involved in Arthurian researches as well as trying to learn what the other 'sides' are up to. This was an ingeniously, intelligently constructed plot with a nice touch of wit, though one critic (undoubtedly innoculated with a desire for 'pace' in spy fiction) commented that 'theorising weighs down action. More war and less jaw needed.' In fact, Anthony Price is very much a thinking man's spy fiction author and much of his work rises well above the average level of the genre because of his sense of humour and wit. Audley and Colonel Butler are the two characters who have supplied a continuity of theme to Price's books since 1944, when they were barely out of their teens as 2nd Lieut. and Corporal respectively.

Sax Rohmer (b. 1883; d. 1 June 1959)
A purist would no doubt object to the inclusion of Sax Rohmer in this book, but one cannot escape the fact that the Dr Fu Manchu stories involve spying (on both sides) and that he marked an era in which all villains tended to be either German or Chinese: it was not until long afterwards that the Russian villain superseded the 'heathen Chinee' whom this popular novelist found it so easy to exploit.

Sax Rohmer was the pseudonym of Arthur Sarsfield Wade, who was born of Irish parentage and who paved his path to success the hardest way possible, according to his own account. In his early days he worked in Fleet Street, but with scant success: 'I "bucked up" interviews with dull people to a point where the victims jibbed,' he said. 'I had written a number of short stories and had papered one wall of my room with editorial regrets.' He was not without a somewhat esoteric sense of humour for he thought up his pseudonym by adapting two Saxon words—*sax* (a sharp blade or lance) and *rohmer* (a rover): in other words 'Sax Rohmer' was a freelance and as such he was determined to succeed in fiction, if not in journalism. 'My earliest interests,' he wrote, 'were centred in Ancient Egypt and I accumulated a large library on Egyptology and occult literature.' But astutely, like the freelance in quest of the timely subject that he was, he switched his attention from Egypt to China: the background of the one was sometimes applied with a total unconcern for accuracy to the land in the Far East and Dr Fu Manchu himself often seems a kind of Egyptian-Chinese hybrid. Pre-1914, while the Western World looked approvingly on the Japanese desire to modernise, they still regarded China as the 'Yellow Peril'. Rohmer struck the appropriate note in 1913 when he published the first of his Dr Fu Manchu stories—*Dr Fu Manchu*. This paved his way out of trouble into fame and wealth: it was, however, all blatantly racist—to use an overworked and often wrongly used modern epithet. But in this instance the epithet was deserved: much of the admittedly photogenic trash which Rohmer turned out was as damaging in its way as any of the anti-Semitic pamphlets of the Nazis. Anita Page said of Sax Rohmer that he 'flashed against richly exotic backgrounds such diabolically ingenious and irresistible villains as one trusts the world has never seen.'

Fu Manchu, the all powerful oriental potentate, had his own spies and methods of spying, but Nayland Smith, the English hero who battles against him for more than a quarter of a century was an improbable mixture for a spymaster or a counter-spy—part amateur detective, part Burmese Commissioner (in the days when Burma was part of the British Empire) and, against all the probabilities of the spy game, a controller of the British Secret Service and the CID, as though these two were combined! Fu Manchu could so easily have been made into one of those fascinating Chinese warlords who had the virtues as well as the vices of his race: instead Rohmer described his 'green eyes' as being 'an emanation of Hell'. Among the books that followed were *Tales of Chinatown* (UK 1922), *Daughter of Fu Manchu* (UK 1931), *Trial of Fu Manchu* (UK 1934),

President Fu Manchu (UK 1936), *Island of Fu Manchu* (UK 1941), *Shadow of Fu Manchu* (UK 1948), while even as late as 1959 we had *Re-enter Fu Manchu*. Book sales rocketed throughout Rohmer's life and in 1955 he is said to have sold the film, television and radio rights in his books for more than four million dollars.

Fu Manchu gradually became a symbol, not of success, but of an awful warning to prospective thriller and spy story writers of what to avoid if their works were to have any credibility or quality. During the Korean War period, when the American witch-hunt against Communists and fellow-travellers was at its height, Rohmer, then living just outside New York, declared that Dr Fu Manchu was 'still an enemy to be reckoned with and as menacing as ever, but he has changed with the times. Now he is against the Chinese Communists and, indeed, Communists everywhere, and a friend of the American people.' Even this ambiguous statement was not explained: of whom was Fu Manchu the enemy?

Angus Ross (b. Cawthorpe, Yorks., 19 March 1927)
Angus Ross claims that 'I got my education by courtesy of the Royal Navy in various ports of the world.' He served in the Fleet Air Arm from 1944–52, after which he worked in the newspaper and magazine field in the provinces and Fleet Street until 1972. His first spy book was *The Manchester Thing* (UK 1970), in which he introduced his central character, Marcus Aurelius Farrow, a newspaperman drawn by chance and against his will into a murder investigation, which leads him in turn to the twilight world of espionage. This first book ended with Farrow's recruitment into the Secret Service. From this followed a whole series of Farrow books: *The Huddersfield Job* (UK 1971), *The London Assignment* (UK 1972), *The Dunfermline Affair* (UK 1973), *The Bradford Business* (UK 1974), *The Amsterdam Diversion* (UK 1974), *The Leeds Fiasco* (UK 1975), *The Edinburgh Exercise* (UK 1975), *The Ampurias Exchange* (UK 1976) and *The Aberdeen Conundrum* (UK 1977).

Ross's view of espionage is that it 'doesn't happen only in Washington, Bonn, Rome and Berlin, but also in places like Leeds and Bradford, Dunfermline and Aberdeen.' His hero, Farrow, reflects this outlook, being a down-to-earth character, but an inherently decent man with humanist principles, who is always clashing with his partner, Charles McGowan, who is totally dedicated to the Service and devoid of compassion.

Robert Rostand (b. Los Angeles, Calif.)
Born Robert Hopkins and educated in Los Angeles, Rostand has
worked as a lecturer in geography at an American university,
managed the Latin-American organisation of a large international
company and served briefly with an arm of the US State Department
in Washington, DC, the Caribbean and the Pacific Islands. He has
lived for long periods in Brazil and England and now makes his
home in Honolulu. Notable especially for his book, *The Killer Elite*
(US 1974), the subject of a major United Artists film directed by
Sam Peckinpah and starring James Caan, Rostand aroused special
political curiosity by his theme. Since he had worked in the State
Department, some astute readers wondered whether that august
establishment really had a special security section named SYOPS
(as in his book) and if they did occasionally indulge in tactics which
savoured more of the CIA. Rostand told how Locken, a SYOPS
agent, was deliberately and viciously maimed by one of the world's
top three professional assassins. Then the American-in-London
chief of SYOPS, a cynical manipulator, asks Locken to do a job for
him—to get an African statesman safely out of London with three
top agents trying to kill him.

Another Rostand book, *The D'Artagnan Signature* (US 1975),
showed a remarkable insight into the Franco-Algerian struggle in a
battle of one relentless set of killers against another. When France
withdrew from Algeria, the men of the OAS, the secret army of the
diehard white settlers, were killed or driven into exile. But the millions of pounds extorted by the OAS to finance its campaign of
terror remained untouched in a Swiss bank. This was why
Alexandre Morin needed the D'Artagnan signature, for the key to
the fortune amassed by the underground army was a power of
attorney vested in a murdered man, Edgar Duret, OAS treasurer,
code-name D'Artagnan. With ruthless single-mindedness, Morin,
former head of the OAS's notorious Delta murder organisation, had
tracked down everyone—old comrades and enemies alike—who
might provide a clue to the location of the crucial document.
Rostand cleverly welded fact and fiction in this convincingly authentic thriller. Another book introducing the character Locken of the
State Department, was *Viper's Game* (US 1974), which was set on
a large Portuguese-administered island in the Pacific, involving
Locken in a battle of wits against not only a band of guerrilla
fighters, but the Sembi, a savage mountain tribe.

Kenneth Royce (b. Croydon, 11 December 1920)

Kenneth Royce says that 'my schooling was constantly interrupted by chronic asthma, so it was virtually nil. The asthma cleared up as soon as my school days were over, and I've been wondering about it ever since!' In the Second World War he served in the 1st Northern Rhodesia Regiment and the King's African Rifles, achieving the rank of Captain. For several years after this he was managing director of a London travel agency which gave him the opportunity to find new settings for his books. His first book was *My Turn to Die* (UK 1958), a spy thriller set in France. This was followed by *Long Corridor* (UK 1960), *The Angry Island* (UK 1962), *The Day the Wind Dropped* (UK 1964), *Bones in the Sand* (UK 1967), *A Single to Hong Kong* (UK 1969) and *The XYY Man* (UK 1970). The last named, which was followed by others using the same hero, introduced for the first time Willie 'Spider' Scott, an ex-criminal who steps out of Wormwood Scrubs with the knowledge that next time he will get ten years behind bars. But an offer from one of those shadowy Intelligence executives whose credentials he finds difficult to refuse involves 'Spider' playing hookey with men in the Chinese Legation, not to mention getting beaten up by agents of BOSS and threatened by an African agent of 'Free Zimbabwe'. This was a thrilling narrative as well as a good spy theme of its kind and deservedly became a Granada TV short serial in 1976. Royce says that 'Spider' is based on an actual cat burglar, or 'creeper' who gave him first-hand advice for background to his stories. *Concrete Boot* (UK 1971), *Miniatures Frame* (UK 1972) and *Spider Underground* (UK 1973) are the three other 'Spider' titles. *The Woodcutter Operation* (UK 1975) was topical in that it concerned an ex-paratrooper who had deserted in Belfast and told how a gang of five men seized a London hospital, in the private wing of which was a high-security patient—the US Secretary of State. *Bustillo* (UK 1976), set entirely in Japan, concerned an American in the CIA who had become disillusioned with the Agency and run away to start an anonymous life in a foreign country. But when he found a little black book full of secrets, his problems started again.

Royce has also written under the pseudonym of 'Oliver Jacks' and one of the best of his spy stories, *Man on a Short Leash* (UK 1974), was published under this name. This gave a new twist to the spy story. Todd, a former CID man, had been lured to join MI6 as a security officer. On one of his days off Todd sees Kuhn, a wanted man. He should have phoned the office for help, but there wasn't time. Instead it wasn't Kuhn who was arrested, but Todd— by the Special Branch. At his trial evidence pointed against him: unknown bank accounts, documents under his carpet. The judge called him a traitor and gave him thirty years! Todd knew he had been framed and he knew he had to escape, even if it was the Russians who sprang him. *Assassination Day* (UK 1976) is another 'Oliver Jacks' story, this time of a plot to kill Leonid Brezhnev on the latter's visit to Britain. Royce once served as an Intelligence sergeant in the 1st Northern Rhodesia Regt., but for one week only.

Rafael Sabatini (b. Jesi, Italy, 1875; d. Adeboden, Switzerland 1950) The son of an Italian musician father and an English mother, he learned English from his mother and was educated in Switzerland and Portugal, coming to England as a young man. Sabatini's first book was *Tavern Knight* (UK 1904) and his novels were mainly historical romances. During the First World War he held a post in the Intelligence Department of the British War Office and in 1918 he was naturalised. Like Conrad, he was writing in a language which was not his own tongue, but he made his greatest success after the war with *Scaramouche* (UK 1921), which was a spy story in the Orczy manner. This was his masterpiece, an epic of patrician virtues in the French Revolution, full of duels, disguises (Scaramouche posed as a clown) and adventure. This book was specially printed in the US for use in schools, a high tribute to the author who had first started to write when he was on the staff of a Liverpool newspaper.

'Sapper' (b. 1888; d. 14 August 1937)
This was the pseudonym of Lieut.-Colonel Herman Cyril McNeile, educated at Cheltenham and the Royal Military Academy, Woolwich. He joined the Royal Engineers in 1907, became a Captain in 1914 and retired at the end of the war to start writing books. Crude and totally unsophisticated thrillers, in outlook they were similar to the sturdy patriotism of John Buchan, but in style, dialogue and construction they were not in the same class. Yet 'Sapper' became famous through the creation of his character *Bulldog Drummond* (UK 1920) who, for a period of some fifteen years, was almost a household world. Drummond, the 1920ish

portrait of a 'clean-limbed young Englishman', was out for adventure and always ready to check the fiendish plots of Carl Peterson and any other 'Hun', 'Wog', 'Dago' or other foreigner. This was the language of 'Sapper': his characters spoke in stilted clichés, expressed right-wing views, frequently indulged in anti-semitism and regarded all lovely young Englishwomen as purity personified. Nobody seemed to raise any objection to this nonsense in the 'twenties and 'thirties and a great deal of 'Sapper' material was filmed, Ronald Colman being an outstanding 'Bulldog' Drummond of the period. Not all the 'Bulldog' Drummond stories were of the spy genre and some, such as *The Dinner Club* (UK 1921), were collections of short stories. There was much that was unpleasant in the 'Sapper' books, sometimes in the violence, more often in the sentiments. In *Black Gang* (UK 1922) 'Bulldog' Drummond tells two Jews 'my friends do not like your trade, you swine' and then beats them up. 'Sapper' introduced many such touches into his stories. The plots of his spy stories were as blatantly right-wing as those of some modern spy writers are left-wing. Russian gold was behind a plot to overthrow the British Government by means of a general strike and famous names in British society were undercover supporters of this. *Four Rounds of Bulldog Drummond*, a volume containing all the 'Bulldog' Drummond stories to that date, including *The Third Round* and *The Final Count*, was published in 1929. The final book, *Bulldog Drummond Hits Out*, was published in 1937. (*See also* Gerard Fairlie.)

Hilary Adam St George Saunders: *see* Francis Beeding

'Sea-Lion' (b. Emsworth, Hants, 7 June 1909)
Educated at the Royal Naval College, Dartmouth, 1923–26, Capt. Geoffrey Martin Bennett was a signals specialist in the Royal Navy and from 1938–40 was Flag Lieutenant to the Second Cruiser Squadron of the Home Fleet, while from 1940–42 he was Fleet Signal Officer, South Atlantic and later Signal Officer to the Admiral commanding Force H for the invasion of Sicily and Italy. His post-war service in the Navy included a stint as a naval attaché in Moscow, Warsaw and Helsinki after he was promoted to Captain in 1953. On retiring from the Navy he took up writing and was City Marshal (London) in 1958–59. Since 1960 he has been

Secretary to the Lord Mayor of Westminster and Hon. Sec. to the London Mayors' Association. His first novel under the 'Sea-lion' pseudonym was *Phantom Fleet* (UK 1946), followed by *Sink Me the Ship* (UK 1947). A number of his books have combined naval and espionage themes, notably *Invisible Ships* (UK 1950), *Operation Fireball* (UK 1959) and the books featuring that engaging character, Desmond Drake—*Meet Desmond Drake* (UK 1952), *Damn Desmond Drake!* (UK 1953) and *Desmond Drake Goes West* (UK 1956).

Donald Seaman (b. London, 25 May 1922)
Donald Peter Seaman was educated at Palmers School, Grays, Essex. In 1946–47 he served as an assistant purser with the Merchant Navy, in order to gather background material for a book on Palestine during the mass migrations there in this period. After a spell in provincial journalism in Shropshire and Northants he joined the staff of the *Daily Express* in 1948, spending twenty-four years with this paper covering wars and insurrections in Cyprus, Suez, Iraq, Syria and Aden, the Arab–Israeli wars, the Indo-Pakistan wars, Bangladesh, Nigeria and other parts of Africa. In 1951 he was assigned to cover the Burgess-Maclean missing diplomats case: 'I worked five years on the story under Lord Beaverbrook's direction trying to break through cover of official silence, denials, half-truths and evasion.' Finally Seaman, with co-author John S. Mather, produced a book on the defection of these men, entitled *The Great Spy Scandal*.

It was this early experience of espionage and treachery that led Seaman to write spy fiction: 'In those years,' he says, 'inevitably I met up with secret agents, defectors and traitors—working on both sides of the fence. Whatever their nationality, I admire the first, pity the second and despise the third: and I hope that something of that deep-rooted feeling emerges in every book I write.' Seaman has produced *The Bomb that Could Lip Read* (UK 1974), a tense and authentic first spy novel, *The Defector* (UK 1975) and *The Terror Syndicate* (UK 1976). *The Defector* is about a reticent couple living in Saddlers Hill; he is a scientist who has defected from the Russians, she the author of books critical of the Soviet régime. Their home is burgled and the scientist shoots and kills the burglar. Inevitably there is a trial, with much publicity, and from then on the KGB relentlessly track down the couple. Seaman can claim to have had the unnerving experience of being watched by the

KGB. In 1962 he became the first Englishman to travel on the Trans-Siberian Railway after the war. 'On my arrival at Nakhodka, near Vladivostok, I was suspected of spying, whereas the humiliating truth was I was probably the only man in the world who knew nothing of the Cuban missile crisis then at its height.'

Seaman served with the British Army from 1939-46 in the Middle East, Italy, Holland and Germany. During his journalistic career he twice represented the *Express* in Moscow and later was chief of their New York bureau, leaving voluntarily in 1973 to write books full time.

Owen Sela (b. Ceylon)

If there is an author of spy stories who *might* be thought to be actively involved in 'the game', it would be Owen Sela, for he shies away from any kind of reference book and replied to a questionnaire: 'I regret that I never provide information to any directories for any purpose.' But any such deduction would be totally wrong. Sela's desire for anonymity and privacy is just that; he's not a spy, or an executive in the Intelligence world. He came to Britain to study chartered accountancy in the late 'fifties and took on British citizenship. In 1963 he qualified as an accountant and eventually went into practice. Then, on a plane journey to Australia, to relieve the tedium, he thought up the story of *The Bearer Plot* (UK 1972). This was a thriller which packed an enormous amount of action into a few days in the life of Nick Maasten, one of those adaptable rogues who are not too squeamish about how they make their money. It involved a quest across three countries. The Maasten character caught on, even if he did seem to lack for a sex life. Sela, however, does not think this is so vital an ingredient for the spy story. Most sensibly, he told Ray Connolly in a rare interview in the *Evening Standard* that 'I don't think there is that much sex for a fellow like Maasten . . . if the character had been driving long distances, been hit over the head and all that, then I don't think he'd really feel up to it. I really think that sex is a bit overplayed in novels.'

It was with *The Kiriov Tapes* (UK 1973) that Sela arrived as a recognised writer of spy fiction. This was one of two books—the other was by Alan Williams—on the possibility that 'Kim' Philby, the SIS officer turned Soviet spy, had become bored with life in Moscow and decided to return to the West. Sela was praised for his 'brilliant research', but Miles Copeland commented that 'spooks like his books for much the same reason that they like Deighton's: they capture the mood and they have the spooks' sardonic sense of humour.' *The Kiriov Tapes* was about an ex-detective inspector, Quimper, who was in charge of security for his Department, a prelude to retirement. He investigates the disappearance of the Kiriov Tapes and so finds out the KGB's best-kept secret since 'Kim' Philby headed Section 9, the anti-communist department of the SIS. *The Portuguese Fragment* (UK 1974) saw Nick Maasten running Custers Bar in Tangier, but this was more of a thriller, just as *The Bengali Inheritance* (UK 1975) was a detective story. One looks forward to a sequel to *The Kiriov Tapes* from this young writer.

Ronald Seth (b. Ely, Cambs., 1911)
Ronald Seth followed his education at Ely Cathedral School, King's School, Ely, and Peterhouse College, Cambridge, by lecturing in English in Estonia, an experience which later he may well have had every reason to regret. In the Second World War he joined the RAF and was a Flight-Lieut. One day his fellow officers were discussing the oil which the Germans were getting from Estonia. Seth suggested the installations could be sabotaged. 'Most of the people who knew about Estonia were middle-aged,' he said, 'so when to my amazement Intelligence asked me if I'd go, I couldn't back out.' Seth was parachuted into Estonia, dressed as a civilian, and with enough explosives in his equipment to blow up a small town: his orders were to sabotage the German-run shale-oil mines. But he landed in the middle of a German patrol with a police dog. The parachutes with his radio and explosives were captured, but Seth managed to escape into the forest. For twelve days he dodged the patrols; then he was captured, jailed and beaten up. Without trial, he was sentenced to death by hanging on the public gallows in Tallinn. But some unknown Estonian patriot had fixed the gallows trap-door so that it wouldn't open. When Seth regained consciousness he was back in his prison cell. He cannot explain why he was not taken to the gallows for a second time. But it might well have been that the Germans felt that a spy who had had such an experience might, through being reprieved, be 'turned' to work for them.

Seth himself told the story in *A Spy Has No Friends* (UK 1952) and he says that later he bluffed the German authorities into recruiting him into their own Intelligence Service to be used as an agent in Britain. He was sent to Frankfurt to the Intelligence HQ of the Luftwaffe and then to the Gestapo. On 14 November 1943, Seth was sent, under guard, to Paris. He was told that the Nazis wanted to use him as one of their own agents in Britain. Meanwhile he was put inside a POW camp for British officers as an 'ear' for the Germans. Seth refused to divulge any information that might harm his comrades but there was no reason why he should not at least appear to agree. So he was introduced into Oflag 79. However the officers there suspected him; some wanted to throw him out of an attic window; one volunteered to be with him all the time to keep him from meeting the Germans. In his book Seth told how he was taken away to be briefed for his trip to England; Himmler, chief of the SS, wanted him to take a personal message to Churchill to the effect that he would seize power in Germany and negotiate peace. Seth agreed, was smuggled across the Swiss border on 12 April 1945, and at once saw the British Minister. 'But,' he wrote, 'I had a feeling that my mission seemed less important than I believed it to be.' And so it turned out. In the end the only use made of his escapade was to round-up a number of Nazi agents who were still hiding out in Paris after the Liberation. Asked afterwards if he would have undertaken such a mission in such circumstances again, Seth replied: 'No. The sacrifice was in my opinion wasted. Even if I'd not been caught I'd have been very little use, for the people who had packed my radio set had forgotten to put in three crystals that were absolutely vital for communications.'

Seth's work has been mainly non-fiction, including a history of the 'Specials', *Defence of Moscow* (UK 1959), *Anatomy of Spying* (UK 1961), *Forty Years of Soviet Spying* (UK 1965), *The Executioners: The Story of Smersh* (UK 1967), *Encyclopaedia of Espionage* (UK 1971) and in 1962 he wrote *Spy in the Nude* about one Alex Marceau, a writer of spy thrillers, who is also a secret agent. He wears disguises at meetings: on one occasion, examining his wardrobe before setting out, he 'murmurs, "The Bertrand Russell, I think" as he takes out a silvery wig'. Other books have been *Patriot* (UK 1954), *The Spy Who Wasn't Caught* (UK 1966), and *The Spy in Silk Breeches* (UK 1968). Seth has been a schoolmaster both in England and Guernsey since the war and now lives in Malta.

James P. Smythe

This entry may perhaps justifiably be regarded as the most controversial in the whole book and some may argue that it is worth no more than a footnote, ruling out Smythe on the grounds that the construction of his one and only 'novel' does not purport to be a novel. Logicians, however, could easily defeat the literary purists in such an argument by asserting that the material would appear to be fiction, gilded by a very vivid imagination.

James P. Smythe, according to an admission made in the American *Who's Who*, is the pseudonym used by William Rutledge McGarry who, according to family records, was born in Grand Rapids, Michigan, in 1868. The *New York Times* obituary of him, however, suggested a much later birth date and stated that he was 'born in New York and educated at Minnesota, Harvard, Yale and Paris'. It also claimed that he was a descendant of four signatories of the Declaration of Independence, but this was largely based on the say-so of McGarry himself, an enthusiastic but somewhat pretentious genealogist. In early life he carried on business as a printer and in 1892 enlisted in the 8th US Cavalry Regiment, receiving an honourable discharge with the rank of private two years later. After that he seems to have dabbled in the law and journalism. He travelled widely and Charles A. Dana, then editor of the *New York Sun*, commissioned him to write a series of articles on a trip around the world. Under his own name he was the author of a sober and factual book, *From Berlin to Bagdad* (US 1912), which made his *Rescuing the Czar* (published under his pseudonym of 'Smythe', US 1920) an astonishing contrast. This book was published by the California Printing Company of San Francisco and purported to be a story of an attempt to rescue the last Czar of Russia and the Imperial Royal Family from the Bolsheviks during 1918–19, the implication being that success might well have attended such an adventurous crusade. In a foreword to this remarkable book, Dr W. E. Aughimbaugh, a celebrated physician, lawyer and explorer, stated that 'an account of the Czar's escape was in my possession on February 10 1920' and he says of the book: 'In a technical sense it is not a story. Nevertheless, while partaking of the nature of a simple diary, it reads like a romance of thrilling adventure upon which a skilful novelist may easily erect a story of permanent interest and universal appeal.'

The book itself is the zaniest example of serendipity of a Czarist supporter ever perpetrated and it may well be that it was the original foundation and inspiration of all the strange tales told since about the rescue of the Romanovs; about the Czarevitch Alexei escaping death and living on to assume the identity of Lieut.-Colonel Mikhail Golienewski of the Polish Military Intelligence, eventually defecting to the Americans in 1964; and the endless legal cases to try to establish whether Mrs Eugenia Smith, of New York City, or Mrs Anna Manahan, of Charlottesville, Virginia, was the Grand Duchess Anastasia. *Rescuing the Czar* has no documentation to suggest it is a non-fiction work and its narrative and dialogue is so unnatural that it seems as though it must be what in modern parlance could be called 'a novel—funny peculiar'. Parts of the story are so obscure that some critics and Intelligence executives have sworn that it is a novel which conceals a coded message. Some sections of the text switch from ordinary type to italics and from lower case to capitals for no obvious reason. The book is supposed to be extracts from two different diaries of different people, both of whom seem to be equally mythical or fictitious. The author writes of his having had to censor some parts of the diaries, but in a most unconvincing manner, and he also mentions a mysterious American called Fox who, presumably, played a part in this fantasy of the Romanovs being alive and free long after they were reported as having been executed at Ekaterinburg. There are some melodramatic passages worthy of Le Queux in the 'diaries': 'I had walked from Euston Station to Madame Tussaud's when the messenger jumped from his motor-cycle and rushed up to me—"Go to Birdcage [Walk] and walk slowly back to Queen Victoria's Memorial. As you pass Buckingham [Palace] observe the heavily veiled lady wearing white lace wristlets who will follow behind. Let her overtake you. If she utters *the correct phrase*, go with her at once to Admiralty Arch and follow the Life Guard to the War Office. Meet number —— there; receive a small orange-coloured packet, *wear the shirt he gives you* and cross the Channel at once." '

On the subject of the Romanovs McGarry seems to have had a very persistent bee buzzing in his head and, according to Guy Richards (*The Rescue of the Romanovs*, 1976), McGarry claimed in a letter that 'both Nicholas and Alexandra [the Czar and Czarina] were encountered in 1923 walking together near the basilisque de Notre Dame de la Garde in Marseilles.' A doctor of philosophy, McGarry made a hobby of studying the fate of the Romanovs and the myth of the rescue of the Czar and his family has recently been resurrected and critically examined by Peter Bessell, the ex-British MP; by Lieut.-Colonel Guy Richards in the US; and by Tom Mangold and Tony Summers in the UK. Much of Smythe's book smacks of lurid spy fiction and some of the diary entries read curiously like portions of the mysterious Chivers Papers which, it is claimed, are written in code and hidden away either in the State Department or CIA records. The 'Chivers Lobby' claims that if these papers could be produced, they would clinch the story of the rescue of the Romanovs for all time. But nobody will confirm their existence either as a romantic fake by some nostalgic Czarist, or some devious and incomprehensible ploy by the KGB or the CIA. Who, in fact, is fooling whom and did McGarry under the pen-name of 'James P. Smythe' fool everybody and invent the legend himself?

John Innes McIntosh Stewart: *see* Michael Innes

Ian Stuart: *see* Alistair Maclean

Julian Symons (b. London 1912)
Before critics can raise their hands and object that Julian Symons is not a spy fiction writer, let it be firmly put on record that Symons himself agrees with them: 'Haven't written a spy story, nothing very near one.' Be that as it may, Symons has all the talents of a skilled writer of the genre and he comes very close indeed to being included if only for *Broken Penny* (UK 1953), of which that distinguished and discerning critic, Anthony Boucher, wrote that the author 'lets himself go on a full-scale Ambler-Hitchcock thriller and without the least sacrifice of brilliance in prose and insight shows a superb command of every trick in the repertory of the spy melodrama.' But apart from this 'near miss', Symons is important to all students of spy fiction in his role of critic and diligent reader of this genre of literature. Particularly to be commended is his work *Bloody Murder From the Detective Story to the Crime Novel: A History* (UK 1972). Though this deals primarily with the novel of suspense and crime, especially the detective story,

Symons does take a brief look at spy fiction over the ages in a highly professional appraisal. For some addicts it may seem too critical and too pessimistic about the future of the spy story, but a dose of Symon's astringent prose is a useful antidote to over-enthusiasm and he supports his criticisms with plenty of well-chosen ammunition.

During his career Julian Gustave Symons has been the secretary to an engineering company, an advertising copy writer, a poet, biographer and critic as well as literary editor of *Tribune* and the founder of *Twentieth Century Verse* (1937–39). He thoroughly deserves inclusion in this book if only for the fact that he has brought to the notice of the public many spy fiction writers who might otherwise be languishing in the darkest basements of Bayswater or wherever unsuccessful spy story writers live.

'Taffrail' (b. Duns, Berwicks, 8 September 1883; d. 1 July 1968)
'Taffrail' was the pseudonym of Capt. Henry Taprell Dorling, RN, who was educated in the old naval training establishment of HMS *Britannia*, which he joined in 1897. He saw action both in the South African War and again at the Relief of Peking in 1900. During the First World War he was awarded the DSO and a Gold Medal for life-saving at sea by the Swedish Government. Having retired from the Navy in 1929 to settle down to a new career as a writer, he was recalled to the Service at the outbreak of the Second World War. For a while he was attached to the Ministry of Information, later serving on the staff of C-in-C, Mediterranean.

'Taffrail's' stories were mainly of sea life pure and simple, but he also produced a few good spy yarns. He had a remarkable talent for telling a story in a lively fashion which won him a wide readership. *The Lonely Bungalow* (UK 1931) was a tale about a young naval commander, a heroine named Calliope Heddon, modestly described as 'quite prepossessing' and a Russian named Boris who is engaged in a secret mission detrimental to British interests. This was followed by *Operation 'M.O.'* (UK 1938), about a master spy discovering an Admiralty secret, and *The Shetland Plan* (UK 1939), set among the fishermen of the Shetlands who become mixed up with spies and a plot to seize one of the islands when zero hour comes. During the Second World War 'Taffrail' produced some excellent narratives of naval actions in that war, returning to fiction when it was all over. *Cipher K* (UK 1932) and *The Jade Lizard* (UK 1951), about an RNVR officer who becomes involved with a Resistance Movement in the mountains of a Mediterranean island, as well as with a Greek heroine, were among his later stories of this genre.

Darwin and Hildegarde Teilhet

For a short spell in the 'thirties the Teilhets were notable exponents of the spy novel and perhaps the only writers of this genre emerging from continental Europe. Their works were published in US and the UK. They wrote books both independently and in collaboration with one another. Darwin Teilhet, whose first work was *Hero by Proxy* (US 1932), made his name with *The Talking Sparrow Murders* (US 1934) which was set in Germany shortly after the accession to power of the Nazis: Julian Symons described it as 'an unusual blend of spy story and mystery'. He also wrote *The Fear Makers* (US 1946) and *The Big Runaround* (US 1947).

Together Darwin and Hildegarde Teilhet wrote *The Feather Cloak Murders* (US 1936), *The Double Agent* (US 1946), *The Assassins* (US 1946) and *Rim of Terror* (US 1947). After the war the Teilhets switched their attention from Nazi Germany to the Cold War and introduced the character of Sam Hook of the US Intelligence in both *The Assassins* and *The Double Agent*. In the former book there was the story of an attempt to set up an American-backed rug factory in Communist China which could also be a base for Sam Hook's Intelligence activities. Both Teilhets seem to have disappeared without trace.

Jerrard Tickell (b. 1905; d. London, March 1966)

Jerrard Tickell had a romantic start to his career as an author. In 1929 it was announced that two young writers, both in their early twenties, were to wed—Tickell and Renée Oriana Haynes, the daughter of E. S. P. Haynes, the writer. Each had had a first novel published the year before.

Tickell is undoubtedly best remembered for his biography of Odette Hallowes Churchill (*Odette* (UK 1949)), the British SOE agent who was sent into France during the Second World War and captured by the Gestapo, and for *Appointment with Venus* (UK 1951), which made an excellent film. Probably his best spy book was *Villa Mimosa* (UK 1960), set in the early spring of 1944 prior to the Allied invasion of Normandy. Major Charles Addison, a British secret agent, alias Charles Bertin, watchmaker, is ordered to report on the activities at the Villa Mimosa, which he enters in the guise of a pianist. He is riding his bicycle along a poplar-lined road in occupied France when he sees a string of feminine garments hung like signal flags on a clothes-line. The house which is flying these revealing pennants is the Villa Mimosa, an establishment which is to arouse the greatest interest in London. Charles Addison swiftly learns that this is the centre of an anti-Hitler conspiracy and a daring and impudent plan is devised and given the appropriate name of 'Operation Sabine'. In his true identity Addison returns dangerously to the Villa to snatch away the ladies and their regular visitors and take them back to England. *High Water at Four* (UK 1965) was about the adventures of a young officer, dismissed from his ship after a collision at sea, who goes on a pleasure trip in an oil tanker and finds himself in an Iron Curtain port where young women are employed to ensnare foreigners.

Tickell's novels were notable for the manner in which he evolved a captivating story from a single, simple incident and for his light touch and evocative dialogue. He was altogether a delightful writer and some of his spy novels—possibly because of *Odette*—frequently raised queries as to how much they were based on fact. Certainly Tickell knew a great deal about operations in France by the SOE and others, though he was most unfairly attacked in *The SOE in France* by M. R. D. Foot in which the latter referred to his biography of Odette Hallowes as 'a popular and partly fictionalised life' and commented on *Villa Mimosa* that it was an 'entertaining, strategically and tactically absurd novel about SOE-CCO co-operation in 1944'. Nevertheless there was more than a hint of the truth in the Villa Mimosa in that it bore some resemblance to the luxurious Villa Isabelle which for months during the war was maintained as the headquarters of 'Spindle', one of the key units in the SOE network.

Nigel Tranter (b. Glasgow, 23 November 1909)
This is the pseudonym of Nye Tredgold. He was educated at George Heriot's School, Edinburgh, and he describes himself as a 'moderate Scottish Nationalist', with the emphasis on better roads

for the Highlands, the safeguarding of personal freedoms and public rights. Tranter started life as an accountant and inspector in the family insurance company in Edinburgh from 1929–39 and did not become a full-time writer until after the Second World War, in which he served in the Royal Artillery, rising to the rank of Lieutenant. His first novel was *Trespass* (UK 1937), but it was after the war that he alternated his Scottish historical novels with some well-constructed stories of espionage. These included *The Man Behind the Curtain* (UK 1959), about a RNVR officer who is both a wild fowler and a skilful navigator and who is sent by the Foreign Office to the island of Bornholm in the Baltic to take a Polish scientist off the Pomeranian coast. One critic said of this book that 'the nightmare of the return home in a storm, hunted by Communist launches, is in the direct tradition of Conrad'. *Cable from Kabul* (UK 1967) concerned a pro-Western espionage group trying to get a defecting Russian scientist out of China and was set, most unusually, in the high Pamirs. Tranter also writes Westerns under his real name, is an authority on Scottish architecture and is President of the Salmon Drift-Net Committee.

'Trevanian'
This pseudonym disguises the true identity of an American professor of English literature who lives in the US. For the truly curious, Trevanian provides one useful clue to his identity at the end of his book, *The Loo Sanction* (US 1973), indicating that it was written at 'London, Essex', presumably some time between 1970 and 1972. In fact he wrote this book while on a sabbatical which was spent partly in London and partly at the University of Essex at Wivenhoe. Some Trevanian addicts in the US insist that the pseudonym is an anagram. It is possible, however, that he took the name from a certain Sir John Trevanian who escaped from Colchester Castle (not far from Essex University) during the Civil War by means of an ingenious plot worthy of the best Secret Service traditions.

Miles Copeland has said of Trevanian that his work contains 'some of the most shocking, brutal fiction in modern literature, but it's also funny—funny, that is, to those who like their comedy a bit sick. Trevanian's characters are real enough and they constantly drop "in" jokes to tell readers among the pros they are not acting out fantasies, but caricatures.' His first novel was *The Eiger Sanction*

(US 1972). A critic said it started 'unpromisingly in a welter of sex, facetiousness and fantastication, but presently when it comes to the climbing settles down to rationality and achieves real grip.' This is an understatement. Trevanian is a real discovery in spy fiction, composing it rather as one would expect Evelyn Waugh to have done, as a merry jape with serious undertones. And the comparison does not stop there: the style is nicely terse, economical and admirably literate in the best sense of that much abused word. Trevanian has the knack of economising in words to achieve a satirical effect in the manner which Waugh employed so effectively in narrating the suicide scene in *Vile Bodies*. Only Trevanian adopts precisely the same method in describing an off-beat sexual encounter between an ageing spinster and her sixteen-year-old protégé, who privately nicknames her 'the Sandpaper Crotch'. Trevanian, having already made a terse note of the nickname, writes how one evening after she has had rather a lot of champagne, the female snuggles up to the youth on a sofa: 'Then she hugged him tighter. By the next morning she had made up a cute little nickname for it and almost every evening thereafter she would coyly ask him to do it to her.'

The Eiger Sanction tells of Dr Jonathan Hemlock, mountaineer, art historian, collector of rare paintings and assassin-designate to an American Intelligence department. The story starts in Montreal where Wormwood, an inept, accident-prone agent of the CIA, having been handed a tiny packet of bubble-gum in the park, believes at last he has safely carried out a mission. He is about to enter his room when he is clubbed to the ground. Thinking he is about to lose consciousness, he has the presence of mind to stuff the bubble-gum in his mouth and swallow it. Doubtless he thinks the microfilm in the packet is safe from the villains who have knocked him out. Such thoughts are rudely disturbed as he feels them rip open his stomach to get the bubble-gum out . . . oh, yes, it's that sort of horror humour, but, mercifully, briefly narrated.

Hemlock wants a huge sum of money to buy himself a picture. He is told that the price will be 'the life of a man in Montreal', the man who killed the unlucky agent, Wormwood. Then it transpires that there is a second man to be bumped off, but nobody is sure who he is. Ultimately Hemlock goes to Switzerland, joins the party making a perilous assault on the north face of the Eiger and plans his assassination exercise. One of his three companions is to be his victim, but when the climb starts Hemlock still doesn't know who. Ruthlessly, he decides to kill all three, just to make sure.

There is perhaps as much sex as espionage in Trevanian's novels, but even this is brilliantly economical, refreshingly un-laboured and full of the most delicious humour. One of the best scenes is the seduction of an agent named Ms Felicity Arce (pro-nounced Arse) by Hemlock. This takes place while Ms Arce is briefing Hemlock on his next assignment; the briefing is beautifully punctuated by her endearing asides, spontaneous verbal reactions to Hemlock's love-making technique and grunts which indicate more or less each stage of intercourse. Trevanian also has a Waugh-like gift for choosing apt names for his characters. Apart from Ms Arce, Wormwood and Hemlock, there are Dragon, the CIA execu-tive, George Hotfoot (a woman), Randie Nickers (another woman) and Anna Bidet, not to mention some really splendid titles for organisations and safe houses within the various Intelligence net-works. To appreciate Trevanian to the full, a study should be made of the appendix of spooks' jargon at the end of this book.

The Loo Sanction refers to a section of British Intelligence called the Loo Organisation which 'provides protection for MI5 and MI6 operatives by the technique of counter-assassination'. It is called the Loo because its headquarters are in a room which was formerly a lavatory and washroom. Hemlock, who appears again, is sent by the American Search and Sanction Division (a section which hires and employs professional killers) to liaise with the Loo in England. The Loo sometimes, in order to protect its own killer agents, pretends to bump them off, discreetly arranging for some-body else's corpse to be left behind as evidence while the agents go into hiding or change their identities. Thus, the Loo is frequently in need of fresh corpses and, for obtaining these and making them suitable, its executives have established a 'Feeding Station' in the English countryside. Hemlock inquires why this most 'un-safe house' has been given this title. The answer is that on this farm the prospective corpses are specially fed: '. . . the Ruskies pump the stomach of a corpse and check its contents. It wouldn't do for a supposed Greek to produce the remnants of a steak and kidney pie.'

Trevanian's espionage jargon is an absolute delight to addicts of this kind of thing. Some of it is extremely witty invention, the rest shows an insight into the strange language of real-life spooks. *The Eiger Sanction* was made into a film featuring Clint Eastwood and contained some of the most daring mountaineering scenes ever photographed.

Antony Trew (b. S. Africa)

Of English descent, Antony Trew first joined the South African Naval Service, leaving it for a variety of jobs in Johannesburg until the Second World War, when he rejoined the Navy and commanded an escort destroyer in the Norwegian and Barents Seas. After the war he was appointed director-general of the Automobile Association of South Africa, at the same time turning his attention to writing. He has drawn heavily on his naval experience and know-how in most of his books, the first of which was *Two Hours to Darkness* (UK 1963), which became an instant bestseller, running into three and a half million copies and sixteen translations. This was the story of a Polaris nuclear submarine: 'When I heard of the capability of a Polaris submarine whose ballistic missiles could take out sixteen of the world's largest cities, I began to think what would happen if the captain of such a sub on patrol began to go round the bend and had his finger on the trigger.'

The book was a dummy run to see if he could make a living from writing. He came to England and settled in Weybridge. Though he has not had anything comparable with the success of *Two Hours* so far, his interest in the links between nuclear warfare and technology and the spy game has prompted such books as *The Zhukov Briefing* (UK 1974), the story of a Russian nuclear submarine aground on a Norwegian island, and *Ultimatum* (UK 1976), a book motivated by a terrifyingly feasible development of a link between the proliferation of nuclear weapons and the ever-rising tide of terrorism. Trew tells how the Prime Minister, the US Ambassador to England and the editors of two British national dailies receive in their morning post an ultimatum: unless the British and US governments accede unequivocally to the demand for an independent Palestine, a nuclear warhead which has been smuggled into London will be detonated within seventy-two hours. Just off Covent Garden, however, an undercover group of Israeli agents has been observing and monitoring nearby premises known to house Palestinians, and it is the Israelis who make the vital discovery. Trew says: 'It *can* happen here, and it is becoming increasingly easy for it to do so. The level of the risk is that something between seven and eight hundred nuclear warheads are on the move in Europe and in this country every day, going from production centres to maintenance centres to distribution units.' Trew is probably the most knowledgeable of all nuclear spy story writers. History has caught up with him more than once. He wrote one novel concerning a war on the east coast of Africa to which the Soviets and the Cubans were supplying weapons. Just as he was finishing it, the Israeli war closed the Suez Canal and thus altered the entire situation. The book could not be published. Yet the fact remains that the author had forecast the then unlikely situation of Cubans actively engaging themselves in African affairs.

Leon Uris (b. Baltimore, Md; 3 August 1924)
Son of a Polish immigrant, novelist Leon Uris did not finish high school and ran away from home at the age of seventeen to join the US Marine Corps in the Second World War. He served in the South Pacific and married a US Marine sergeant. After the war he joined the *San Francisco Bulletin* as a district manager for the home delivery of newspapers. His first book, *Battle Cry* (US 1953), was about life in the Marines, but it was with *Topaz* (US 1962), a novel about a Soviet espionage network inside French governmental circles, that he made a sensational impact in more ways than one. This book seemed to be an ultra-realistic spy story, telling how the head of the KGB's anti-NATO bureau defected to the Americans and revealed the existence in Paris of a Soviet spy ring code-named Topaz, of which the two key members were a senior French official and a close adviser—code-name Columbine —of the French President. *Le Canard Enchaîné*, the satirical French weekly, suggested in its columns that Columbine was an accurate portrait of one of de Gaulle's most trusted Intelligence advisers. Shrewd observers of the Intelligence game paid rather more attention to *Le Canard*'s allegations than did the general public. They noted that the various spy rings organised by the Russians against NATO were known to use the names of jewels for their code-names. The ring organised against the French was actually not known as Topaz, but as Sapphire. Then it was realised that Philippe Thyraud de Vosjoli, formerly head of French Intelligence in Washington, had been a friend of Uris, and in 1968 de Vosjoli, who had been chief liaison officer between the French Secret

Service and the CIA, made some astounding allegations which were highly damaging to French prestige.

Nevertheless, though *Topaz* was undoubtedly based on certain elements of truth, it was a work of fiction in that the truth had been gilded out of all recognition except to those in the Intelligence game. The French were able officially to pooh-pooh the *Topaz* legend. De Vosjoli had angered his French employers by showing rather too much enthusiasm for collaborating with the CIA, whose favourite Frenchman he was. He was also consulted by the CIA on revelations made to them by the Russian defector, Dolnytsin. When ordered back to Paris, he refused to go and resigned from the Service. It was then that de Vosjoli gave as his reasons for leaving the French Intelligence organisation that they had been infiltrated by Soviet agents. So what started with the publication of a novel eventually grew into an international scandal and de Vosjoli maintained that not only was the French Secret Service infiltrated by the Russians, but that there was a 'French Philby' inside de Gaulle's own entourage. In Paris de Gaulle ordered a searching inquiry into the existence of NATO spy rings, as a result of which Georges Paques, a French press attaché with NATO, was arrested and sentenced to imprisonment for spying. The French official view was that the de Vosjoli affair was a CIA plot aimed at embroiling de Vosjoli and exploiting anti-French sentiment in Washington, its ultimate object being the discrediting of de Gaulle himself. Another view was that it was a deliberate ploy by the KGB, that its object was to stir up anti-Americanism in Paris by involving de Vosjoli with the CIA and discrediting the French in American eyes. If one compares the two viewpoints it is clear that the Soviet Union stood to gain more from such a contrived plot than did the CIA or the US Government. It was also suggested that behind these allegations was a KGB plot—probably planted on the CIA—to discredit one of the ablest Intelligence advisers in Paris, Jacques Foccart, officially the Secretary-General for Madagascar and African Affairs, but unofficially de Gaulle's chief adviser on all Intelligence matters and watch-dog on counter-espionage. A side issue of all this was Foccart's support for Biafra during the Nigerian Civil War which the Russians, who were backing the Nigerian Federalists, wanted to check. De Gaulle loyally stood by Foccart, but when he left the Elysée Palace, M. Poher, who became the interim President, dismissed Foccart from office. There was an outcry against this and when Pompidou became President Foccart was restored to his post. This is one of the most extraordinary examples in modern times of a novel having such far-reaching effects on trans-Atlantic politics—and it all started from a mischievous, if amusing review in *Le Canard Enchainé*.

Gerald Verner (b. 1897)

At one time the favourite author of King Edward VIII, Gerald Verner 'graduated among crooks and gangsters to make my books live', according to his own account of how he started to write. Making Soho his 'village', he actually lived as a down-and-out with race gangs and cocaine traffickers and worked with policemen on underworld beats. 'My first novel was written on lavatory paper among down-and-outs on the Thames Embankment,' he declared. During the nightclub boom of the late 1920s he was making £200 a week running a nightclub in Soho. His spy novels include *Ghost Squad* (UK 1936) and *Faceless Ones* (UK 1964).

Gore Vidal (b. US, 3 October 1925)

Educated at Phillips Exeter Academy, New Hampshire, Gore Vidal served in the US Army from 1943–46, rising from private to warrant officer. In 1960 he offered himself as Democratic Liberal candidate for the US Congress and in the same year was appointed to President Kennedy's Advisory Council of the Arts. His first novel was *Williwaw* (US 1946) and he has mainly written mildly satirical and sometimes humorously wicked commentaries on modern life. *Myra Breckinridge* (US 1968) created a sensation when it was published and was described by one critic as 'a virtuoso exercise in kinkiness'. Yet though he excels in sexual comedies, Vidal often has a serious message. To a large extent this was true of *Burr* (US 1973), which, though few would call a spy story, nevertheless reconstructed as a novel the story of Aaron Burr, the third Vice-President of the US, and one of those enigmatic figures of early American political intrigue and espionage. Vidal has highlighted an eighteenth-century Watergate and the undertones of secret service and counter-espionage which existed, despite the fact that there was then no kind of federal police system and no organised military intelligence. It is the skullduggery in high places, the espionage and picayune imbroglios which Vidal puts into perspective with more imagination and objectivity than any historian yet. The book also introduces the devious spy Major Benedict Arnold, who crossed over to the British forces. Burr killed Alexander Hamilton in a duel in 1804. His adventures along the Spanish border—supposedly with separatist intentions—led to his trial for treason and eventual acquittal in 1807. Burr then sailed to Europe where he tried to draw England and France into his plots to capture Spain's American colonies. He died in obscurity in 1836. Vidal turns this whole story into a superb historical peepshow.

Kurt Vonnegut Jr (b. Indianapolis, Ind., 11 November 1922)
Kurt Vonnegut came from a family with a long tradition of being architects, but his family insisted that there was no longer any money in such a career and he went to Cornell University and studied chemistry for three years. In the Second World War, he says, 'I was the battalion scout and so I was very easily taken prisoner in Germany.' As a result of this Vonnegut endured the terrible ordeal of being 'a prisoner in a meat locker under a slaughter-house during the Dresden air raid.' When it was over he worked as a 'miner of corpses'. After the war he went to Chicago University to study anthropology. Then came the diverse jobs of police reporter on the *Chicago City News* Bureau and work in the research laboratory of the General Electric Company. His first novel, *Player Piano* (US 1952), was, in fact, a sly dig at GEC.

Vonnegut is a highly original writer who, in his own way, has created a similar cult among the young as did Tolkien with his make-believe people. His first spy novel was *Mother Night* (US 1960) about an American spy in wartime Germany who manages to survive because he plays the role of a Nazi so convincingly and makes such virulent and vile anti-semitic broadcasts. There is no doubt that Vonnegut has a message in this book and, though the theme would be not unfamiliar to Le Carré, Vonnegut turns it into a novel of ideas as well as of spies. His theme is that 'we are what we pretend to be, so we must be careful about what we pretend to be'. Underlying this thought-provoking message is some judicious satire handed out impartially and directed towards Nazis, right-wing Americans, Jews, Negroes and the American left-wingers. Graham Greene described Vonnegut's *Cat's Cradle* (US 1963) as 'one of the best novels by one of the most able living writers'. It was the story of a Caribbean island dictatorship in

179

which the author repeats his message about the dangers of pretence, this time dealing with a religion called Bokononism, through which one is introduced to 'useful lies which make you brave, kind and happy'. Out of this book a Vonnegut cult has sprung up, a phenomenon that has attracted some attention in France and Germany as well as in the US.

Arthur Sarsfield Wade: *see* Sax Rohmer

Walter Wager (b. New York, 4 September 1924)
Educated at Columbia, Harvard and Northwestern Universities, Walter Herman Wager obtained both law and arts degrees. He has had a varied career calling for great versatility of talent. After being an editorial research director of Aeroutes Inc., New York, he was awarded a Fulbright Fellowship in 1947 and went to the University of Paris. This was followed by a spell as diplomatic adviser to the Department of Civil Aviation in Tel Aviv (1951–52). He then worked in the United Nations Secretariat, as a writer for TV documentary films for NBC in New York, as editor of *Playbill* (1963–66) and in a wide range of other jobs, including at least one in a New York State investigation.

His earliest book was a spy story, *Death Hits the Jackpot* (US 1954), which was about dollars stolen from an OSS courier killed in Madrid in 1944 showing up at a Chicago gambling club in 1953, and the efforts of the CIA to solve the mystery. This was followed by *Operation Intrigue* (US 1958), *OSS: A Short History* (US 1963) (non-fiction) and *I Spy* (US 1965). *Sledgehammer* (US 1970) was the story of four ex-OSS men who learn of the death of an old comrade and, determined to avenge him, use the skills they acquired during the war to undermine the rule of a gang boss in a small US gambling town—not quite a spy tale, but not entirely unassociated with it. Wager seems to have a nostalgia for the OSS. *Telefon* (US 1975) was a more orthodox novel of this genre, telling how Russian 'sleepers' and others acting as undercover agents on the quiet are planted near key installations in the US, waiting for the signal to destroy them. Wager then develops a most skilful and ingeniously constructed plot which provides an entertaining glimpse at life inside the CIA. The top Soviet agent takes off with a book of triggering signals and sets the destroyers off one by one. By doing this he hopes that the US will retaliate and attack Russia. His efforts to set off World War III bring out the spy-catchers from all sides like maggots out of cheese: the ensuing three-cornered chase is tersely and competently narrated. *Body Count*, his latest book, is due to be published in 1977.

Wager has two favourite characters—Captain Garrison in SWAP, a tough Green Beret who is very independent and versatile on a private mission to get a little Jewish orphan out of Russia, and a very glib and violent CIA man code-named Merlin in Wager's latest opus. Merlin is very worldly, wise-cracking and so professional that his real name never emerges. One of the themes that recurs in Wager's spy stories is how headquarters Intelligence bureaucrats meddle and resist field agents. To put it in his own words, he tries to demonstrate 'how stuffy and nervous the desk commandos are'. And, adds Wager, 'I often try to show that The Other Side has some decent people, too.' He is a 'great and outspoken fan of other writers of spy fiction, especially British writers who,' he says, 'are almost surely the best.' The most likeable quality about Wager is his frank, outgoing personality; his refusal to dodge questions and issues is exemplified in his reply to inquiries about any associations with the world of Intelligence. 'I have had friends in The Game, including one US Naval Intelligence officer officially ordered never to see me alone lest I try to worm out secrets. Idiotic! I was offered a job in OSS, declined in order to finish my law training when told in May 1944 that the war would end soon. I try to visit the places I write about, but when I can't I'm a dynamite researcher with guide books, travel films etc.'

Edgar Wallace (b. London, 1875; d. 10 February 1932)
Adopted by an East End family, Edgar Wallace was educated at the local Board School. He served for six years as a private soldier, first in the Royal West Kent Regiment, then in the RAMC. He went out to South Africa and there obtained his discharge from the Army. A bright and adaptable young man, willing to try any adventure, he became a journalist and during the Boer War was a war correspondent with Reuter News Agency from 1899–1900. He founded the *Rand Daily Mail* and then returned to London, working first with the *Daily News* and then with the *Daily Mail*. During this period Wallace was probably one of the first newspapermen to come up against an example of the long arm of the

Russian (then Czarist) counter-espionage unit during the Russo-Japanese War. The Russian Fleet had been ordered to sail east to destroy the Japanese Fleet and as the Russian ships were stationed in the western ports they had to sail from the North Sea to the Mediterranean and then on to the Far East. A heavy fog descended when the Russian ships were bearing down on the Dogger Bank and, in a moment of panic, due no doubt to the low state of morale and incompetent leadership, the Russians opened fire on a British fishing fleet in the belief that it was the Japanese Navy. The incident strained almost to breaking point relations between Britain and Russia and the *Daily Mail* sent Wallace to Vigo, the next port of call for the Russians, to ascertain what had happened. In Vigo Wallace found two petty officers from the Russian Fleet and they explained that the fog had created the utmost confusion, that the fishing vessels had made no response to signals and that the Russian officers had been convinced that a small detachment of the Japanese Navy had deliberately tried to trap them in the shallows. Wallace's report of this incredible story was wired to London. The *Mail*, not unnaturally, found the story rather thin and unconvincing, so they ordered Wallace to proceed to Tangier, the next port of call for the Russian Fleet, to obtain more facts. When he got there he learned that the petty officers had been executed and buried at sea. The Russian counter-espionage in Vigo had obviously acted swiftly. Some years later Wallace told Colonel Thoroton, RM, head of Intelligence at Gibraltar, that he had discovered that the Russians had been using as an informant a smuggler who operated around the coasts of Spain and Portugal and who employed some thousands of men. Laughingly, Wallace added that he thought the facts were so incredible that they could only be used as a short story, which he had written. But the story never appeared, nor (according to Wallace's daughter, Miss Penelope Wallace) can it be found even in manuscript form. It is said that Thoroton vetoed any use being made of the story because the smuggler was also one of his own chief informers and later, in fact, kept Gibraltar informed of all German submarine movements. So it is possible that Wallace destroyed the manuscript at Thoroton's request.

Wallace did not start writing books until 1905 when his first crime story, *The Four Just Men*, was published at his own expense. He was without doubt one of the unluckiest gamblers who ever lived, both in racing (his great passion) and in business. In this first book he gave no solution to the problem of how the Foreign Secretary had been killed, so he offered a prize of £500 for the correct solution. Alas, several correct solutions were sent in and this factor plus the already heavy costs of publishing and advertising, meant that he suffered a heavy loss. But Edgar Wallace never lacked either courage or determination and all his life he fought against odds with relentless drive. Of his imaginative talent there was no doubt whatsoever; ideas poured from his fertile mind and they nearly always clicked into shape as tidy and effective plots. Altogether he wrote 173 books, most of which came into the category of crime and detective stories. Margaret Lane, his biographer, has said that, when writing serials, he rarely knew what was going to happen in the next instalment. Did it matter? The reading public gave a resounding 'no' and the fact is that Wallace's experience as a crime reporter had given him a remarkable insight into life in the underworld and the *patois* of criminals. He also had a shrewd and imaginative eye for the theatre and his plays such as *The Ringer* and *On the Spot* showed a flair for creating atmosphere with skill and adroitness.

His most famous spy story was undoubtedly *Code No. 2*, which first appeared in the *Strand Magazine* of April 1916, then in the sixpenny paperback, *The Little Green Man*, and in various anthologies and collections of the world's best spy stories. What is most remarkable about this story is that in essence it anticipated the technological developments of a quarter of a century later—the computer-controlled hidden camera and infra-red photography. The story could, with a few changes of detail, almost entirely technical, be re-written perfectly adequately for today. It told the story of a Swiss clerk working in the 'Intelligence Department' in London who, on the eve of the First World War, disappears after having systematically deceived the ageing Chief of Intelligence. Schiller, the Swiss, had designed a new wireless receiver and, while working on it each day, obtained his Chief's permission to place it in the latter's safe each night. In this safe had also been placed the Department's top secret code—Code No. 2—and when Schiller vanished a member of the staff suspected that the wireless receiver was something quite different from what it purported to be. The Chief and the staff man sat up all night, with the safe door open, just watching: 'Immediately beneath the box [the receiver] was Code 2, enclosed in a leather binder, the edges of which were bound, for durability sake, with a thin ribbon of steel.

Now, slowly, the cover of the book was rising. It jerked up a little, then fell, leapt back again and fell back, as though something inside was struggling to get free. Then of a sudden the cover opened and remained stiffly erect, forming, with the contents, the letter L, the upright of which was the cover. There was a "click", and the interior of the safe was illuminated with a soft greenish radiance. It threw a glow upon the top page of the code which lasted for nearly a minute. Then it died away and the cover of the book fell . . .'

An ingenious little story and the suspense was well maintained right up to the trapping and killing of Schiller in German-occupied territory and the final denouement in London. Other pre-war Wallace spy stories were *Heine the Spy, Green Rust* and the series of stories about Major Haynes—*Major Haynes of the Secret Service* in *Thomson's Weekly News*, later revised for publication in the US as *The Adventures of Major Haynes (of the Counter-Espionage Bureau) with Some Additional Stories*. The Major Haynes stories, combined with those about Hermann Gallwitz, the German spy, also appeared in *Thomson's Weekly News* under the title of *My Adventures as a German Spy*. Another series in the same paper was that of *The Secret Service Submarine*, featuring John Dudley Frazer and his exploits in submarine Z1.

After the First World War Wallace seemed to drop the spy story and concentrated more on crime and detective books. He became chairman of the British Lion Film Corporation and, a few months before his death, he stood unsuccessfully as a Liberal candidate at Blackpool in the General Election.

Evelyn Bridget Patricia Ward-Thomas: *see* Evelyn Anthony

Edward Weismiller (b. Monticello, Wisc., 3 August 1915)
Educated at Swarthmore College (1931–32), Cornell College and Oxford University, where he was a Rhodes Scholar at Merton College from 1938–39, Edward Donald Weismiller then went to Harvard University where he was a post-graduate student until 1943. He soon won for himself a reputation as a poet of distinction, his first work including such poems as 'Deep Woods in Winter' and 'Frog' being published in *The Deer Come Down* Yale Series of Younger Poets (US 1936). From 1943 until the end of the war

he served in the US Marine Corps, receiving the Bronze Star and the *Médaille de la Reconnaisance Française.*

'At that time,' he says, 'things moved very rapidly. I was picked up by a secret intelligence organisation and trained in secret camps outside Washington . . . by December 3 I was in London beginning another intensive period of training at the hands of British Secret Intelligence . . . The Commandant of the Marine Corps is said to have snapped that "this is the first time I have ever been asked to commission a god-damned poet in the Marine Corps." To demonstrate to my superiors such skills as I had acquired I had been set loose in a vast industrial city with instructions to spend two days getting as much specific information as I could that would be of use to the enemy. I was, it might be argued, testing the city's security. I pretended to be a freelance writer, down from New England, his identifying papers in his other suit, intent on collecting material for an article on the magnificent things being done by industry on behalf of the war effort . . . The information I managed to pick up still makes me shudder when I think of it. I got with ease into numbers of top-secret places; I got photographs, I got figures; I learned "off the record" things which in the hands of the enemy could have been used in a matter of hours to set back our war effort for months.'

Weismiller's one and only spy novel is nevertheless one of the most important of the genre and, indeed, should be compulsory reading for anyone making a study of this type of fiction. This is *The Serpent Sleeping* (US 1962). Norman Holmes Pearson has said of this book that it 'is one of the few accounts of the handling and psychology of a turned agent, in this case after the invasion of France, when German agents attempted to operate behind the American lines.' Weismiller himself describes it as 'a novel of counter-espionage', adding that 'all the characters in *The Serpent Sleeping*, French and American, young and old, good and evil, are, I suppose, among my selves. In John Peale Bishop's magnificent poem *Ode*, occur the lines "I have been as many men, as many ghosts/As there were days", and I have tried to show some of the ghosts.'

This may seem somewhat arcane to the uninitiated, but to understand what Weismiller is trying to say it is necessary to study his wartime activities and experiences. In July 1944 he was sent to Cherbourg and in France had to become involved with a Nazi agent, the object being to use him in what came to be cynically called 'the Double Cross System'. Weismiller explains that the agent in question was used 'against the Nazis as though he were working freely, as though he were not under our control. Of course we had to give the Nazis information; of course, though our ultimate purpose was deception, some of the information we sent had to be verifiably true, and this meant that we had to betray our own forces, a little, in the interest of the greater good. Fortunately it was someone at Supreme Headquarters, not I, who had to decide how much betrayal, of whom, was acceptable on any given day. But in order to build up my double-agent so that ultimately he would be able to deceive and damage the enemy as much as possible, I had of course to press constantly to give away as much good information about our own troops as could be thought, in balance, not too unsafe . . . In the end we caught most of the spies the Germans had trained and left behind to work for them in France. Many of these I interrogated, or came to know in other ways. One of them all was, I think, an evil person; a few of them were morally empty, had become, somehow, human trash. Most of them were decent men and women—not strong, not heroic, but basically decent—whom the German Intelligence Service had manoeuvred into impossible situations, had subjected to impossible pressures.'

This was the background to *The Serpent Sleeping*, a book which germinated gradually over the years in Weismiller's mind. It all started partly out of a story called *The Green Place*, which he began to write. Then, having read Rebecca West's *The Meaning of Treason*, he turned his attention to *The Serpent Sleeping* in which he introduced the same boy and the same girl, but in different situations. In 1950 he obtained his doctorate in philosophy at Oxford and went to Pomona College to teach. Then in 1953 he received a fellowship from the Fund for the Advancement of Education, Ford Foundation, 'a fellowship for which I had applied so that I might complete the novel'. But Weismiller now felt that his work up to date needed revision and to tackle this effectively he returned to Cherbourg in 1957–58 to learn 'certain facts I needed to know about what had gone on in that city during the German Occupation . . . By this time my characters were as real to me as was my own family; I had to find out about them, not invent them.'

Weismiller has been a Fulbright Lecturer at the University of Leiden in Holland and in 1967–68 was a Fellow of the Center for Advanced Studies, Wesleyan University, USA.

Dennis Wheatley (b. 8 January 1897)

Dennis Yeats Wheatley was educated at Dulwich, but modestly describes his education as having been received at 'HMS *Worcester* and Germany'. He joined his father's wine business in 1914, but in September of that same year was commissioned in the RFA (T), City of London Brigade. He transferred to the 36th Ulster Division in 1917 and, after being gassed, was invalided from the Army in 1919, when he rejoined his father's firm. In 1926 he became sole owner of this firm, which he sold in 1931 before settling down to writing.

His first book was *The Forbidden Territory* (UK 1933), which was later filmed. This story was set in Soviet Russia and introduced three of Wheatley's most famous characters, Rex Van Rhyn, an American, Simon Aron, a Jewish financier, and the Duc de Richelieu, a French aristocrat. Wheatley's early works included such diverse subjects as *Old Rowley* (UK 1933), a 'private life of Charles II', *The Eunuch of Stamboul* (UK 1935) and *They Found Atlantis* (UK 1936). Though a late starter in the writing game, Wheatley soon achieved a prolific output of books which mostly enjoyed enormous sales in several languages. Some critics seem to have envied him his success, as one finds frequent references to his 'outdated' style of writing—'reminiscent of a boys' adventure paper in the period before World War I'. It is true that much of his work suggests old-fashioned extrovert writing at great speed, but Wheatley has been a meticulous researcher of historical background and in the mid-'thirties he was also somewhat of an innovator. In collaboration with J. G. Links, he launched in 1936 what he described as 'Crime Dossier Murder Fiction' with the publication of *Murder off Miami*. This was a revolutionary attempt at realism in crime and detective fiction, as the book comprised typewritten police dossiers and memoranda, handwritten letters in facsimile, telegrams and hair, matches and pills in cellophane envelopes attached to the pages (these last-named being the clues). This novel kind of detective story, while attracting considerable publicity at first, was less successful with later books. Perhaps, with the Second World War approaching, Wheatley would have done better if he had created a realistic dossier book of spy fiction. On the other hand, censorship in wartime might well have ruled out anything so ambitious.

Nevertheless, Wheatley turned his attention to spy fiction later on, introducing two recurring characters, Gregory Sallust and Roger

Brook. The former was based on an Army friend of Wheatley's and first appeared as a lone wolf British Secret Service agent in *The Scarlet Impostor* (UK 1940), then in *Faked Passports* (UK 1940). Wheatley made the Sallust stories topical by dramatising the 1939–45 war up to the end of the Russo-Finnish campaign and then in *The Black Baroness* (UK 1946) covered the period from the Norwegian campaign to the fall of France. Sallust, a romantic character, appeared again in *V for Vengeance* (UK 1942).

Meanwhile, however, Wheatley was employing his vivid imagination and perpetual motion enterprise to some effect in the national interest. In 1939 he had toured England as a member of Sir John Anderson's team of speakers on the subject of National Service. But 'Wheatley's War', as his friends in clubland jokingly called it, began with a lunch at the Dorchester Hotel in London three days after the surrender of France to the Germans. Sir Louis Greig, Wing-Cdr. Lawrence Darvall and a Czech armaments manufacturer were in the party with Wheatley, the object being to discuss a paper the author had written, giving his own, unofficial and highly original ideas for repelling a German invasion. He was asked to develop his theme and for the greater part of the rest of the war he was installed in Churchill's secret underground fortress off Whitehall, the only civilian member of the Joint Planning Staff. Later he was re-commissioned as an officer in the RAFVR. He not only worked out his own projects, but provided some of the background details for two such successful Intelligence coups as 'The Man Who Never Was' and the creating of General Montgomery's 'double' to put in an appearance at Gibraltar to fox the Germans. 'Making myself think as a Nazi,' as Wheatley said afterwards, he initially wrote a 12,000-word plan for the conquest of Britain, as it might have been prepared by a member of the German General Staff. Then, having contrived an invasion plan with Teutonic thoroughness, he thought up moves to counter every plan the Germans might have, such as the blacking-out of the names of railway stations on the platforms and the uprooting of sign-posts as well as a 230-mile barrier of fishing-nets to foul the propellors of Nazi landing-craft. Not all his ideas were accepted: many were rejected on the spot, but he had a fair measure of success. One of his pet ideas was a plan to invade Sardinia. He remains convinced that the war could have been won at least a year earlier if Sardinia had been invaded instead of Sicily, but 'Operation Brimstone', as the project was called, though said to have been favoured by Eisenhower, was finally turned down by Sir Alan Brook, the CIGS. Amidst all this Wheatley still found time to pour out his books—*Codeword Golden Fleece* and *Come into my Parlour* (both UK 1946), the latter bringing in not only Gregory Sallust, but an uproarious parody of an old-fashioned Intelligence Chief, Sir Pellinore Gwaine-Cust. After the war Wheatley put together his hush-hush wartime papers and published an account of his work in *Stranger than Fiction* (UK 1959).

Since the Second World War he has taken a particular interest in the theme of black magic, claiming that half the drug-pushing in Britain is done by people belonging to the nation's witch covens. A number of his books of recent date have been devoted to witchcraft. But in the post-war period Wheatley has created a highly popular new character, another British secret agent, and a series of spy stories set in the Napoleonic era. In this kind of a setting Wheatley is much more at home and totally uninhibited. His first book of this series was *The Launching of Roger Brook* (UK 1947) in which a sixteen-year-old Brook, disenchanted with the Royal Navy, runs away to France (perhaps an echo of Wheatley himself here, for he switched from being a naval cadet to being a gunner in the First World War, and also ran away from school), and does a spot of discreet spying in between amorous escapades. There is a blatant, but none the less effective plug for the series at the very end of this first book: 'Consider yourself launched, Mr Brook. England and I have a hundred uses for a man like you,' says the redoubtable William Pitt, addressing the hero.

In *The Shadow of Tyburn Tree* (UK 1948), which followed, Roger Brook continues as a secret agent for Pitt, still freely indulging in his love life. It is then that the 'lovely Lady Georgina' tells him: 'Since that day long ago when I turned you from a schoolboy into a man, I've made no secret of the fact that I was born a wanton and will take my pleasure where I list.' The list of Roger Brook's *inamorata* is extensive: in *The Dark Secret of Josephine* (UK 1955) he is involved with Napoleon's first Empress; in *The Sultan's Daughter* (UK 1963) he is nearly shot by a firing squad, almost dies of plague and just misses being turned into a eunuch, while it is Zanthe, the Sultan's daughter, who saves him from some of these fates. Other Roger Brook stories are *Evil in a Mask* (UK 1969), which Wheatley wanted to call 'Enter a Nympho'; *The Ravishing of Lady Mary Ware* (UK 1971), in which the hero is an ADC to Napoleon, still spying, this time for the Duke of

Wellington, heavily involved with Portuguese bandits and a new love affair; and *The Irish Witch* (UK 1973), the witch being an Irish spy chief who is supplying information to the French. But by *Desperate Measures* (UK 1974) the Roger Brook saga has moved on as far as the Congress of Vienna which Brook, now an Earl, attends. This was the twentieth book of the Roger Brook series.

Wheatley was one of the first spy story writers to introduce uninhibited sex as an underlying theme. He has sustained a faithful readership over more than forty years, an undoubted tribute to his cynical humour and quick brain. For one who produces books at such a pace it is worth noting that he writes them all by pencil, 'frequently using a rubber'. He was said to be King George VI's favourite novelist.

Stewart Edward White (b. US, 12 March 1873; d. 18 September 1946)

Stewart Edward White was for much of his life an adventurous eccentric. So much of his career was hearsay and legend that it is almost impossible to separate gossip from fact. As a young man there were stories of his having undertaken hair-raising missions for the US Treasury Intelligence during the Spanish–American War and later in Guatemala. The *New York Times* said of him that he was a 'pioneer by inheritance and instinct' and that 'he possessed a brilliant talent for interpreting the spirit of pioneering to newer generations'. For the last seven years of his life, spent in retirement at his estate in Burlingame, California, he wrote books, which, so he claimed, were dictated to him by the spirit of his wife after her death.

His early books were mainly on the pioneering theme; such works as *The Silent Places, The Blazed Trail, The Forest* and *The Mountains*, were written before and just after the turn of the century. He travelled across America, describing his adventures in the Sierra Nevada Mountains, and giving instructions on how to live off the land and make the most of camping. It was the First World War which caused him to turn his attention to the spy story. *The Leopard Woman* (US 1916) was the nickname of a Hungarian countess who was the head of a strange tribe in Equatorial Africa and who took sides with the Germans in the war. White told of the struggle between her and Culbertson, a British agent, to secure the support of an African chief, M'tela. Though there was nothing specially remarkable about White's writing, he consistently held his own as a bestseller on both sides of the Atlantic and he must have been one of the longest serving authors of Hodder & Stoughton's lists. An unusual type of spy story— in a sense perhaps one of the first of the industrial spy species —was *Pole Star* (US 1936), which took the actual figure of Baranov, head of the Russian Fur Company, from the history of Alaska, and dealt with the intrigues with which he was surrounded, including spies sent to watch his every move and plots to destroy him.

Alan Williams (b. 1935)
Son of the actor and playwright Emlyn Williams, educated at Stowe, Grenoble and Heidelberg Universities and King's College, Cambridge. While still a student at Cambridge, attending a world peace conference in Warsaw, Alan Williams helped to smuggle a Polish refugee out of the country. He also witnessed the Hungarian Revolt of 1956 and had to masquerade his way into and out of East Germany among other adventures. Williams is no stranger to the Intelligence game; he worked for a period for Radio Free Europe, the anti-communist radio station at Munich which had close links with American counter-intelligence, and which was eventually infiltrated by and unmasked by Soviet Intelligence through a Polish agent, Capt. Andrzej Czechowicz in 1971. Later Williams entered journalism in Britain, working for the *Western Mail* and then the *Daily Express*. He covered the wars in Algeria and Vietnam as well as the revolt in Czechoslovakia and the civil war in Ulster. Some measure of his diligence and objectivity as a war correspondent may be gleaned from the fact that, when in Algeria, both the Algerian and the French forces complained about him and suspected he was a spy!

Williams, who is still a freelance journalist, has been praised for his spy novels, all of which are topical, relevant to today's problems and have strong, factual backgrounds. *The Tale of the Lazy Dog* (UK 1970) was a para-military thriller set in Laos, Cambodia and Vietnam and about a roving Irish journalist who learns of a US shipment of a billion and a half used dollars out of Saigon. But it was *The Beria Papers* (UK 1973) which first attracted the attention of a wider readership. This book postulated the discovery of a diary belonging to Lavrenti Beria, former head of the Soviet secret police from 1938 until his execution in 1953.

The diaries told of Beria's seductions, intrigues and rapes and, in concocting this item of fiction, Williams certainly kept close to the truth, for after Beria's death a great deal of evidence of his sinister habits was provided by those who had previously been too frightened to talk. Beria would in real life prowl the streets of Moscow at night in his bullet-proof ZIS limousine and when he saw an attractive girl—usually a teenager, but sometimes even younger—he would have his chauffeur pull up alongside and order the terrified girl into his car. Alan Williams' book describes how an American publisher was worried about the authenticity of the Beria Papers, and indeed it transpires that the papers are fake, their authors an unsuccessful English novelist, Mallory, and Boris, a temperamental fat Russian exile who works in Munich for Radio Free Europe.

More unusual and intriguing was Williams' *Gentleman Traitor* (UK 1975), which had for its hero none other than 'Kim' Philby. This imaginative twist to a spy thriller was based, says Alan Williams, on a friend's interview in Moscow with a drunken but still cunning Philby who said he was 'fed up with Russia and wanted to leave'. In the novel he did just this, and, bored, drunken and embittered in Moscow, agreed to accept a seedy job in Rhodesia for British Intelligence (still apparently riddled with old traitor chums of his always willing to lend a helping hand). So he escaped from Russia and appeared again on behalf of the SIS on a special mission to Rhodesia, having 'lost' his identity as part of the bargain. Philby himself was vividly portrayed in this exciting and highly intelligent story. In the end he died of a heart attack when on the point of letting all sorts of inconvenient information out of the bag.

One of the most important lessons of Alan Williams' ultra-realistic spy novels is that they are not just mere entertainment, nor are they, like some of this genre, mischievous realism. Each book takes a slice of history and builds around it with real and fictional people a credible story that really could have happened. Yes, even the Philby story . . . well, not in 1977, perhaps, but ten years ago such an incident would not have been as inconceivable as it sounds. And quite a few nervous executives in the British SIS would have gladly done a deal with him, had the chance occurred. It is the making of the incredible credible that is Alan Williams' great talent as a spy story-teller.

Valentine Williams (b. 20 October 1883)

The son of a former Chief Editor of Reuters News Agency, Valentine Williams was educated at Downside School and privately in Germany. He joined Reuters as a sub-editor at the age of nineteen and in 1904 became Reuters' correspondent in Berlin. It was in this period that he gleaned much of the material that was later to form the basis of so many of his spy stories. In 1909 he resigned to become Paris correspondent of the *Daily Mail*, a post he held for four years before covering the Balkans as a war correspondent. In 1915 he was appointed as the first accredited correspondent at British GHQ in France and later in the year was commissioned in the Irish Guards. He was wounded twice and won the MC. He represented the *Daily Mail* at the Versailles Peace Conference and was afterwards made Foreign Editor of that paper. His first novel, *The Man with the Club Foot* (UK 1921), introduced his German Secret Service character and was an instant success. This was followed up by *The Three of Clubs* (UK 1924), and in 1925 *The Red Mass* and *Mr Ramosi*, a novel based on the Luxor excavations, a story which Williams covered for the *Daily Mail*.

Some of his later spy stories he based on the subterranean intrigues which in the 'twenties fermented beneath the ruins of European ex-monarchies. A secret society known as 'the Three of Clubs', for example, intends to proclaim the Archduchess Valerie as Queen of Hungary. One wonders whether the idea for this plot was not developed from his *Daily Mail* experiences, as the first Lord Rothermere, then proprietor of that paper, was deeply involved in Hungarian imbroglios. In *The Crouching Beast* (UK 1928) Clubfoot was again brought back, this time into the period of that summer of 1914 immediately preceding the war. A lonely English girl in a German household suddenly finds herself swept into the dangerous currents of the British Secret Service. She is given a mission by a fugitive British spy whom she never sees again. The mission takes her to Berlin and a prolonged duel with the Kaiser's master-spy, Clubfoot. Clubfoot pops up, too, in *The Return of Clubfoot* (UK 1923), *Clubfoot the Avenger* (UK 1924), in which the ubiquitous German spy-master is engaged in a campaign of revenge against the British Secret Service agents responsible for his past discomfitures, *The Gold Comfit Box* (UK 1932), and *The Spider's Touch* (UK 1936).

A new spy-master was introduced in *The Fox Prowls* (UK 1938), in which Don Boulton, of the British Intelligence, is detailed to pick up the trail of Alexis de Bahl, known in Rumania as 'The Fox'. In the same year Williams' autobiography, *World of Action*, was published. During the Second World War he was engaged in confidential work for the British Government in Britain and the US. Eventually he was included in the ranks of the PWE (Political Warfare Executive) at their 'black propaganda' sanctum at Woburn Abbey. 'Kim' Philby, who met Williams at Woburn Abbey and once travelled back to London with him, commented: 'I would have liked to talk to him about Clubfoot. But we had lunched well and he slept all the way.' Even during the war, while serving as a double-agent, Philby's main interest for that hour's journey was to discuss a fictional spy!

Ted Willis (b. London, 13 January 1918)
Educated at Tottenham Central School, the son of a London bus driver, Ted Willis left school at fifteen and became in turn office boy, delivery boy, baker's roundsman. Later, while unemployed, he tramped the country working on farms and doing other casual labour. During the Second World War he served in the Royal Fusiliers, achieving the rank of Lance-Corporal. Subsequently he paved the way to success as a scriptwriter for films and television by working as a writer of War Office films and documentaries. His most notable and long-lived success in the sphere of television films was undoubtedly that of the *Dixon of Dock Green* series. Eight of his plays have been produced in the West End of London and many of his films have won him international fame. His own personal favourite among his television scripts was the cycle of four plays called *The Four Seasons of Rosie Carr*, which was a great success in Britain, Australia, Japan and Germany, and was, he says, based loosely on the life of his own mother. He was founder-member and first chairman of the Writers' Guild of Britain. A stalwart supporter of the Labour Party, he was created a life peer in 1963 as Lord Willis of Chislehurst.

In the field of television he has entered the world of spy fiction with his *Virgin of the Secret Service* (ITV). More interesting was his contribution to spy fiction in 1975—*The Left-Handed Sleeper*, all about the efforts of the British Secret Service to trace the whereabouts of Mark Ritchie, MP, suspected of being a spy for the Russians. Party politics were not entirely forgotten in this book: Lord Willis made his villain a Conservative!

A Fellow of the Royal Society of Arts, Ted Willis is also president of the Churchill Theatre Trust and the Police Dependents' Trust.

Diana Winsor (b. Belfast, 1946)

Diana Winsor went to school in Hong Kong, Bath and Dunfermline before moving to Portsmouth with her Service family. If she had been a boy, she says, she 'would have gone into the Navy'. Her elder brother had the chance instead; he went to Dartmouth, but hated it so much that he bought himself out before the year was up—just before the Dartmouth Ball which Diana, at fourteen, had been looking forward to for months. But Diana's consolation all along has been writing; she published her first story at the age of fifteen and a year later she wrote her first novel. Success in writers' competitions in the *Sunday Times* and *Daily Telegraph* encouraged her to try to write seriously. Ships are still her first love, but she also loves painting, animals, Paris and Italy. She undertakes commissions for paintings: 'The worse was for a dalmatian, with every spot having to be in the right place.'

Her father was working in the Navy Department at Bath when Diana's first novel was published, *Red on Wight* (UK 1972), and, yes, you have guessed right: it was about espionage in the Royal Navy. 'I wrote it when my father was with the Admiralty in the weapons department in Portsmouth and I got a lot of information from him. But he's not worried. He is a very untypical civil servant and he does not have access to top secret information. Anyway, I had the book unofficially vetted to make sure I wasn't giving anything away.' Coincidentally the book was published at the same time that Sub.-Lieut. David Bingham was jailed for twenty-one years for selling naval secrets to the Russians. *Red on Wight* was about a KGB plot to immobilise the NATO fleet when the Russians invade Africa. But it is an attractive heroine, Tavy Martin, who comes to the rescue of the Royal Navy when ships at Portsmouth start blowing up in mysterious fashion. Tavy was no superwoman. She lived in a room over a pub, worked in the Naval typing pool, went to Naval cocktail parties. But, in framing the part of Tavy, Diana Winsor was working on facts. She says that it is easy to find out what's cooking, especially in Portsmouth: 'Of course, if you turn up in a trenchcoat and a slouch hat, nobody's going to talk to you and occasionally you get someone who clams up and says "Can't talk about that", but on the whole you can find out about anything just through dinner party conversation in pubs and bars.' Diana has been around quite a bit. At nineteen she joined the *Times Educational Supplement* and after two years in London spent a year on Bath local newspapers and then worked in a magistrates' court and ran a company magazine for IBM. She is fascinated by technology and therefore understands what she hears rather more than most girls. She reads the *Scientific American* for fun and to find out what new developments are in the pipeline and actually enjoys visiting oil refineries and battleships.

Diana Winsor's new approach to spy fiction suggests that much else that is good is still to come from her pen. *The Death of Convention* (UK 1974) again brought forward that nice, bright and by no means unsophisticated girl Tavy for further adventures. Maurice Richardson in the *Observer* described the book as 'ultrareadable'. It told how Tavy, the girl from the MOD, went to Amsterdam to keep an eye on a convention of conservationists. The chief attraction was a defecting Soviet physicist who appeared to know rather more than was good for him or anybody else.

Leslie Charles Boyer Yin: *see* Leslie Charteris

Andrew York (b. Guyana)

'Andrew York' is the pseudonym of Christopher Nicole. Under his real name he writes historical fiction, but, as Andrew York, he has made a reputation through his creation of that lone Secret Service hired assassin, Jonas Wilde. Not surprisingly, as he hails from the Caribbean area, he was a keen cricketer in his youth, but now, in the Channel Islands, he spends more time on chess and bridge, at least when he is not travelling—in search of exotic backgrounds for new books.

It was in 1966 that he launched Jonas Wilde in the first of his ten novels on espionage themes. This was *The Eliminator*—an apt description of his character, Wilde—which the *Guardian* described as having 'everything that James Bond had and perhaps more'. The book was filmed and the whole series of Wilde books has been successful in the US and in translation into many languages. *The Eliminator* was followed by *The Predator* (UK 1968), *The Expurgator* (UK 1972), and *The Fascinator* (UK 1974), among others. Jonas Wilde has the sinister code-name, The Eliminator, and in *The Fascinator* Andrew York tried to put him 'out to grass'. But where does a professional assassin retire? How does he forget? Jonas Wilde chose the island of Ibiza, where he hoped to lose himself among the crowd of tourists and lose his memory in endless bottles of wine. One would have thought that once a professional killer takes to the bottle, his usefulness is ended. But Wilde, apparently, was too valuable to be forgotten. His old employers, his old enemies and others who only know of him as the most dangerous man in the world, all wish to discover if he can still be put to use. So he becomes involved in one of his most bizarre adventures, with the oil-rich prince of Xanda, a man who is as deadly a character as Wilde himself. But in *Dark Passage* (UK 1976) York has sought a new character of a totally different type, big Tommy Angel, a born loser. The signs are that Andrew York is turning away from the spy novel with this character switch.

Jeremy York: *see* John Creasey

APPENDIX

List of Abbreviations, Titles and Jargon Used in Espionage in Fact and Fiction

AG & FISH Refers to the British Ministry of Agriculture and Fisheries which, in the Second World War, was sometimes used as a cover address for 'resting' Intelligence operatives. Alexander Foote, the double-agent who worked for Russia and Britain, had a desk there for a period. 'Ag & Fish' came to mean 'gone to ground' in the early 1950s.

AMTORG Soviet Trade Agency overseas: sometimes a cover for spies.

BIOGRAPHIC LEVERAGE CIA jargon for blackmail. Used by 'Trevanian' in *The Eiger Sanction*.

BLACK OPERATIONS This covers several illegal operations such as murder, blackmail, extortion and kidnapping carried out by Intelligence Agencies.

BLACK TRAINEES The nickname given to foreigners recruited for CIA undercover training at the hush-hush 'Farm' in Virginia. These trainees were at one time allegedly not supposed to know they were on US territory.

BLEEP-BOX Used by some agents for both telephone tapping and obtaining calls to anywhere in the world without paying. In its primitive form this has been extensively used by agents in Europe and especially in Britain. The Chinese have developed a more sophisticated device called a multi-frequency-simulator, a machine for generating tones or frequencies used on various telephonic networks by which they have cracked the secret numbers of various organisations round the world—and so gained much useful information.

BLOWN The phrase used to describe an agent whose cover has been broken, or a network of spies which has been infiltrated. When an agent deliberately gives away to the opposition details of his sub-agent, wife or mistress for some devious reason, he is said to have 'blown his own strumpet'.

BOSS Bureau of State Security of the South African Government. This is a new favourite with some writers of spy stories, probably due to the wild tales told about it and the mysterious but un-substantiated innuendoes of Sir Harold Wilson.

BPR A joke reference for many years to CIA headquarters in Langley, Virginia. The only indication as to the address in that area was a signpost bearing these initials which were supposed to signify Bureau of Public Roads. Eventually the signpost was substituted by one stating 'Fairbanks Highway Research Station'. But the CIA has many establishments in Washington, New York, Chicago, San Francisco, New Orleans and other US cities.

c The initial given to denote the head of the British Secret Service. The full initials are CSS.

CACKLEBLADDER Secret Service slang for the method of disguising a live body to look like a corpse after having induced an enemy agent to hit or shoot the 'dummy'. As a general rule, the blood of poultry is used for smearing over the corpse. Though this may sound more like spy fiction than fact, it is a ploy adopted more often than would be supposed in real life, usually for blackmail purposes or forcing a confession from an agent.

CANNON Name given to a professional thief employed by an Intelligence Agency for the sole purpose of stealing back from an enemy agent or target some object given to him or her by another agent in order to make a deal or buy information. Often practised by Intelligence units short of funds, especially in wartime.

CASMS Abbreviation for Computer-controlled Area Sterilisation Multi-Sensor System, a highly sophisticated area of the modern Intelligence game and a revolutionary development of electronic eavesdropping which was tried out in Vietnam. Hundreds of small, self-contained bugging devices are dropped by aircraft in a certain area. They can pick up the movements of troops or individuals hidden in the jungle, or tanks and armoured cars.

CAT Civil Air Transport, the CIA's private air service. Founded in 1946 in China and later based at Taiwan from whence it supported clandestine air operations in Korea, Vietnam and other Asian states.

CELD Central External Liaison Department, an important branch of the Chinese Secret Service which is concerned with the analysis of foreign Intelligence.

CENTRE Refers to KGB headquarters in Moscow.

CHENG PAO K'O Chinese counter-espionage service, employed against foreign agents and to keep watch on the Chinese overseas. Not to be confused with *Chi Pao K'o*, the Internal Security Section.

CIA American Central Intelligency Agency. South Korea also has its own CIA.

COBBLER A forger of false passports.

COMPANY Nickname of CIA.

CONDEMNED SPY A Chinese Secret Service term which has sometimes been wrongly interpreted into English. Literally, it means: 'Ostentatiously doing things calculated to deceive our own spies, who must be led to believe that they have been unwittingly disclosed. Then, when these spies are captured in the enemy's lines, they will make an entirely false report, and the enemy will take measures accordingly, only to find that we do something quite different. The spies will thereupon be put to death.'

CONTROL QUESTIONS A system of checking used by the KGB. These questions are known only to the Centre, the Resident Director and the agent concerned and are employed to verify his identity should he appear in an unexpected place.

COVERT ACTION CIA jargon for attempting to influence the affairs of another country.

CUT-OUTS These are Intelligence officers who come directly under the area Chief Intelligence Officer (or, in the case of the Russians, the Resident Director). They are talent spotters and recruiters and act as go-betweens for agents and the Resident Director or Chief Officer.

DEFECTORS There is, of course, the genuine defector from one side to another; more complicated are the forced, or kidnapped defector and the bogus defector. The WALK-IN DEFECTOR is the person who arrives unannounced, bringing information with him. The DEFECTOR-IN-PLACE is one who stays on ostensibly as a defector, but in reality as an undeclared agent who sends back information as and when he can.

DEMOTE MAXIMALLY To purge by killing. 'Trevanian' mentions this phrase as an example of the CIA bureaucracy's 'new-speak'.

DI5 The new title for MI5, though even old hands in the Intelligence world still use the old title.

DI6 The British Secret Service, controlling overseas agents, formerly known as MI6. Also known as the SIS.

DIRTY TRICKS Usually applied to the 'black operations' of the CIA and covering a wide range of espionage and counter-espionage skulduggery. It is a phrase sometimes applied to breaking into premises illegally to install bugging devices, also called DIRTYING.

DISINFORMATION   The technique of discrediting one's opponents by manufacturing evidence, or smear tactics.

DOCTOR   The police.

D of I   Director of Intelligence (RAF).

DMI   Director of Military Intelligence.

DNI   Director of Naval Intelligence.

DOUBLE-AGENT   In the past a double-agent was usually a freelance Intelligence agent working for two sides without either knowing about the other. He could be working for two powers who were allies, or two at war with one another. In recent times it often means an agent who appears to be working for two sides, but in fact is being deliberately and knowingly used as a double-agent by one side, both to obtain information and to fob off false information on the opposition. Sometimes, though more rarely, there are TREBLE- and even QUADRUPLE-AGENTS, but their careers are normally brief. The exception was Englishman Sidney Reilly, who worked for at least four powers during more than thirty years in Intelligence.

DOUBLE-CROSS SYSTEM   This is the system by which one country either plants her agents on the enemy, or captures enemy agents and 'turns' them (converts them to their side) with the object of misleading the opposition. This system was adopted by the British in the Second World War with great success.

DROP   This word has two meanings. In CIA ranks it denotes success in a 'black operation'. Inside the KGB it refers to a 'letter-box', or hiding-place for secret messages, sometimes a crevice in a wall. See also DUBOK.

DST   *Direction de la Surveillance du Territoire*, the French Internal Security organisation.

DUBOK   Name given to secret hiding-places for agents' messages inside both the GRU and KGB. Curiously, for a nation so sophisticated in espionage, Soviet agents sometimes adopt the kind of hiding-place used by schoolboys for their secret notes. For example, a Soviet sub-agent in the Colonel Abel case told the Americans that he had been using a hole in a flight of steps in Prospect Park in Brooklyn. Park workers had noticed the hole and filled it in with cement.

ECM   Electronic-counter-measures. Special gear for producing these measures is installed in NATO power submarines engaged in round-the-clock anti-submarine warfare watch—today the front line of espionage.

E & E   Escape and Evasion. Specialist agents in the CIA are used for these tasks—e.g. sending a man in to rescue a captured agent, or preparing an escape route.

ELINT   Electronic Intelligence. Information obtained by planes, ships, submarines, space satellites, electronic intercept stations and radars. This is handled and interpreted by SQUAWK HAWKS, officially known as substantive Intelligence analysts.

FBI   Federal Bureau of Investigation: USA's counter-intelligence organisation.

FIA   NATO power Intelligence Agencies' name for the West German Federal Intelligence Agency, known in Germany as the *Bundesnachrichtendienst*.

FIELD   'In the field' means an agent actually on assignment in foreign territory.

FIRM (the)   Sometimes used by British agents to describe their Secret Service.

FIX   This is a word used in CIA phraseology, usually relating to a situation where somebody is singled out for being compromised or blackmailed, or possibly just conned. Those seeking out the possibilities of employing such tactics talk of a 'low-key' fix or an OK fix; the latter is actual blackmail.

FORTRAN   Formula Translation Language. This is an abbreviation used both by Ted Allbeury and Len Deighton and it refers to computer language with special reference to engineering and scientific matters.

FUMIGATING   Checking premises suspected of having been planted with listening and other devices and de-bugging those which actually have been so treated.

GAME (the)   A person who works in Intelligence is said to be 'in the game'. Not to be confused with 'on the game', though occasionally the two are combined!

GOING PRIVATE   Leaving the Secret Service: this applies both to DI6 and the CIA. Not, of course, to the KGB!

GRU   *Glavnoye Razvedyvatelnoye Upravlenie*, founded by Trotsky as the Fourth Department of the General Staff of the Red Army, a highly professional military Intelligence-gathering organisation.

HARMONICA BUG   A tiny transistorised eavesdropping gadget which can be placed inside an ordinary telephone.

HOSPITAL   Prison.

ILLEGALS   Soviet espionage élite agents sent, usually on false

205

passports, into foreign countries where there is a death penalty for espionage. They are mainly deployed by the GRU. Referred to in Intelligence circles as 'singles' or 'doubles', the latter meaning married couples who are 'illegals'.

JIC Joint Intelligence Committee (British), a body comprising representatives of all the Intelligence Agencies.

KGB *Komitet Gosudarstvennoy Bezopasnosti,* an organisation of vast ramifications covering both espionage and counter-espionage on behalf of the Soviet Union.

LADIES A euphemism for female members of an Intelligence team out to compromise one of the opposition. They set out to ingratiate themselves with the male 'target' for treatment, sometimes, but not always seducing him. Often the 'Ladies' are, as implied, out of the top drawer of society.

LAMP-LIGHTERS If you hear this phrase used by somebody claiming to be 'in the game', suspect him at once. It is a spy fiction title for a certain type of agent, used (and probably invented) by John Le Carré.

LION-TAMER When an agent is sacked, he sometimes goes berserk and makes threats. One of the Agency's muscle men is then called in to soften him up. The Lion-Tamer is also used to cope with recalcitrant or double-crossing 'Ladies', or 'Sisters'.

M The initial used to denote the head of the British Secret Service in the James Bond series. This gave rise to the mistaken idea that the initial denoted the surname of the chief, because Mansfield Cumming (First World War) had been known as 'C' and in the Second World War General Sir Stewart Menzies was the head. Probably Fleming's Service training made him jib at using the true initials for the head of the SIS, which had been 'C' for more than seventy years. The head of the SOE was known as 'M' for a brief time.

MAGPIE BOARD A small board or pack of keys, wire, knives and other odds and ends for aiding escape. In more sophisticated packs benzedrine tablets, compasses, maps and even miniature radio transmitters are included.

MEASLES The term applies to a murder carried out so efficiently that death would appear to be due either to natural causes or an accident.

MI 1C The original initials of the British Secret Service before this was changed to MI6; hence the use of C for the head of the Service.

MI5   The old title for DI5, Britain's counter-intelligence service, operating primarily at home.

MI6   Initials of the British Secret Service, which operates abroad, after discarding its original title of MI IC and before it was changed to DI6.

MI9   Initials of the wartime organisation set up by the British for planning escapes and escape routes for Allied prisoners-of-war.

MISINFORMATION   Baffling and misleading the opposition by planting false information. The technique was brilliantly employed by the British during the Second World War through the Double-Cross System and in modern times has been effectively employed by the Russians in creating mistrust and ill-feeling between Western Allies.

MOKRIE DELA   In Russian this means literally 'wet or bloody affairs' and refers to espionage missions actually involving bloodshed, violence or death. The CIA refer to a killing in the course of business as WET WORK.

MUSICAL BOX   A wireless transmitter.

NEIGHBOUR   Soviet operatives use this phrase to refer either to the local Communist Party or a member of it. Westerners would call a neighbour a 'fellow traveller'.

NEIGHBOURS   Warsaw Pact Powers.

NEWS   News in the Intelligence game is usually bad, and this term is used for passing the word to a contact or 'target man' that he is on the spot—i.e. that he must either deliver the goods (which can mean anything from revealing information to carrying out a mission) or face exposure or blackmail. The 'news' is usually conveyed subtly and not directly so that it will slowly sink in and the victim can ponder the alternative. Occassionally this is done merely to keep a 'target man' on ice, that is, to hint that he may eventually be required to perform a task for his mentors or tormentors—in CIA language be 're-activated'.

NID   Naval Intelligence Division (British).

NSA   National Security Agency of the US.

OKW   *Ober Kommando Wehrmacht* (German military Intelligence organisation in the Second World War).

ONE-MAN BAY OF PIGS   This was the nickname given to the unlucky and incompetent agent in Trevanian's *The Eiger Sanction*, Wormwood, who was killed in Montreal. It refers, of course, to that catastrophic CIA operation against Castro during Kennedy's presidency, and no doubt has been used in real-life Intelligence about any disastrous and accident-prone agent.

ONI Office of Naval Intelligence (US).

ORCHESTRA A term coined by Lenin to refer to the creation of a team of potential long-term agents, people selected without being told but allowed to remain dormant until ultimately they could be bullied, blackmailed, cajoled or compromised into collaboration. Usually the people chosen were those who had access to secret information or to important individuals or offices (this would apply as much to cleaners as to people inside the Establishment or a high-level social clique) and had weaknesses which could be exploited—perversions, homosexuality, alcoholism, marital infidelity etc. Sometimes the term is applied to a network, though this is mainly because in the Second World War the Germans nicknamed the Soviet espionage network in Belgium *Rote Kapelle* (Red Orchestra) when they discovered that a radio-operator in Soviet espionage terminology was a 'musician' and a transmitting-set was a 'musical box'.

OSS Office of Strategic Studies, set up in the US in the Second World War under General 'Big Bill' Donovan. The forerunner of the CIA.

PAVEMENT ARTISTS A surveillance team, or an agent keeping watch on a house. It is used by Le Carré, but does not appear to be employed outside fiction.

PEEP The name given to both an espionage photographic specialist who can take good (useful) pictures in conditions of great difficulty, and a planter of secret cameras.

PFIAB President's Foreign Intelligence Advisory Board (US).

PIANO CONCERTO Message, e.g. 'See my 43rd concerto'.

PIANO STUDY Radio operating.

PLACE OF CONSPIRACY A Soviet term for a secret meeting place, usually in a nearby country where an agent may in certain circumstances make contact with his 'side' on fixed days.

PUDDING A sarcastic term applied by Intelligence agents in the Western World to the United Nations. 'In the pudding club' means inside UN headquarters.

PZPR Polish Secret Police & Intelligence Agency.

QUEEN ANNE'S GATE Many spy fiction writers have and still do refer knowledgeably to Queen Anne's Gate. Allbeury, for example, writes of 'one of those beautifully panelled little set-ups that MI6 finds so necessary to its trade in Queen Anne's Gate'.

An Intelligence Branch of the War Office was started at Queen Anne's Gate in 1871. It was moved to Adair House in Pall Mall in 1874 and then back to Queen Anne's Gate in 1884. DI6 developed out of this and for many years its principal address was at 21 Queen Anne's Gate and the telephone number was listed under a sub-branch of the Ministry of Land & Natural Resources.

QUESTORS   Investigators of Section Q of the CIA.

RABCOR   A system of 'worker-correspondents' (*rabcor* in its abbreviated Russian form) was one of the first forms of Soviet espionage and was set up in France before the Second World War and revived afterwards. It consisted of developing a system of industrial espionage in factories and elsewhere. During the early 1950s there were said to be more than 800 *rabcors* in France, all supplying information to Soviet Intelligence.

RADAR BUTTON   A gadget which can pin-point its carrier's position back to base at any given time, which means the agent can be shadowed by the controller and aid sent to him if he is in trouble.

RESIDENT DIRECTOR   In the Soviet Secret Service the Resident Director of a spy network does not as a rule live in the country against which the network is directed, but in an adjacent or nearby territory. He usually has diplomatic status, but not always.

RESIDENTURA   Refers to the spy network controlled by the Resident Director.

SAFE HOUSE   A hide-away, where agents and defectors can be accommodated. More often the term is applied to a place where agents and suspects are interrogated.

SANCTIFICATION   An American term, bluntly described by Miles Copeland as 'blackmail for the purposes of extracting political favours from a victim, not money'. A Russian translation of this word is applied to tactics of the KGB and GRU in winning defectors from the Roman Catholic priesthood. When they secure a priest as an agent, the KGB say he has been 'beatified'.

SANCTION   To 'sanction' a man means that his killing (usually for revenge or other counter-measures) is sanctioned by an Intelligence Agency. Trevanian makes use of this word in the titles of his two books, *The Eiger Sanction* and *The Loo Sanction*. The phrase is used sometimes in CIA circles. Trevanian has given it a special department—the Search and Sanction Division of C II—which is a counter-assassination organisation aimed at removing the opposition's killers.

SCALP-HUNTERS Specialists in the whole subject of defection and experts in telling who is genuine and who is a fake defector. Their job is to keep their ears open for news of any diplomat or priority 'target' in the enemy camp who seems anxious to defect. They are given top priority in such instances over other Intelligence operators.

SDECE *Service de Documentation Exterieure et de Contre-Espionage,* the French Secret Service. Many writers of spy fiction, past more than present, have fallen into the error of calling the *Deuxième Bureau* the French Secret Service and Ian Fleming even described it as the French counter-intelligence agency—wrong again. The *Deuxième Bureau* began as a branch of military Intelligence within the French Army. Today it is still a military service, but one which co-ordinates Intelligence Services interested in national defence.

SETTING-UP The jargon used for framing or trapping an individual by secret agents. A diplomat, for example, is said to be 'set-up' when he is lured into a bedroom, fitted with hidden cameras and microphones, to be seduced by one of the 'Ladies' or 'Sisters'. The KGB are pastmasters at 'setting-up', but these tactics have been used by Western Intelligence Services as well.

SHOE A false passport.

SIFAR The Italian counter-espionage service.

SIS Secret Intelligence Service (British). Another title for DI6, but sometimes wrongly used as a blanket term for DI6 and DI5.

SISTERS The lower ranks of the 'Ladies': they usually get the tougher assignments and invariably find themselves bedding down with the opposition regardless of their inclinations.

SOAP Nickname for the truth drug, specially treated sodium pentathol, known for short as SO-PE.

SLEEPER A deep-cover agent planted in opposition territory with orders to lie low and work up contacts over a period of years. Gordon Lonsdale (Konon Molody), the Soviet spy caught by the British in London in 1961, was a typical sleeper, having been planted in Canada in the 1930s.

SMERSH An abbreviated combination of two Russian words, *Smyert Shpionam* (Death to Spies), used to describe the Soviet organisation James Bond was fighting. In fact, Fleming, writing in the late 1950s, was somewhat out of date in talking of SMERSH.

An organisation of this name existed in the 1940s, but was incorporated into the OKR (*Otdely Kontrrazvedki*) counter-espionage service in 1946.

SOE Special Operations Executive. Second World War British-sponsored organisation for aiding and collaborating with Resistance movements in Occupied Europe.

SOFTWEAR Official jargon for the programming and designing of systems for use on computers in Intelligence.

SON ET LUMIERE This is the amusingly apt phrase used to cover the obtaining of evidence from a 'setting-up': it means that the seduction of the victim by a 'Lady' or a 'Sister' is recorded by hidden cameras and microphones.

SPECIAL FORCES CLUB Mentioned by a number of spy fiction writers, notably by Allbeury in *A Choice of Enemies*: 'It's quiet and friendly and, unless we have another war soon, it's going to run out of members.' The club actually exists at 8 Herbert Crescent, London SW1, and membership is open only to those who have been 'in the game'—SIS, SOE, SAS etc.

SPECIAL PROJECTS CIA jargon for the tougher and more unpleasant side of the Intelligence game, including anything from murder to para-military operations, but sometimes this covers illegal bugging as well. Watergate was a 'special project'.

SPOOK A professional Intelligence executive or agent. Also covers spy-catchers.

SPOOKS' CLUB A somewhat esoteric club, whose members, if elected, must not only be recognised writers of spy fiction, but have other qualifications, one of which is to have been 'in the game'. They operate internationally and have 'drops' on both sides of the Atlantic, but are London-based. Their meeting-place is known as 'The Safe House', but the address is not normally publicised.

STABLE The list of 'Ladies' and 'Sisters' available for 'setting-up' operations in an allotted territory. This sometimes included 'Taxis', or 'Fairies'.

STATION CHIEF Top CIA official under diplomatic cover in a US Embassy.

STUCEN According to Len Deighton (doubtless with tongue in cheek) this is the War Studies Centre, London, and situated in Hampstead: see his war-gaming, nuclear submarine-cum-espionage book *Spy Story*. For more sober inquirers there are the Royal College of Defence Studies, 37 Belgrave Square,

London SW1, the Study of Conflict Centre, Northumberland Avenue, London WC2, and the International Institute for Strategic Studies, 18 Adam Street, London WC2.

SWEETENER   Any method used for softening up a 'target' either by gifts or inducements.

TAXI   Cover word for 'Jacksie', a homosexual member of the Stable, but now somewhat dated as even 'Taxis' tend to be called 'Ladies' or 'Sisters'. As one SIS executive told a British Minister during a recent sexual scandal involving another Minister: 'We are all bisexual these days and when our Stable-mates say that have "got the whips on", they aren't talking in parliamentary language.'

TARGET   Someone selected for 'sanctification' by the Americans and, in British parlance, for 'special treatment', in other words a person usually in the enemy camp on whom incriminating evidence is needed so that a hold on him (or her) can be acquired. But it can also refer to someone marked out as a likely defector who needs just that last push to be lured across.

THERMAL DETECTOR   A gadget which makes it possible to discover where people have been sitting or lying and even how many clothes they have been wearing.

TOBY (Doing a)   An 'in' word in NID and some other British Intelligence circles in the Second World War, meaning to be involved in devious procedures. It originated from Lieut.-Col. 'Toby' Ellis, an Intelligence executive in Tangier notorious for his sometimes incomprehensible imbroglios.

TURNED AGENT   An agent of an enemy power who is either captured or comes over voluntarily to the other side and is used by that side to feed false information to the enemy and obtain Intelligence from them.

TWISTED BALLS   Originally a Russian expression to indicate an agent who had at some time previously been given electric shocks in the genitals. Such a man was considered relatively an easy subject for further interrogation.

WAR OF DIVERSION   This is a Soviet term for carefully calculated sabotage of Western installations and factories. This is hardly ever indulged in on a large scale, but is intended mainly as a 'diversion' and a probe and sometimes is done under cover of such terrorist movements as the IRA. It used to be controlled by the 9th Section for Terror & Diversion of Soviet Intelligence.

XX COMMITTEE   The Double-Cross (usually referred to in Code as 'The Twenty') Committee, set up in the Second World War to control and exploit double-agents by BI A Section of MI5.

Y SERVICE   Wireless deception.

ZETA MEN   Name given in some circles to graduates from St Antony's College, Oxford, who have joined DI6.

Bibliography and Acknowledgements

Before listing works and sources consulted in compiling this book it should perhaps be made clear that, in the case of living authors, a great deal has been supplied by the authors themselves, occasionally in interviews, sometimes in their own response to questionnaires. Where apt, their own comments have been given in direct quotation. Various authorities on espionage in real life have also been consulted: many of them are so impressed by the spy fiction of today that they have sometimes said that the fiction very often puts on paper what they themselves think. A great deal of research on earlier writers has been done at the British Library and I should like to record my appreciation to the London Library for helping to provide a detailed catalogue of spy fiction from 1900 onwards.

I am especially indebted to Hodder & Stoughton for enabling me to inspect all their catalogues from 1900 to the present time—an invaluable source of inspiration—and to Miss Livia Gollancz of Victor Gollancz for assistance in tracing some pre-war authors; to Macmillan, William Heinemann, Weidenfeld & Nicolson and Blond & Briggs for suggestions and information; to Mr Gerald Austin of the Hutchinson Group for all manner of help and answering of queries over several weeks; and to Miss Marian Babson, of the Crime Writers' Association.

Books specially consulted and which can be recommended to any student of the genre were:

Amis, Kingsley, *The James Bond Dossier* (Jonathan Cape, London 1965).

Barzun, Jacques & Taylor, Wendell Hertig, *A Catalogue of Crime: Being a Reader's Guide to the Literature of mystery, detective and related genres* (Harper & Row, New York 1971).

Masterman, Sir J. C., *The Double-Cross System in the War of 1939–45* (New Haven, Yale University Press 1972); see foreword by Norman Holmes Pearson.

Steinbrunner, Chris & Penzler, Otto, *Encyclopaedia of Mystery & Detection* (McGraw-Hill, New York 1975).

Symons, Julian, *Bloody Murder From the Detective Story to the Crime Novel: A History* (Faber & Faber, London 1972).

Weismiller, Edward, *Serpent's Progress: The Writing of a Novel* (Center for Advanced Studies, Wesleyan University 1968).

Wiseman, Sir William, *The Private Papers of Sir William Wiseman* in the *E.M. House Collection*, Yale University Library, New Haven, Connecticut.

Also consulted: *The Dictionary of National Biography, Contemporary Authors, Who Was Who, Everyman's Dictionary of Literary Biography, English & American*, as well as book reviews in *The Times, New York Times, Sunday Times, Daily Express, Evening Standard, Washington Post, Times Literary Supplement, Daily Telegraph, Daily Mail, Le Monde, Private Eye* and various magazines.